Israel Today

Israel Today

LAND OF
MANY NATIONS
REVISED EDITION

by *Ruth Gruber*

WITH PHOTOGRAPHS BY
THE AUTHOR

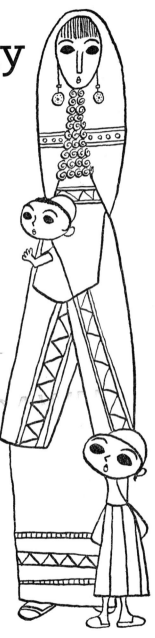

HILL AND WANG
NEW YORK

To my husband, Phil Michaels, and to Celia Joyce and David

Contents

Illustrations

Foreword

It is the joyousness of Israel's youth that strikes you the moment you set foot on her soil.

It is her laughter and her dynamism that envelop you.

Here the beauty and nobility of three thousand years of religious faith have been enriched by the joyousness of the Return. From seventy-nine nations, Jews have returned Home.

In writing this book, *Israel Today: Land of Many Nations*, I have sought to record some of the laughter and the spirit of youth that marked the character of Israel's life. There have been problems, to be sure, grave ones, and I have recorded those too.

For this paperback edition, I have added the dramatic and often poignant story of Israel's role in Africa and Asia, the birth of new regional developments in this decade of the Negev, the archaeological discovery of the Bar Kochba letters, the continued flowering of art and culture in the International Music Festivals and the Casals Competition, the Chagall windows, the gifts of sculpture from Jacques Lipchitz, Billy Rose, and the estate of the late Sir Jacob Epstein, Nasser's new weapons, and the latest travel information.

In June 1963, just as this revised edition was going to press, David Ben-Gurion announced his retirement, and his old comrade-in-arms, Levi Eshkol, former Minister of Finance, became the Prime Minister of Israel. Not only was it too late to change the text; but Ben-Gurion promised, as he had done once before when he resigned, that he would come out of retirement "if a crisis arises."

For the opportunity to continue discovering Israel, I wish to thank the editors and publishers of the New York Herald Tribune. For permission to reprint material and photographs that they first used, I thank the New York Herald Tribune, the Reader's Digest, the National Broadcasting Company and "The Eternal Light" program of the Jewish Theological Seminary, This Week, Commentary, The Hadassah Magazine, The Zionist Quarterly, and Look.

And to all the friends in Israel and America who helped in shaping this book—my husband Phil Michaels, Katherine Bregman, and scores of others—my unending gratitude.

R. G.

June 1963

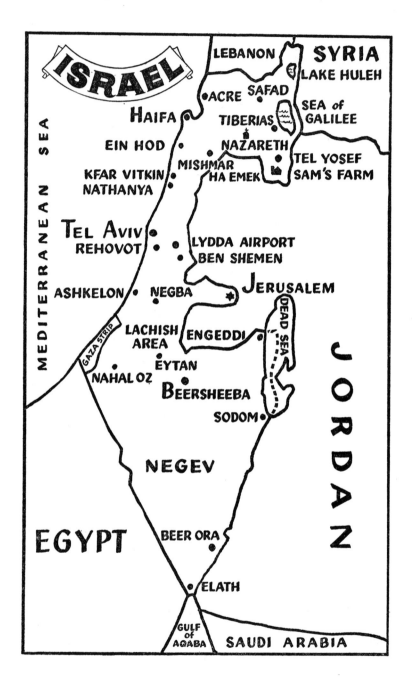

1: A State Is Born

ON A FRIDAY afternoon, the fourteenth of May, 1948, in a museum room in Tel Aviv, David Ben-Gurion, a short, stocky leader with a strong face and a cowl of white hair, read Israel's Proclamation of Independence. Israel was born.

It was built out of chaos. It was built by men and women whom many people considered a little touched with madness. "You don't have to be crazy to believe in Israel," they said, "but it helps."

Within a few hours, President Harry S. Truman recognized Israel. Within minutes, Egyptian planes dropped bombs on Tel Aviv. Within twenty-four hours, seven Arab states with a population of forty million people marched against a country of six hundred and fifty thousand Jews, and Israel, born of a majority decision in the United Nations, had to fight for its life.

In the middle of that war, I asked Prime Minister Ben-Gurion what he thought Israel would be like in the future—after the blood had stopped flowing and the immigrants had come home.

He leaned back in his desk chair. His eyes, tired and red with the business of fighting a war and setting up a government, suddenly lost their tiredness. He brushed his hand against his cowl of white hair and for a few moments the man of the people became a visionary.

"There will be no more desert," he said. He looked off into space as though he could see this future land that he, perhaps more than any living man, had helped shape. "There will be no more sand. Everything will be fertile. Irrigation will make everything bloom. There will be trees on every hill. The sky will be full of planes. The sea will be full of ships."

The room was silent. His loyal young military aide sat like a disciple at the foot of the master. Some of the vision of the stocky, beloved prime minister reflected itself in the younger man's face.

3

Ben-Gurion went on. "There will be cottages all over the country. No skyscrapers. We are a little country; we don't need big skyscrapers like those in New York and Chicago. We'll have towns and villages filled with flowers and trees and lots of children. Children are our future."

I had heard him say that many times before: "Children are our future. Children are Israel's future."

"Our children will have every advantage of education and modern science. We will develop science to the last degree. We will use our only advantage—brains. We will use science for creation, not for destruction."

"And what," I asked, "will be your philosophy of life? What will be your Bill of Rights?"

It was the question I had been asking ever since I first became interested in Israel. The country was creative, exciting, the most exciting country on the map in the postwar years, but where was it going, what did it see as its place in the world, what promise did it make to its own people?

"It takes many words in English," he said. "In Hebrew it takes only three, Veahavta re-ekh'a kamoh'a. They mean 'Love your fellow human as yourself.'"

I have returned to Israel almost every year since Ben-Gurion made that prophecy, and each year I have watched it come true. Today the sand is disappearing in the Negev. From the road all the way to the horizon lush green fields of cotton wave gently. New immigrants are raising the food they eat on land where once there was not a blade of grass. There are trees on nearly all the hills. Small towns have mushroomed across the country from the hills of the Galilee to the plains of the Negev. There are planes in the sky, ships in the sea, white cottages all over the land, and beautiful children.

Nor have the Israelis forgotten that Bill of Rights—to love their fellow human as themselves. Since 1948 a nation of six hundred and fifty thousand Jews has taken in over a million new immigrants, until now there are more than two million citizens. In forty years, Moses led some six hundred thousand Jews out of slavery in

Egypt to freedom in the Promised Land. Israel, in ten years, had topped Moses and led the largest migration in history to any country, big or small, in so short a time.

Rescue was the greatest achievement after Israel's war of independence. But there were also achievements in politics, in industry, in agriculture. A once broken people and a once broken land were being repaired. After two thousand years the gates were thrown open for progress to march into the Middle East. The land that gave the world the Bible, had for two thousand years remained like the Bible. The poorest of the Biblical people, like the shepherds of Judea or the wandering tribes of patriarchal times, seemed still alive in the men and women who moved slowly across the desert sand. In Ecclesiastes, Koheleth the Preacher spoke of "the crackling of thorns under a pot" and at the rebirth of Israel you could still see Arab women cooking in the fields with little fires of crackling thorn-bush twigs set beneath their black pots.

Against this background the modern, progressive Republic of Israel began to emerge half a century ago. A black-bearded first-rate journalist and second-rate playwright, Theodor Herzl, dreamed a dream that was to inspire hundreds of thousands of Jews to sacrifice, idealism, undreamed of heroism, and a complete upheaval of an ancient pattern of life. An outpost of Western civilization was established in the heart of the backward Arab world.

The Jew who comes from the Diaspora to Israel is transformed there into a new type of man. The moment he sets foot on the land he is a citizen—a first-class citizen. Slowly he learns to shed the immemorial fears, the heritage of two thousand years of restriction, quota and pogrom. Under his hand, released from fear, an ancient land is now changing.

For over a thousand years Israel was a country with a few cities, ancient settlements, and vast stretches of desert where there was not a tree, a shrub, a blade of grass; where the sun rode the sky in fierce and often terrible loneliness.

The terrain varies from the mountains to the Dead Sea; the weather from winter cold and even snow to tropical rains. In a country little larger than the state of Vermont, you can travel in an hour from winter to summer, from the mountain air of Jerusalem to the hot plains of Tel Aviv.

No one word can capture Israel's color and mood. You think of the cypresses that spread cool shade, or the cactus plants whose thorny arms and delicious red pears line the roads for miles. You think of the blue Mediterranean, the Arab mud villages, the domes and golden steeples of Jerusalem. You think of the mauve and pink mountains of the Galilee and the Huleh, the Beverly Hills white cottages and pink-tiled roofs of the *kibbutzim,* the collective farms. But mostly you think of rocks and stones, the rocks and stones of the Hills of Judea as you go up to Jerusalem, the rocks and stones of the farm lands that the pioneers dug up with their bare hands.

Stones generally mark the beginning and the end of a civilization. The stones of the Aleutians look like a new world forming, like the first day of creation. The stones of the Hills of Judea, the boulders and relics of old terraces, look like an ancient world almost dead. The rocks of Jerusalem are small and broken, sunning themselves in the sunset. Now, on the Hills of Judea, in the Galilee, on the Plain of Esdraelon, the new settlers are beginning all over again, clearing the stones to make way for green growth, planting trees, rebuilding lives.

You think of stones, of orange trees, of lovely terraced hills, of purple grapes and mosques, of cactus and pomegranates and palm trees, of the blue-washed nights of Jerusalem and the promise of the sunrise on Mount Carmel. You think of a narrow, elongated country that lies beside the Mediterranean, a country that runs from the mountains to the sea—and immediately you think of the word *tiny.*

Israel is a little country. Compared with the Rocky Mountains or the Alps, the mountains of the Galilee are little hills. Jerusalem is still a little town. Tel Aviv is no London or New York. The Yarkon River in Tel Aviv would be hardly more than a creek in America.

History, legends, childhood stories have made the land seem gigantic. Yet Israel is so small that sometimes you can hardly find it on a map. Sometimes the mapmakers sneak its name into Egypt, or they use an asterisk and Israel becomes a footnote.

Geography is her lifeblood, for she is a tiny border country. Geography is her politics. Geography makes up her sinews of war and peace.

Yet you cannot measure Israel with a ruler. You have to measure it in height and depth, in history and dreams, in hills old even two thousand years ago, in roads that only now are being traversed, in mysterious valleys where once only Arab bands roved and where now Jews are building settlements.

It is the soul of the country that is big. It is the soul of a people who have known death and outwitted it. This is the key to Israel: that it was built on a Biblical vision and the cremated bones of six million dead.

This is its strength: that it is a creative country, built in our time by a creative people. It is a country built out of death for life. This is its strength: that it has the broadest arms in the world, welcoming home every homeless Jew.

2: Gather Yourselves Together

GREAT RIVERS of Jews began to pour home into the sea that was Israel. They rushed in from the Displaced Persons camps. They came from the prison camps on Cyprus. They flew home from Yemen and from ancient Babylon, now called Iraq. They came from North Africa, from India, from Egypt, from Hungary, from Poland and Russia—from the lands trapped behind the Iron Curtain. Wherever there was the shadow of terror, the Jews fled to the Land of Israel.

Like streams of people painted on a Renaissance canvas, Jews poured out of Europe and Asia. Ancient Jewish populations uprooted themselves entirely.

Today there are white Jews and yellow Jews and black Jews. There are Jews from Paris, Afghanistan, and Rome; Jews from Abyssinia, China, and India. Like Whitman's America, Israel is a nation of nations.

Israel is not a melting pot, they say jocularly, but a pressure cooker. New immigrants from Hitler's Europe ride the buses and walk the streets. Heavy, serious-faced Germans plod Tel Aviv's streets, lugging their brief cases. Sensitive-faced Yemenites, dark-skinned Jews from Cochin and India, Poles, Russians, Hungarians, Moroccans, Tunisians, Algerians, and Bulgarians—all have squeezed themselves into the pressure cooker, some in search of refuge, some in search of faith.

For thousands of years a nucleus of Jews had lived in Jerusalem, Safad, and other holy cities. For hundreds of years solitary Jews came to pray and remained to die. But the first of the migrations that built the new Israel came in 1882, when seven thousand people left Russia and eastern Europe during a wave of pogroms. Among them were a little group of intellectuals who took an oath to work on the land and who called themselves, dramatically, *Bilu*, from the Hebrew of the Biblical verse "House of Jacob, come let us go!"

8

This was the first *aliyah*—a beautiful word that in the Bible means
"The ascendancy, the going up," the going up from Egypt into the
Hills of Judea. *Aliyah*, the word for immigration, is perhaps the
most important word in Israel today.

The country was built on aliyah. The second aliyah came after
1900, after Herzl. The third came after the Balfour Declaration
of 1917. The fourth came in 1925. The fifth aliyah was Hitler's.
Jews who could escape from Germany and Hitler's Europe rushed
into Palestine.

Ironically, it was the British who helped give birth to a new
aliyah, called *aliyah beth*, illegal immigration. In 1939, after the in-
famous White Paper, the British, who controlled Palestine under
a mandate from the League of Nations, restricted immigration to
fifteen hundred a month, in effect condemning shiploads of Jews
fleeing from Hitler to death. Aliyah beth continued through World
War II to 1948. The people of aliyah beth were concentration
camp graduates, unafraid of guns and bayonets. Dachau and
Auschwitz had steeled them. Nothing could stop them in their
flight home. Aliyah beth reached its climax in the tragic voyage of
the *Exodus 1947*, when forty-five hundred Jews broke their way
through the British blockade and then were sent back to Germany
—the death land.

The sixth aliyah was Israel reborn. In 1948, with every farm
settlement turned into a beachhead and the streets of her beloved
cities turned into front lines as the Arab states invaded and attacked, Israel opened her gates to a tide of fleeing people.

In that first year of life, Israel took in a hundred thousand Jews
from the Displaced Persons camps in Germany, Austria, and Italy.
Another forty thousand came from the prison camps of the island
of Cyprus, where the British had held the Jews of aliyah beth. Now
there were no more illegal people and illegal ships. The legally
homeless were brought home on legal ships to a legal land. The
long night of martyrdom had ended, and a new era of nationhood
and aliyah began.

1949 was the fateful year when Israel was admitted to the United
Nations. The nations of the world voted to make the one-year-old

democracy a member state. The Jews now had a voice in world affairs. Moshe Sharett, Israel's first foreign minister, flew to the United Nations to raise the blue and white flag of Israel, to speak the words that were in the hearts of all his grateful people: "I can only pray that we may prove worthy of the dignity that has been restored to us."

Israel went on gathering in the exiles. In 1949 she rescued the entire Jewish community, fifty thousand strong, living under slavery in the Arab kingdom of Yemen. American planes, paid for by the United Jewish Appeal, brought these deeply religious people home on the "eagles' wings" that Isaiah had prophesied.

In 1950, the Iraqi government, still officially at war with Israel, since she had never signed an armistice agreement, ordered the Jews of Iraq to get out within a year or be trapped forever. Twenty-five hundred years ago, the Jews captured in Jerusalem by King Nebuchadnezzar had sat in exile weeping by the rivers of ancient Babylon. "By the rivers of Babylon," they sang, "there we sat down, yea, we wept, when we remembered Zion." The Jews of Babylon weep no more. Once again American planes rescued Iraq's one hundred and twenty-two thousand Jews. In the largest human airlift in history, a thousand Jews a day were flown from the ancient valleys of the Tigris and Euphrates to the new land of Israel.

In 1951 there came a migration from behind the Iron Curtain. Rumania's ill-fated dictator, Ana Pauker, herself a Jew, announced that the Jews could go. Eighty thousand escaped. Others came from Hungary. They came from Czechoslovakia. The entire Jewish communities of Bulgaria and Yugoslavia came.

The epic story continued. Each exodus was the Bible Exodus retold. From 1952 to 1956, Jews poured in from North Africa, from Libya, from Morocco and Tunisia. In 1957, as Israel approached her tenth year of independence, she took in almost a hundred thousand refugees. They came from Hungary, crossing the borders into Austria during the ill-fated uprising. Others came out of Egypt. In 1962, 62,000 came. They fled from North Africa and Eastern Europe, from war-wracked Algeria, from Castro's Cuba, and Argentina.

One of the strangest migrations had come from Poland. It was kept secret to prevent the Arabs from pressuring Russia to stop it. Wladyslaw Gomulka, the leader of Poland, told the Jews they could go. In one year, some forty thousand rushed out of Poland. Planes flew directly from Israel to Warsaw. Ships left Stettin and traveled to Le Havre; there the people boarded trains for Marseille and sailed on Israeli ships to Haifa.

For a few weeks, there was a railroad strike in France. The only trains that moved were those carrying the refugees from Poland to Israel. "There is no strike when it comes to saving refugees," one of the French trainmen said. "We know Israel. We'll help the Jews get there."

Doctors, lawyers, judges, engineers, a new class of skilled workers, came from Poland to be added to the pressure cooker. They were leaving Poland because anti-Semitism had never stopped, and their children, born since the war, were its newest victims. Golda Meir, Israel's foreign minister, told me one day of a Polish immigrant who had come to her office.

"I want to tell you," he said, "why I have come. You know that during the war, many of us stayed alive in Poland by living underground as Christians. When the war ended, I found it easier to go on living as a Christian. I married and had a son, and I never bothered to tell him that he was not a Christian. Then one day his teacher called me to his school. She said to me, 'Look. I hate the Jews as much as you do. And I understand why we treat them the way we do. But your son—he's absolutely inhuman in the way he treats the Jewish boys in the class. Can't you teach him that Jews are human beings?'

"I decided then that you never stop being what you are. I took my son out of school and we came to Israel."

Each migration was different from the others, each aliyah brought its special problems to the young state. The Jews coming from North Africa and the Oriental countries brought illiteracy and sickly, undernourished bodies. The Jews of Egypt came, shocked and stunned that this had happened to them. The Jews of Poland and the lands behind the Iron Curtain came, filled with suspicion of everyone and everything. Government was an evil word. Their only interest now was survival, personal survival. They had survived Hitler. They had survived Stalin. Now they were determined to survive anything the world could throw at them. Israel was a last stand.

The Bible had said, "Gather yourselves together." They were being gathered. They were helped by Jews and Christian friends in America, through the United Jewish Appeal. They were helped by Jews and Christians in England and Canada and South Africa and South America. They were helped by money raised through the sale of Israel Bonds. They were helped by United States grants-in-aid and by reparations money from Germany.

But it was the people of Israel themselves who made the greatest contribution and the greatest sacrifice. The world gave of its resources, the people of Israel gave of themselves. There was not enough food for the newcomers. Somehow Israel fed them. There was not enough housing. She set up tents and aluminum huts. Thousands of new immigrants began their life in transient villages, in maabaroth. The newcomers came from strange countries with strange languages and strange customs for the Israelis to assimilate. They came ill in body and in mind for the Israelis to heal. There were no riots against immigration. There were no protests, no cries of indignation. They were welcomed into the country by the simple Law of the Return, the first law that the young state enacted.

The people of Israel greeted each new wave of immigration with their eyes open, knowing that it meant higher taxes, lower living standards, tent cities, a return to rationing. Knowing that it might even break their economy. But knowing, too, that it meant rescue.

They knew the price of rescue. They had smuggled Jews out on sealed trains. They had ransomed Jews, flown them out on planes that picked them up almost at the thirteenth hour. They knew each dictator's price. But after the extermination of six million Jews by Hitler, every life was valuable. There was no price on human life. There was only life itself.

The world has known great shifts of population before. The

world has seen hordes of people marching. But there has probably never been such a march of people into any land in so short a time. And there has surely never been such a tiny country bursting its seams to take in the homeless. Each of the people brought its own genius, its own culture, its own ingredients. The pressure cooker is working overtime to cook them all together into one nation.

The last ingredient, and of course the most important, is the child born in Israel, the native-born, or *sabra* (pronounced sah-bra). He is the basic stock. Even now the whole is flavored by him, for it was the sabra, in the farm settlements and in the cities, who was the backbone of the Haganah, the Jewish self-defense movement. In the 1930's, the British under General Orde Wingate had organized the Jews of Palestine into night squads under the Haganah to fight against Arab riots. In the 1940's, it was the sabra in the Haganah who helped bring in the "illegals." It was the sabra who helped defeat six Arab states, and who held the soil so that it could blossom again and become a land without tears.

The sabra, named after the local cactus—thorny outside, but sweet within—is a new face in the Jewish world. He is daring, sassy, afraid of nothing, with the assurance of an American at home in his land. Wearing his khaki shorts with studied carelessness, singing as he swaggers down the street, he makes the country thrill with pride.

When the sabras fought in tiny numbers against the armies of the Arabs and won, the people said, "Our sabras are afraid of nothing in the world—except their mothers."

For out of the land has come a new man whose mother tongue is Hebrew, who knows no home but Israel, no sea but the Mediterranean, no desert but the Negev. In a few years the Yemenites' spindly little thighs developed into sturdy legs. The eyes of the Kurds lost their Tartar fierceness. The fear of persecution of the Rumanians disappeared. The children grew tall and broad, like athletes, their faces toasted golden brown, tawny like the hills in summer.

There is space here in which to grow, and hills and blue sky. Some of the boys look like young Greek gods, with their stomachs tight, their hips lean, their shoulders broad. The girls grow shorter than the boys—soft, full bosomed, and full hipped.

The old caricatured Jew, the pimply-faced, hungry scholar, has disappeared. Even the city children have the look of the land. Almost as soon as they can toddle, they are taken in little nursery-school groups to the beach or the fields. They grow up full of sunshine and orange juice. They become scouts, go on long overnight hikes, prowl through the country exploring hidden trails mentioned in the Bible, the Book used as a living text in their schools.

The old "intellectuals" had thought of their sabras as lovable *enfants terribles*, not cultured as Europeans understood culture, diamonds in the rough—who, of course, accepted without a single reservation the life their parents had begun for them in the Home Land. The sabras are proving, in a flood of published diaries and letters, that their parents were wrong. They are as sensitive, well informed, and searching as most adolescents and young adults anywhere in the civilized world.

As new ingredients are added to the pressure cooker, from Europe and the Oriental lands, the sabra will undoubtedly take on new flavor. But on the horizon of Israel a new man has already emerged, born of the country's climate and landscape and history, healthy, laughing, secure in his newly won strength and love of life, realistic, questioning, ready to fight for his soil.

3:   Haifa, the Sunrise City

THE GREEKS had a word for it. A city-state. A city that guarded its personality and integrity more jealously than a French mother guards her marriageable daughter. A city that had nearly the autonomy of a state.

Israel has three such cities: Haifa, Tel Aviv, and Jerusalem. And like the Greeks and the latter-day Californians, they have their partisans, apologists, and detractors. For me, each of the cities has its own magic. The three are like the cycle of a day. Haifa is a sunrise city; Tel Aviv is a city of daylight; Jerusalem is a sunset city.

Haifa is an early-morning city, a city of brawny young men and women, pushing out to their jobs in the factories, the oil refineries, and the harbor. Haifa is at its most beautiful as the sun rises.

Tel Aviv is high noon, the city of frenzied commerce and even more frenzied traffic, the city of cafés and baby carriages, the largest all-Jewish city in the world. Travelers who fly into Israel from New York and Paris come straight into the hurly-burly of Tel Aviv.

Jerusalem is the sunset city. Jerusalem is the eternal Going Home. Every trip to Jerusalem is a pilgrimage, an ascendancy. Every journey to Jerusalem is a maturing and an illumination. I have never seen anywhere else the phenomenon of a sun that seems always to set, not in red or lavender, but in solid gold. In Jerusalem the sun seems to set from within the stones.

Haifa, once the port where most of the illegal ships docked, on whose quay so much blood and tears had been spilled, is now the "point of first joy," for it is here that most of the new immigrants and travelers who come by ship first see the Holy Land. People know that Israel is a pioneer country. They know that it has been reclaimed from the desert. But the beauty, the sheer civilized beauty of Haifa comes as a shock to most travelers.

From the harbor, Haifa is a white city of stone staired up a Biblical mountain, Mount Carmel, whose literal translation is said to be "The Vineyard of God." Modern white apartment houses catch the warm sun. Here and there, throwing shadows in the midst of the stony whiteness, are green trees and brown shrubs.

From the mountain, you see the blue crescent of the Mediterranean, two incongruous, giant, milk-bottle-shaped oil refineries, and a vast, flat horseshoe of land near the sea, on which new stone houses for immigrants are being thrown up swiftly. You see ships flying most of the flags of the world, docking, loading, unloading, their cranes swinging in mid-air.

Though Mount Carmel was known in the Bible, Haifa is a young city, the city of Israel's industries and future, called in Hebrew *Ir Ha'atid* (City of the Future). It is built like a three-layer cake. The bottom layer is the bay and dock area. The middle layer is *Hadar Hakarmel*, which means "The Beauty of the Carmel" and which spreads over the slopes of Mount Carmel. The top layer is *Har-Karmel*, the top of the mountain itself. Each of the three layers has its own life, its own shops, its own tempo. The bay has the harbor, the factories, and many of the government offices. The Hadar has the commercial life, the municipal buildings, the cafés, movie houses, and year-round hotels. The top of the mountain has the better residences, summer hotels, more cafés, sanitaria, and rest homes. For Haifa is the convalescing spot of Israel and Mount Carmel is the Magic Mountain of the republic.

It is also the Magic Mountain of technology, for here, on a campus with a magnificent view and in buildings that are a modern architect's dream, is housed the new Technion, Israel's school of engineering. Its teachers come from all over the world; its graduates serve the air force, the road builders, the vast project of waterways, the mineral research in the Dead Sea and the Negev, the building program that never catches up with the needs of the new immigrants.

Haifa varies from white beaches along the Mediterranean to rambling forests and rolling hills. Like all of Israel, Haifa loves music, and the people of Haifa listen to Beethoven under a cloud-

less blue Mediterranean sky. One of the most beautiful buildings
in Haifa is the temple of the Bahai faith, the world center for the
followers of Baha'ulla. The shining gold dome of the Shrine of
the Bab, set above the Bahai's exotic Persian gardens, glistens in the
hills.

It is a teeming, healthy, happy city, a tribute to its mayor, Abba
Hushi. He has been called a dictator by his enemies, and like any
strong man he has accumulated a horde of enemies. But to his ad-
mirers he is a great administrator.

He has been Haifa's mayor since January, 1951, and in that time
he has not only dreamed an ideal city but has gone about hammering it into shape. He is indefatigable. Up every morning at five-
thirty, he drives around the city to make sure the street cleaners
are keeping his streets clean. About six-thirty he goes to his office
"because those first two hours of planning and thinking are the
best hours of the day." Often he works until eleven at night.

"You remember," he said, driving me around Haifa, "a few
years ago we had a plan for developing the city into three parts,
industrial, residential, and commercial.

"Now we are living by this plan. Our town planning area is
twenty-five per cent bigger than Paris. Rome was built on seven
hills. Haifa has eight hills. We are building on each hill, tying all
of them together. We have two hundred thousand people and we
have reserved four thousand acres for industry. Amsterdam, with
seven hundred and fifty thousand people, has a thousand acres for
industry. We have to plan big—because we are planning for the
future."

Late one evening we drove on Panorama Road and looked down
at the incredible sight of this port and mountain city, with its new
blue street lights, the yellow headlights of cars, the electric lights
in all the homes, and the spotlights in the harbor. It was unforget-
tably beautiful. But Abba Hushi was not yet satisfied. He had his
own philosophy of city life.

"I think a big city is bad. It pulverizes people. It estranges them.
In Haifa we have people from forty-eight countries—from China,
from Abyssinia, from everywhere on the globe. We want to create

of this human Diaspora a people. Noisy streets can't do it. People like beauty.

"If people walk among flowers and trees, they smile. Even flowers can shape the character of people. That's why we built public gardens in front of all their houses. Now people call our gardens 'generators of smiles.' "

The next morning he showed us the gardens and they were beautiful. In a few years he had built over a hundred city gardens, parks, and playgrounds, each with its own character, its own intimacy. One park, called Mother's Garden, had a special section for the "golden age," where we saw old people sitting on benches in the sun. Mothers and babies had their own section. The third part was for children, with gay rocking horses and special equipment to develop the children's muscles.

Overlooking the harbor was Memorial Park, commemorating those who fell in Israel's war of liberation in 1948. It had been built on the site of an old Crusaders' fortress.

"A park," Abba Hushi said, "is like a lung for a man. This park is in the midst of thirty thousand of the poorest people of Haifa. They live in tiny apartments. Every night you will find eight or nine thousand people in this park.

"I said to our gardener—he is a young man of thirty-one, the best gardener in the country—'Remove all the signs that say, "Don't walk on the grass. Don't pick flowers." Speak to people in a human way.' "

The signs indeed spoke in a human way. In a lovely pond where goldfish were swimming among the water lilies, a sign showed two fish talking: "Dear children," the sign said, "don't give us anything to eat. We have enough and more will hurt us."

"Because we are building a city for the future—which means a city for the children," Abba Hushi said, "we set up a committee with youngsters, fifteen to seventeen years of age. We asked them to plan the kind of city they wanted to live in. Our engineers and architects were astonished. They hadn't even dared suggest most of the things the children had thought of. But we implemented their planning. They told us how to build a school, where to build it, how to build a playground, even how to build a bus station so people would be happier waiting for a bus."

Still concerned with children and young people, Abba Hushi took us to David Stadium, dedicated to David Dubinsky and built with funds that came from the International Ladies' Garment Workers' Union. "About forty to fifty thousand young people come into the stadium every week," the mayor said. "So here, too, we can mold character."

With all its emphasis on beauty and children, Haifa remains the workers' city, the center of Israel's industrial life. Here is the Kaiser-Frazer assembly plant, with workmen welding, painting, spraying, riveting in a plant that looks like Detroit-on-the-Mediterranean.

One of the great open sesames to Israel's future is a plant called Fertilizers and Chemicals Limited, its huge sulphur boilers and giant steel pipes looking like some prehistoric animal against Haifa's blue sky. Its managing director, Alexander Goldberg, a dark-haired chemical engineer who left his native England to become an Israel citizen, took me through the plant.

"One of the reasons for the success of this kind of operation," he said, "is that Israel is one of the rare countries in the world that has all the necessary products for a basic chemical industry within its own borders. In order to give a plant like this all the food it needs, you must give it phosphate, potash, and nitrogen. In most parts of the world these three are thousands of miles apart. Here they are just tens of kilometers. Nitrogen is in the air. We get the phosphate from our own mines in the Negev in the Makhtesh Hagodol, literally the 'Great Canyon' of Israel, and bring it out on trucks. We're planning to build a narrow-gauge railroad at the mine, with ropes to pull the cars because the canyon is so steep there. We estimate there are a hundred million tons of phosphates in the Negev, or about six hundred years' supply. We get the potash from the Dead Sea; the old potash corporation is a shareholder in our firm. The only raw material we have to import is pyrites, which we get from Greece and Cyprus, countries that are right on our doorstep."

New industries spring up constantly along Haifa's coast: industries built by private capital, government funds, German reparations, and money raised through Israel Bonds.

At the end of the working day, residents of Haifa who live on top of Mount Carmel climb into crowded buses and ride along Panorama Road, which curves snakelike up the mountain. Or they take walks on roads overlooking the harbor. It is there, in the shiny, white, new Jewish ships, the *Israel*, the *Zion*, the *Jerusalem*, in the Israel cargo ships and the Israel navy, that the future of Haifa is written too.

Here the Israelis captured the Egyptian warship *Ibrahim al Awar*, as it attempted to shell Haifa during the Sinai campaign in the fall of 1956. Here the battered hulks of illegal ships that the British had smashed in 1946 and '47 were overhauled. Here the flags of the nations of the world now fly on ships visiting or trading with the young state.

In 1942 Ben-Gurion had written prophetically of his dream of a Jewish navy—a dream that had come true:

Jews as a seafaring people may seem fantastic to those who know the Jews in Europe and America. . . . A few years ago there was not a single Jewish sailor on the seas of Palestine, although the main sea trade was Jewish. Now . . . Jewish ships manned by Jewish captains and sailors traverse the seven seas. It was a Hebrew-speaking tribe who gave the world maritime trade and navigation: the people of Tyre and Sidon, who founded the great empire of Carthage. Tyre and Sidon perished and disappeared. But the descendants of the Jews, who fought the Romans, are very much alive. Many of them are back and more are to come. They went back to the soil. Now they are going back to the sea. Israel is a small country. But the two seas of Israel, the Mediterranean and the Red Sea, are big, and Jewish sailors and fishermen will add the large seas to Israel and the Jewish people will take part among the maritime nations of the world.

4: Shabbat in Tel Aviv

ISRAEL LONGS for peace. That is the thing a traveler feels keenly in Tel Aviv. Israel wants peace and you know it best on *Shabbat*, the Sabbath.

On Shabbat, several hundred thousand tired, nerve-strained people forget their urgency and purposefulness and greet each other with the warm, slow ancient greeting "*Shabbat shalom*" (Peace to you on the Sabbath).

All week Tel Aviv shrieks, honks its horns, grinds its brakes—whose oil dries out in the hot sun—beats its Persian carpets like the rat-tat-tat of a machine gun, blares its radios, backfires its ancient jalopies. But by two o'clock on Friday the offices are closed; by four most of the shops are closed; and by sundown the buses have stopped running completely. The hustling city of Tel Aviv becomes a village again.

All Friday afternoon you smell the city preparing for its Shabbat. The odor of floors being scrubbed, the rich herb odor of gefillte fish, and the richer odor of fat rendering from chickens pour out of the open windows.

Men hurry along the streets carrying two or three gladiolas wrapped in tissue paper for their wives or sweethearts. Sometimes a man carries a bouquet in one hand and in the other a little bundle of sticks to heat the hot-water boiler for his afternoon bath.

Friday afternoon before Shabbat is when Tel Aviv's husbands absolve their guilt; all week they have involuntarily neglected their families, busy with the work of earning enough money to feed them, and bringing new immigrants into the land. On Friday afternoon, Abba (Papa) takes a shower, puts on a fresh white shirt, puts the spotlessly clean baby in the spotlessly clean modern

21

baby carriage, and takes him out for a stroll. On Friday Abba walks
the baby while Ima (Mama) makes the gefillte fish.

On Friday afternoon, the people who have worked late or
shopped late—the good housewives do their shopping for Shabbat
in the market place on Thursday—queue up for the last crowded
bus home. Traffic cops, standing on little safety islands, wave their
white-sleeved arms like semaphores. Nerves, already tattered, go to
pieces—and are healed again with jokes.

Every life current that made this land and these people has left
a deep furrow across this city, built completely by Jews. The big
Polish immigration of the turn of the century is in the architecture of the newspaper kiosks and the large courtyards. The Germans brought their Bauhaus architecture, their silver industries
and fine leather goods, which fill the shops along Allenby Road.
The Viennese brought their sweater factories and tailored clothes.
And now, new immigrants from everywhere in the world, swelling
the city to three hundred and ninety thousand, are writing all
their dreams—conglomerate, confused, and noble—into the face
of Tel Aviv. In Lev Tel Aviv (Heart of Tel Aviv), a Chinese
pagoda stands flimsily near a solid bourgeois modern German house.
And running through the center of fashionable Rothschild Boulevard is a soft green narrow park with benches, candy-bar stands, fish
ponds, and lawns for the incredible number of beautiful babies.
Abruptly the park's character changes at the intersection with
Allenby, where the men who love to talk and the men who love to
listen run their Israel version of Hyde Park or Union Square and
argue, cajole, dispute, shake their fists, and make or lose converts.

On Friday afternoon, the public forum reaches a reluctant climax
as the men go home. The newsboys, running down the streets
shouting "Maar-eeeef, Maar-eeeef," disappear. The shoeshine men,
most of them Georgian exiles from Russia, with mustaches like
Stalin's, pick up their shoeshine boxes. The skinny cats and the
well-fed boxers vanish. All week Tel Aviv is a noisy young giant,
bustling, loud, gay, and excited, forever bursting out of itself. But
on Friday afternoon it whittles itself down to size.

Just before the sun sets, ancient bearded men ride through the

streets of the city in ancient cars, blowing trumpets to announce
the Sabbath. The single-noted purposefulness of the trumpet rises
above the traffic noises. The last shopkeeper closes his shop. And as
the Sabbath crier, whom the children call "Joshua and his
trumpet," drives off, the orthodox men go to the Great Synagogue
or the small synagogues and bare rooms and pray. The air is full
of the sound of young boys' voices reciting the psalms and singing
a sixteenth-century poem written in Gaza comparing the Sabbath
to the bride and the people of Israel to the bridegroom. "Oh,
bridegroom, go and welcome the Sabbath bride," they sing, "Oh
go and welcome the Sabbath queen."

After the services, the men walk home slowly. Tradition says
that angels accompany them on their way home, so on their arrival, they sing a song of welcome to the angels, "Shalom aleikhem,
malakhei hashalom" (Peace to you, angels of peace).

Tel Aviv is a noonday city, but it is at its loveliest on Friday
night. There is the night sound of the Mediterranean beating
against the shore, the palm trees waving their fronds, and glowing
lights in the windows of the houses as up and down the streets
friends who have worried about meeting the rent and paying the
taxes and keeping the children in school put their burdens aside
and go visiting. For Friday night is visiting night in Tel Aviv, just
as Saturday night is movie night.

There are no movies open on Friday night, but there are cafés
and hotels where one can eat and dance, some lectures, and variety
shows. But mostly Friday night is visiting night and all over Tel
Aviv people who love company and good talk hold open house.

All week, Tel Aviv's workers and owners may go to bed late,
but they get up early. By six on weekdays Tel Aviv is wide awake.
But on Shabbat, people sleep even until ten. Shabbat morning
breaks quietly and peacefully all over the land.

On Saturday morning the orthodox men go back to the synagogues to pray; about eleven, when the services are over, they
emerge to walk about the streets until lunch time, carrying their
prayer shawls in velvet bags with the Shield of David embroidered
in gold.

In the Talmud, they play with the word *Shabbat*—they play with the idea that on Shabbat you must rest and sleep. The good and holy people, of course, will sleep after the Shabbat lunch; the evil ones must sleep too, because when they rest the whole world can rest. Right after lunch, Ima gets into a clean washable housecoat, Abba takes his shirt off, the children lie naked, and the whole family takes its Shabbat nap.

About five, the family gets dressed again in its best Shabbat clothes and walks leisurely to an outdoor café to drink iced coffee or tea and to visit with friends. The mark of Tel Aviv is its cafés. There are women in Tel Aviv who form small café-sitting cliques that outsit any café-sitters in the world.

Tel Avivians have their favorite cafés and many of the cafés have their own clientele and often their own language. Some cafés are pure Warsaw, others are Berlin or Budapest or Vienna. Ima and Abba drink their coffee with a piece of cake and order a plate of ice cream for the children.

On Shabbat, the beaches of Tel Aviv are packed with bobby-soxers. Soldiers and sailors and Air Force boys walk arm in arm with their girls, or sit holding hands on the slippery rocks. Chubby sunburned children, holding hands like a daisy chain, run swiftly along the beach.

People walk along the concrete promenade, assaulted by delicious odors of sweet corn and the shouts of vendors wearing white aprons, selling drinks and food in little shops that look like boardwalk stands in Atlantic City. One man has a Hebrew sign on his showcase, proclaiming himself THE FELAFEL KING. Felafel is an Arab kind of tortilla, a flat Arab roll filled with a small fried ball of chopped vegetables and herbs, garlic, pepper, with diced tomatoes and cucumbers on top. It is served on *peeta*, a flat, unleavened Arab bread, and is as essential a part of a visit to the beach as frankfurters and sauerkraut at Coney Island.

Jaffa, the former Arab city that now houses thousands of Jewish immigrants and Arabs, curves around the sea at Tel Aviv like a painting of an old medieval stone city. On the edge of Jaffa there is a long, white-sanded beach called *Bat Yam*, or Daughter of the

Sea. On Shabbat, Jews from Tel Aviv and from all over the world come to Bat Yam; whole groups come in trucks from villages and nearby housing developments.

Everyone gets into the holiday spirit. I saw a little boy of about four run near the feet of one of the truck drivers and sing out, "I don't have to pay. I'm a little boy." The driver put his hands on his large hips, looked down like a jovial giant at the chubby child, and said, "Such a hero. A hero in Israel." He lifted the child up and swung him into the van.

The pressure cooker of Israel comes to a slow, smooth boil on the beaches on Shabbat. People from every part of the world swim, play ball, and ride bicycles and jeeps on the broad white sand. Dark-skinned Jews from India play soccer while lovely Indian girls in saris watch, or play with their babies. The bathing suits are styled from everywhere in the world, in all degrees of Oriental dress and Western undress. Long-robed Arabs walk on the sand leading donkeys whose saddle sacks are filled with sabras (cactus pears) for sale.

All along the beach at Bat Yam enterprising new immigrants have built pavilions, cabañas, and cafés on the sand. Middle-aged or old ladies and men, especially from Bulgaria, carry trays filled with powder-covered Turkish delight. Men, shouting "Sh'keidim" (almonds), hold trays of shelled almonds that in the sun look naked. Others walk up and down with wooden boxes shouting "Eskeemo, Eskeemo" and for about ten cents you get a good Israel replica of an Eskimo pie.

Late one Shabbat afternoon I sat on the veranda watching the people walk through the park that runs through the center of Rothschild Boulevard, wondering how you could capture the pulse and feel and movement of this city and its shutdown on Shabbat. How you could put down the quiet of people sitting in shirt sleeves, sipping tea on their balconies. How you could describe a city with hills, gray and still and barren, at one end and a sea at the other in which the sun sets like a flaming ball every evening. The sun began to sink in sudden fierceness into the sea. The sound of children in the synagogue across the street, singing a happy song, "Artza alinu" (We went up to the land), told the story that the quiet of Shabbat was ending. In the synagogue old men singing the prayer of *Havdalah* held a glass of wine near candelight.

Street lights came on; fathers wheeled their baby carriages home; suddenly the buses were running again, grinding their ancient brakes; motorcycles whizzed down the street; truckloads of soldiers drove by, shouting and singing; horns began to honk; red and blue neon lights twinkled among the yellow electric lights of the city.

Thousands of people queued up to go to the movies, blocking traffic on Ben Yehuda Street. Cafés squeezed more chairs together to hold more people. Jazz bands screamed. People laughed. Tel Aviv was its old noisy self again. Tomorrow was a working day and Tel Aviv would have its Monday blues on Sunday morning.

5: Sunset in Jerusalem

IN JERUSALEM, as before all sunsets, man throws a long shadow.

The ties to Jerusalem are sunset ties and the worship of God, though it goes on with prayers in the morning, with prayers before washing the hands, prayers before eating, prayers before entering a house, is essentially a sunset worship. At sunset on the evening of Shabbat, peace floods the faces of the people, no longer tense on Shabbat. The holiest of all holidays seems doubly holy in the Holy City.

The ancient maps put the Land of Israel in the center of the world and Jerusalem, the Holy City, in the center of Israel. On Shabbat, the ancient maps seem to come close to life. You can find nearly every religious Jewish community in the world living in a miniature counterpart of its native habitat. In ten minutes on Friday night in Jerusalem you can walk from the Middle Ages of Yemen through Bokhara and the Caucasus of the nineteenth century into the little village ghettos of Poland and Russia of fifty years ago and, by turning a corner, emerge suddenly into the twentieth century of a city with broad streets, modern houses, beautiful gardens, telephones, electricity, and private elevators.

In Rehavia and the new sections of the New City, Shabbat has much the same rhythm as Shabbat in Tel Aviv. It is in the old quarters of the New City, in Mea Shearim especially (whose name means the Hundred Gates), that Shabbat in Jerusalem has a flavor extracted from the whole world of little Jews.

Down the alleys, no clothes hang in the setting sun. In tiny rooms in stone houses sinking with age the light of candles shines diffused through white window curtains. Inside the little rooms, you see women fresh from the mikve (ceremonial bathhouse) wearing clean white head kerchiefs and sitting at tables covered with a still life of white Shabbat bread, white candles, and bottles of

27

red wine. Some of the women read their prayer books; others chat softly as they wait for their men to return.

Bearded patriarchs walk the winding roads, sometimes hurrying alone to reach the synagogue early, sometimes strolling with other men in black *kaftans*, velvet or satin robes, and *streimels*, mink-tail hats. Young pale men with earlocks, the kind that fashionable young men wore in England in the days of Queen Elizabeth and James I, hurry down the streets with their lovelocks flying in the wind.

This whole quarter is a world apart in a city apart. On Shabbat, there is eloquent silence in Mea Shearim and Makhne Yehuda, the market place whose name means the Camp of Judah, where all week fishwives and peddlers shriek their wares. Even the children are still.

With a group of friends, I walked through the miniature worlds of Jerusalem one Friday night. One of the men was a seventy-year-old visitor from England. His eyes shone. He greeted the people with a spontaneous "*Shabbat shalom, Yiden*" (Peace to you on the Sabbath, Jews).

Dominating a narrow street, the Great Synagogue of the Bokharian Jews was actually a small square Oriental room. Wooden benches ran around its walls, covered with magnificent rugs. In the center, a man with a white brocaded kaftan stood in a pulpit singing.

Slender old men with high cheekbones and Tartar faces sat on the benches, wearing long white kaftans and little Caucasian embroidered caps. One of them wore an elegant kaftan of green Scotch plaid, a new note in a Bokharian house of worship. The robe was buttoned up to his neck in Russian fashion, ending right under his small pointed beard. A young man sat beside him—wearing Western clothing with a hand-embroidered Caucasian cap as his nod to his origins.

There was a wooden balcony in the tiny "Great Synagogue" for the women. But no women sat there. They were in the doorway, wearing the costumes they had brought with them out of the mountains of Asiatic Russia—long cotton skirts, little floral-patterned caps, and soft white woolen shawls. As they approached the synagogue, they touched the *mezuzah*—the little holy scroll nailed on the door—then touched their foreheads and their hearts and shut their eyes for a second of divine worship. Close together, they sat in the small passageway on the floor, listening to the men sing and watching the sun set over the hills and the houses of glowing stone.

These are a sunset people, I thought, who came to Jerusalem for the sunset of their lives. They did not come, like the pioneers or the workers or the new immigrants, to build a nation of Jews. They came to die. There was sweetness here, and gentility, and a yearning for Zion. On their front wall, in the wine-red-carpeted house of worship, there was a painting of a simple ship with the Hebrew words IF I FORGET THEE, O JERUSALEM, MAY MY RIGHT HAND FORGET ITS CUNNING. For them there was no place but Jerusalem, and Israel, the new Jewish state, might have been five thousand miles and a hundred years away.

A few streets away, we entered the synagogue of the Cabbalists. Their synagogue was a single square room too, but without the Oriental beauty and unity of the Bokharians'. The men, dressed in kaftans and red turbans, covered their eyes with their hands in the profound aloneness and oneness of their worship of God.

All week, most of them were beggars in the streets of the Holy City, but on Friday night, their tattered sackcloth coats covered with the Shabbat kaftan, they stood and swayed and walked around the pulpit chanting their greeting to the Sabbath queen.

One of the old men, looking like a Chinese mandarin, squatted Buddha-like on his bench, his face turned to the window. He put his hand across his eyes and prayed with the gestures and postures of a man blinded by the golden sunset of the shining city of God.

The Yemenite synagogue, a few streets away, was small and beautiful, like that of the Bokharians. But the Yemenites had no benches. They sat cross-legged on pillows. Oil from silver filigreed lamps lit the room. Of all the worshipers in all the temples, they were among the happiest. They had returned.

Just as in the Yemen, there were little groups of readers with a smiling man in each group holding a Bible before him. The others sat around him, some reading the Bible sideways, some obliquely, some upside down. It was the way a people hungry for learning could pray from a single book.

They swayed back and forth as they squatted, looking like camel-riders. In Yemen, they were forbidden to ride camels. So they pretended to ride in their synagogues, as their act of equality, and they chanted their prayers to the tune of the camel-drivers' songs.

They sat against the walls, singing the prayers with the joy of children singing a song that delighted them. The old men with kaftans and turbans and beards like Solomon's lifted their voices in triumphant glory. They laughed out loud, pointed to their books, taught the children while they sang, and spent the sunset of the Sabbath in triumph and wild, unbounded jubilation.

We walked down a warren of alleys and stairways, past old stone houses, into the miniatures of Poland and Russia. Here the synagogues were a beehive of small bare rooms, each with a few benches, a reading table, a cupboard holding the Torah, and closely packed men chanting, shaking, bowing, weeping, praying. "God's Cossacks," some were called. They were the "army" of the Gerer Rabbi from Poland. They wore mink hats, long black socks, and silk coats, with tightly curled lovelocks hanging down to their shoulders.

Most fanatic of the worshipers in the Holy City, a small group called the Watchmen of the City (Nturei Karta), chanted not with joy but with almost unbearable sorrow and bitterness. They covered their eyes, not because they were blinded with the sun of the glorious city, but as if they could no longer tolerate their own misery. Every country has its fanatics and its own enemies. The Watchmen of the City are the professed enemies of the Jewish state. A year after independence, they announced to the world that they would rather live under the Arabs than under the modern Jews. The new Jew had grown too secular.

Theirs was the ancient Jewish tragedy of exile. They were like a man who has yearned for years for a woman who has been denied him. When at last she is offered to him as his bride, he can no longer accept her. His bitterness and torture have poisoned his love. There can be no bride who is called Zion, because the bridegroom has been mutilated. There can be no joy on earth.

The sun had set. The men hurried home for the Sabbath wine and the Sabbath supper.

We walked down Abyssinian Street, then down the Street of the Prophets, where Hadassah, the Women's Zionist Organization of America, once had headquarters for healing the sick. In the hills of Ein Karem the magnificent Hadassah-Hebrew University Medical Center, with its school and hospital, had taken shape. But now there were only memories of the hospitals that Hadassah had set up after the Arabs slaughtered a convoy of doctors and nurses on their way to the hospital on Mount Scopus.

Many years had passed since Jerusalem had lain under siege, but the marks of that agony were still in the Commercial Center, where the Arabs had first launched their attack. In the quiet of Shabbat, we walked silently past the yet broken walls and ripped-up streets, each of them a landmark in the siege, remembering how every shell had torn the city like a talon of a beast tearing at the city's throat; remembering how Jerusalem had been like a man with creeping paralysis sitting on a mountaintop; remembering how the children had picked grasses for food; remembering that any community but a community of madmen would have given up. But they held on. And now we were celebrating the Shabbat.

We walked on to Zion Square, past all the new projects for improving Jerusalem that the late Mayor Gershon Agron, publisher of the Jerusalem *Post*, had begun. Tomorrow night after sunset, Zion Square would look like New York's Times Square on New Year's Eve. Most of Jerusalem's hundred and seventy-one thousand people, newcomers and old residents, seem to come into Zion Square to end Shabbat. They go to the movies, sit in the cafés, window-shop, or just see who else is out walking. New immigrant mothers proudly wheel their baby carriages in the road; and youngsters walk six or seven abreast, arms locked, singing at the top of their lungs. Few cars can drive through this sea of swarming humanity on Saturday night. But now, on Friday, no car drove in the quiet of Shabbat.

"Who would have dreamed," the visitor from England asked, wonderingly, "that I would live long enough to see these sights?"

He turned to some strangers walking down the Sabbath-filled street and said, as though this were the most joyous prayer in the world, and the word *Jew* a word filled with new dignity:

"*Shabbat shalom, Yiden.*"

6: Hebrew as She Is Spoke

THE OFFICIAL language is Hebrew. Not Yiddish, the language of the Middle High Germans, which the Jews adopted in the Middle Ages and enriched in their migrations, but Hebrew, the language of the Bible. The historic connection with the land meant a connection with the language too. They took the tongue of Solomon's love songs and Moses' Laws and made it the language of a new state, of bus drivers and farmers and statesmen. They made it so alive that it could be used by soldiers on the Arab fronts and by diplomats in world assemblies.

A ride in a bus in Israel is like a ride through Biblical Babel. Straphangers hanging on for dear life speak French, German, English, Hungarian, Bulgarian, Polish, or Yiddish. Arabs in *keffiyehs* (head kerchiefs) and Yemenite women in embroidered pants, talking Arabic, sit next to people who speak Hebrew with all accents, including the Scandinavian.

The effort to make everyone speak Hebrew brought on a crop of humor. During the fighting with the Arabs in Jerusalem, an old lady sat huddled in a bus while Arab shots whizzed all around. She put her hands to her head and shouted indignantly:

"*Dort schiesst man, un hier redt man Ivrit!*" (Over there they're shooting and here they're talking Hebrew!)

Some of the Germans of Hitler's aliyah found Hebrew an almost impossible language to master. They tell the story of a German Jew drowning in the sea at Nahariya who shouted "*Ezra, ezra!*" (Help, help!)

Another German Jew, walking along the beach, saw him and shouted back:

"*Ivrit hast Du gelernt? Schwimmen hättest Du lernen sollen!*" (Hebrew you've learned? You should have learned to swim!)

Yet Israel, just as America, had to have a single language. Even before the modern pressure cooker began to whistle, the Jews of the various aliyahs spoke not only Hebrew but about twenty-seven other languages. The two main ones were Yiddish and Ladino, the language of the Sephardic Jews, who were driven out of Spain in 1492 and who settled in the vast domains of the Ottoman Empire. The Western Jews spoke no Ladino, the Sephardim no Yiddish.

It took a dreamer and a fanatic, Eliezer Ben Yehuda, to prove to the Jews that the people of the Book should speak the language of the Book. The Jews had never stopped studying and reading Hebrew; now they began to use it to buy bread and sugar and shoes. Newspapers appeared in Hebrew. In a single generation, Hebrew became the language of the Jewish population of Palestine.

The people began to change their names into Hebrew, largely to remove the stigma of old ghetto names. Soon there were so many thousands of changes that some wit suggested putting out a book to be called Who Was Who. The trend toward Hebrew names was started by the prime minister, who had long ago changed his name from David Green to David Ben-Gurion (Ben in Hebrew means "son of"). After independence, name changing took place almost every day, with personal notices in the newspapers to let friends and creditors know. Moshe Shertok, the first foreign minister, became Moshe Sharett (Sharett means "servant"—servant of the people). Ambassador Eliahu Epstein became Eliahu Elath; Rabbi Fishman became Rabbi Maimon. Golda Myerson, the former schoolteacher from Milwaukee who became a chicken farmer in Palestine in the 1920's, then Israel's first minister to the U.S.S.R., and then the world's only woman foreign minister, changed her name to Golda Meir.

The greatest change, of course, was in the name of the land— from Palestine to Israel. The name Palestine came from the Philistines, who disappeared some three thousand years ago after their defeat by David. The name Israel first occurred in the Bible when Jacob wrestled with the angel. He changed his name from Jacob to Israel, which means literally "contender with God." Later it became the name of the northern Hebrew kingdom. Before the new name was decided on, there was the usual avalanche of discussion, debate, approval, and dissent. In the end Israel was selected—since the land had for thousands of years been called in Hebrew *Eretz Israel* (The Land of Israel).

S. Y. Agnon, generally considered Israel's greatest living novelist, made a startling statement to me one day in his home in Jerusalem.

"I think the creation of Hebrew," he said, "is an even greater miracle than the creation of the state."

Many people would disagree with his emphasis, but to Agnon the Hebrew language was almost as dear as life itself. He simplified and purified literary Hebrew by modeling it after the pure, limpid "neo-Hebraic" prose of the Mishnah, the traditional doctrine of the Jews.

Born in 1885, old and almost crushed by the siege of Jerusalem, Agnon is now living in complete asceticism. He has almost no furniture; his five thousand books are packed in a cellar in town. "I don't want to be a book slave," he said. Moving slowly between his old dark desk and a writing stand, he has been rewriting his earlier works that are out of print. Some of his books, including *Bridal Canopy*, *In the Heart of the Seas*, and *Days of Awe* have been translated from Hebrew into English.

"When you think of it," he said, "it is like something divine. Our poets who write in Hebrew are like monks. They have a very small reading circle. Yet they dedicate themselves to their divine service. Someday, I hope, Hebrew will be a world language and more and more people will read it and speak it everywhere."

The majority of immigrants do not know Hebrew. They are studying it in quick courses given everywhere—in the schools, in the army, even at the police stations. They need it, of course, for jobs, just as new immigrants in America needed English to get work.

A new type of school for teaching basic Hebrew to adults, called *Ulpan* (which means teaching), has had remarkable success. It is based on the method worked out by the U.S. Army in World War II to teach soldiers foreign languages. Some of the Ulpan courses are given in the evening for working people. Others are held at regular boarding schools, like the one in Nahariya, where new immigrants who are doctors, lawyers, and engineers spend several months of intensive work learning to read and write and eat and sleep in Hebrew. Mothers who come to child care clinics often are taught the language while they wait to have their children examined.

In a few days, every visitor and new immigrant picks up the most commonly heard words in the land. Shalom (peace) is the greeting that you hear more than any other word in Israel. "Goodbye, Mr. Chips" became on a movie marquee SHALOM, KHAVER CHIPS. "Thank you" is toda raba, and one of the expressions a visitor needs most is rega ekhad (pronounced ray-gah-hot), which literally means "one minute," but which can mean anything from an hour to a day. To get off a bus, you break a path toward the door, shout "Rega, rega, rega" as loudly as you can, run like mad, and jump off.

A tourist can get along quite well with English, very well with Yiddish and German, and, if he knows even a little Hebrew, he can find himself far along the road toward making friends.

But even if he knows Hebrew, he has to learn two things. First, the accent may be strange to him. He has probably been speaking Hebrew with an Ashkenazic accent, the accent of the West. In Israel, Hebrew is spoken with the Sephardic accent.

Second, he soon realizes that the language of the bus drivers and soldiers and children on the street is not so much Ivrit (Hebrew) as Sabrit, the language of the sabras, or native-born, a brand-new language called by some of the soldiers "Sleng."

Sleng, which, of course, is Sabrit for slang, is a wonderful language that is built while you run. Any good explosive onomatopoetic word can be dropped in the grab bag. It is made up of English, French, Russian, Yiddish, German, Arabic, and any other language, with a switch into Hebrew syntax.

Sleng can be divided into three categories.

1. Pure Hebrew of which the meaning is corrupted. E.g., "Nidback l' shinaim" means literally "It's glued to the teeth." In Sabrit it means "delicious."

2. English words, phrases, and idioms translated whole into Hebrew. E.g., "Get cracking" becomes tistadek, which means

"Split yourself up in small pieces." During the early days of the Arab-Jewish War, American students, mostly ex-G.I.'s, who had been studying at the Hebrew University, spent their evenings translating American slang into Hebrew Sleng. Phrases like "big wheel," "eager beaver," and others have become part of the new language, literally translated.

3. Words brought over intact from another language with varia-tions on the accent and a jovial broadening of the usage.

One of the most common words is *puntcher*, from the American "puncture," though it has nothing to do with a tire. Anything that goes wrong, from putting a slip on backward to being fired, is a *puntcher*.

A hitch-hike is a *tremp*, from the British "tramp," and a *trempiste* is a boy who rides on his thumb. Transportation is such a problem in the new state that the roads are full of *trempistim* (note the *im*, Hebrew plural ending for nouns) who queue up at various points, while an M.P. stops every military vehicle and any civilian vehicle and gets the *trempiste* a *tremp*.

Qvacker, pronounced like "qvack" in Donald Duck, is the name for almost any cereal. It comes from "*Qvacker* Oats."

A *schwitzer* (from the German *Schwaetzer*, for a man who talks a lot) is someone who runs around in a fury, talks constantly of how much he does, makes everyone mad, and gets practically noth-ing accomplished.

For me, the most descriptive word in the language is *nudnick*. Brought over by the Russian Jews, the word is used for anybody who is a bore. There are wonderful variations on *nudnick*. A *phud-nick* is a *nudnick* with a Ph.D.; a *shudnick* is a *nudnick* who says "Should I—shouldn't I?"

The most accomplished Slengists are the Israel soldiers. They look down with rare contempt upon the grammarians who are building modern Hebrew out of the Bible and who thumb through the Old Testament to find something in Isaiah or Jeremiah that resembles a jeep, which in Sleng is a "jip."

"So what?" or "Never mind" is *malesh*, which every G.I. in

Cairo or Casablanca learned, and which must be spoken with the Arabic shrug of the right shoulder.

Here is a list of words and expressions built from languages all over the world and spoken by accomplished Slengists:

artiste n. A man who never does any work and gets away with it. In the Israel army there are two kinds of people, *artistes* and soldiers.

beck-ex n. The back axle of a car. A *beck-exel* is a small *beck-ex*. A front axle is a *front beck-ex*, and a small front axle is a *front beck-exel*.

Ben-Gurionchik n. An affectionate name for a child born at the time the British slowed down Jewish immigration. Ben-Gurion, then as now the political leader, urged mothers to defy the British by having large families. It was a kind of immigration from within.

blintze n. (Russian) A pancake. But since nothing is simple in Israel, there is a constant lively debate on whether to call a pancake *blintze, melintze, blinitzi, blintshe, blintzke,* or *blintsess.*

bnei dodenu n. (lit. the sons of our uncles) Arabs.

chizbat n. (from the Arabic *chizib*) Tall stories told especially by soldiers; derived from the Arab custom of sitting around a campfire telling true stories—but with rich embroidery.

Chizbatron n. (from *chizbat* and the Hebrew *teatron,* the theater) The U.S.O. of Israel.

dreher n. (German, lit. a twister) A man who wangles himself in and out of situations, usually with success.

eisen a. (German) Colossal, terrific, "super."

eisen beton a. (lit. iron concrete) Supercolossal.

festukes n. (Italian, pistachio) Peanuts; what little boys call little girls.

finjan n. (Arabic) An Arab coffeepot. Young Israelis sit around a *finjan* the way young Americans sit around a campfire.

fresh n. Salmon, because in some farm colonies all the salmon cans from America had a large word, FRESH, printed across them.

jedda n. (Arabic) A smart fellow, a sharp cookie.

jip n. The most popular vehicle in Israel.

jokair n. (English, joker) An Englishman.

khabibi n. (Arabic) Darling, sweetie; "Ya *Khabibti*"—"Hi toots."

khevre n. The gang.

khutzpeh n. A combination of cheek and guts; sassy; a man who murders his father and mother and then pleads for mercy on the grounds that he is an orphan.

kolbo n. (Hebrew, lit. all in him) A department store; in a kibbutz, the communal dish for olive pits, these being tossed into the dish from all ends of the table, with a sharpshooter's ping.

kolboynick n. (from *kolbo*) A jack-of-all-trades. A kolboynick differs from an expert, who knows more and more about less and less, in knowing less and less about more and more.

kumsitz n. (German, lit. come sit) Informal gathering, usually around a *finjan*.

leekhol puzmaq v. (Hebrew, lit. to eat a stocking) To be bitterly disappointed.

lekaleps v. (English) To collapse.

lekashkesh bekumkum v. (Hebrew, lit. to drum a teakettle, translated from the Yiddish *hacken a chaynik*) To talk nonsense.

lenadned v. (lit. to rock) To bore, to annoy by being a nudnick.

letsaftsef v. (Hebrew, lit. to whistle) Not to give a hoot.

lo fidaltee (from the Yiddish *nit gefeedelt*, lit. not playing with the violin) Sour grapes; so I didn't succeed; a fellow can try.

masmayr n. (lit. a nail) A man whom everyone hammers on the head, a poor fool. See *schlimmazel*.

matsav ruakh n. (Hebrew, lit. state of mind) The blues.

mea akhuz a. (lit. 100 per cent) Mission accomplished, everything O.K. *Eisen mea akhuz* is supercolossal.

meshuge a. Crazy.

meshugayim l'sport n. Sport fans.

messtink n. Mess tin.

namier n. (lit. a leopard, a word formed from the first letters of *nudnick madrega rishona*) Nudnick first class.

nudnick n. A pest, an ear bender. The difference between a summer *nudnick* and a winter *nudnick* is that you can tell a summer *nudnick* right away, but it takes a little longer with a winter *nudnick*. You have to wait until he removes his coat.

nylon n. Terrific, marvelous. See *eisen*.

paskudniak n. (Polish) Nasty fellow, good for nothing. (Was used recently with great effect in the Knesset, the Israel parliament.)

pkak n. (Hebrew, lit. stopper, cork) In a kibbutz, a man who has no specialty and is used for odd jobs, particularly as a "stopper" to replace others.

puntcher n. (English, puncture) Everything that goes wrong.

Qvacker, n. (from Quaker Oats) Nearly any cereal.

sabra n. (lit. cactus) Native-born Israeli, thorny outside but sweet and juicy within.

Sabrit n. The slang of the sabras.

schlemihl n. (German) Bull in a china shop.

schlimmazel n. (German) A poor fool who has only bad luck. The difference between a *schlemihl* and a *schlimmazel* is that a *schlemihl* is the man who spills the hot soup on the *schlimmazel's* pants.

schwitzer n. (German) A man who talks but does nothing.

tremp n. (English, tramp) A lift, a hitch-hike.

trempiste n. The man who takes a *tremp*.

Tziyonut n. (pronounced Tsee-o-noot) The boring conversation of an intellectual *nudnick*, derived from the word *Zionism*, which you almost never hear in Israel except in this connection.

Yecke n. German Jew.

yotze li mehaaf (Hebrew, lit. it comes out of my nose) It bores me (because of repetition).

zift n. (Hebrew and Arabic, lit. pitch) Mess; it reeks.

Another language spoken in Israel is Pinglish. Pinglish is Palestine English, born during the Mandate; it is English translated from Yiddish or German or Hebrew idioms. It is seen at its best on signs printed in both Hebrew and Pinglish.

A butcher has the gory information strung across his shop: I AM KILLING MYSELF TWICE A DAY.

A billboard on a road in Haifa, showing a torso properly bras-sièred and corseted, announces: CORSET SALOON.

A woman's dress shop declares solicitously: WOMEN CAN HAVE FITS HERE BY APPOINTMENT.

A doctor calls himself: SPECIALIST FOR WOMEN AND OTHER DIS-EASES.

Another doctor's shingle reads: DR. BLIND—EYE SURGEON.

And in a Jerusalem garden, a corsetière's sign says: CORSETS MADE TO ORDER. ENTRANCE FROM THE REAR.

Ivrit, Sabrit, Yiddish, English, Pinglish, and good humor are all applied rigorously to the situations and problems of life in Israel.

In Tel Aviv, they tell of two lions who escaped from the zoo. One of them said to the other, "Now you go to the Negev. There are a lot of people there; you won't have any difficulty getting food. I'll stay here and see how I make out around Tel Aviv. We'll both meet at this same spot in ten days and discuss our plans some more."

After ten days, the two lions met. The Tel Aviv lion was fat; his face was content. The Negev lion's ribs stuck right through his skin.

"What happened to you?" the Tel Aviv lion asked. "You look famished."

"Well, the Negev had a lot of people, like you said. But they had guns. It's dangerous. They can shoot you. So I starved. But what happened to you? You look wonderful."

"Oh, I had a fine time. Every morning at eight I went to the government offices and ate five officials and nobody missed them."

An elderly couple arrived in Jerusalem during the water rationing. The wife complained to her husband that the apartment they had received was fine but that water flowed from the tap only one day a week.

Her husband was reassuring. "Don't worry, dear," he said. "The rest of the week the tap is reserved for milk and honey."

Reilly, an Irishman from America, went to Israel to live. One day an old friend from America arrived and saw Reilly drinking an Israel brandy and soda.

"Reilly," he said, "and what are you doing in Israel?"

"I'm living the life of Cohen."

Some months after independence, an American visitor brought a blue-blooded boxer pup from Israel to America. At the proper time, he took it to a kennel club on Long Island.

"I want to breed my dog," he told the manager, and presented the papers from Israel, showing the dog's long pedigree.

"I'm terribly sorry we can't help you. The American Kennel Society hasn't yet recognized Israel."

The late Chief Rabbi Isaac Herzog, once Chief Rabbi of Ireland, was talking with his good friend Eamon De Valera.

"A basic trait that our people have in common," Rabbi Herzog said, "is that the Irish don't know Gaelic and the Jews don't know Hebrew."

Austerity in Israel, called *tzena*, became a way of life. Queues formed all over the country and became, inevitably, material for humor.

A new immigrant complained to another new immigrant: "I'm sick of it. I queue up for food. I queue up for a ration book. I queue up for a medical examination. I'm going to shoot Ben-Gurion."

The next day his friend met him on the street. "Well, how did you make out?"

"I took my gun. I waited until dark. Then I went to Ben-Gurion's house. But there was such a long queue waiting to shoot him that I got disgusted and went home."

The Israelis are forever poking fun at the way they are seen in the eyes of the rest of the world. They sent a few jet pilots to England for a brief period. An English officer saw their insignia, I.A.F., and asked what it stood for.

"The Israeli Air Force," they said.

"Isn't it the Royal Israeli Air Force?" he asked.

"No. We're an independent state now."

"Of course. I remember you kicked Farouk out a couple of years ago."

The borders of the state are so close together that the conductor of the railroad that connects Haifa, Tel Aviv, and Jerusalem walked through the cars crying: "Ladies and gentlemen, please do not put your heads out of the state."

During the Sinai campaign, when the Israelis captured an Egyptian warship, the *Ibrahim al Awar*, which was attempting to shell Haifa, one Israeli asked another, "What's happened to the Egyptian crew?"

The other Israeli answered, "We sent them back to Egypt to bring us another warship."

One of the stories that swept Israel and the United States was that Kennedy and Khrushchev were about to sign a peace treaty.

"There is only one condition left," Khrushchev said. "You must publicly announce that Adam and Eve were Communists."

Kennedy said he would have to think about it. He telephoned the Cardinal, who said he would have to give it some thought. "Why don't you call the Pope?" the Cardinal suggested.

But the Pope, too, wanted to give it some thought. "Why don't you call Ben-Gurion?" he suggested. "He's an expert on the Old Testament."

Kennedy telephoned Ben-Gurion, who answered without hesitation, "Of course Adam and Eve were Communists. They walked around naked; they ate only apples; and they thought they were in Paradise."

During the fighting in Sinai, Russian-speaking Israeli troops in the Israeli spearheads were able to converse easily by radio in Russian with Russian tank commanders mixed with the Egyptian forces, sources said. One Israeli officer started this conversation by radio, in Russian:

"How are you?"

"Terrible over here," replied a Russian, in Russian. "How are you?"

"We're doing fine, just fine," replied the Israeli.

"Well, for goodness sake come on over and help us," replied the Russian.

A young soldier back on leave from Sinai was talking about his adventures. "And you know all the people who ran the job were young. My commander was twenty-four."

His father was a little piqued and pointed out that Mr. Ben-Gurion, who was responsible for the campaign, was seventy.

The boy said, "No, you know what they say of him in the army? He's just two young men of thirty-five."

The Russians come in for a great deal of kidding. There is a story that soon after Krushchev revealed Stalin's anti-Semitism, he sent a cable to President Eisenhower. "Ike, will you take Stalin's body?"

President Eisenhower cabled back: "We don't take Commies, dead or alive."

Krushchev sent a cable to Anthony Eden: "Will you take Stalin's body?"

Eden cabled: "Sorry, but we're embarrassed by the Suez affair. Can't take body."

Krushchev sent a cable to Ben-Gurion: "Will you take Stalin's body?"

Ben-Gurion answered: "Of course we'll take his body. But remember this is the country of the Resurrection."

Krushchev cabled back: "No go. Have decided to keep body in Kremlin."

An operations officer of an unnamed country suffered a nervous breakdown and started the atomic war. Civilization was totally destroyed. Only one small monkey survived, somewhere in the Middle East. When the noise died down he crept out of a cave looking for something to eat. Presently a female monkey came out of another cave. "I'm so terribly hungry," said the first monkey.

"Oh, I've got an apple here, have a bite," she said.

"Good heavens," said the first, "are we going to start all that again?"

A man from one of the frontier villages came to Jerusalem to consult an official in one of the national institutions. It was afternoon and he wandered down a long passage with open doors to empty rooms. At last he found a woman washing the floor. "Don't they work here in the afternoon?" he asked.

"Oh, no," she answered, "it's in the morning they don't work, they just sit at desks. In the afternoon they don't come."

An American tourist asked an Israeli, "How do you say hello in Hebrew?"

"*Shalom*," he said.

"How do you say good-by?"

"*Shalom*," he said.

"Then how do you know whether you mean hello or good-by?"

"That's just it. We don't know whether we're coming or going."

Two people are talking. One is an optimist, one a pessimist.

The pessimist says, "I can't see how we can get out of this mess."

The optimist says, "Look at Germany. She lost the war. Then the U.S. sent Marshall Plan aid, Point Four, built up her economy, and she's better off now than she was before. So let's declare war on the U.S. After we lose, they will give us the same aid they gave Germany."

The pessimist says, "And what if we win?"

During the Sinai campaign, a British officer approached Ben-Gurion to ask if Britain could borrow Israel's chief of staff, General Moshe Dayan, for a week.

Ben-Gurion was furious. "If I let you have Dayan, you'd need him for only twenty-four hours."

A woman went to see a psychiatrist in Tel Aviv.

"What is wrong with you, madam?" the doctor asked her.

"I talk to myself all the time."

"That's nothing. Everybody talks to himself at some time or other."

"But Doctor, you don't know what a nudnick I am."

Russia's Sputnik, of course, did not go unnoticed. Israel, according to the latest top-secret information, is now launching not one but two flying saucers. One for meat, and one for dairy.

In Czechoslovakia, according to the Israelis who would like to help the people escape from the Iron Curtain, a schoolteacher was enlarging on the marvels produced by Mother Russia. "This year," she said, "we have produced a satellite moon that flies in outer space around the world. But that is not all because next year we will probably be able to fly to the moon. And in the year after we will be able to go to Mars. And even that is not all, because in three or four years we will be able to go to Venus, or even to Jupiter."

At this point a small boy raised his hand and said, "And when can we go to Vienna?"

A delegation from Burma came to Israel with the Burmese prime minister, U Nu. They were greatly impressed by the progress they saw everywhere. Their problem, they pointed out to the Israelis, was to clear the jungle, while Israel's problem was to conquer the desert. When they were taken to the Hills of Judea, where tens of thousands of tiny trees were being planted on the ancient eroded soil, the Burmese said solicitously to the Israelis, "Pull out those little trees right away. If you let them grow big, you'll never get them out."

Israel adores its army, but the people cannot resist poking fun at it. "Do you know," they ask, "how Safad, the second holiest city in Israel, was saved during the war of independence?"

"How?"

"In a natural way, and in a miraculous way."

"How is that?"

"In a natural way—God helped us. In a miraculous way—the army chased the Arabs out of the city."

7: The Kibbutz

THE FARMS of Israel are like farms nowhere in the world, shaped by a people hungering for roots and the immortality of land.

To most of its pioneers, the thing of greatest beauty in Israel—its very meaning—lies in the kibbutz, the unique farm pattern the Jews developed. The kibbutz, a small or large village of farmers (and pronounced, not like the sidewalk superintendent at a card game, but with the accent on the butz) is Israel's mark of achievement. The return from the ghettos was essentially a return to the land. And because these were idealists who were returning, they chose a form of communal life based on perhaps the most Christian ideals in the world. No one was to grow rich from the sweat of another man's face.

In the kibbutz, the farmers live as one family. They eat their meals together in a communal dining hall; their children sleep together in children's houses; they work in groups together all day in the fields and in the kibbutz industries; then they meet again at night for discussions and self-probing, for lectures and committee meetings, for recitations by visiting actors of the poetry of Nathan Alterman or Leah Goldberg or other living Israel poets, for communal songs and the wild, high-spirited joining of hands in the hora, dancing round and round, faster, wilder, more breathless, until they fall into their chairs in laughing, red-cheeked exhaustion.

The people who come to live in the kibbutz are tall or short, lean or fat, fair or dark. Some are serious-faced and intellectual-looking, as though they had just walked out of the lamp-lit reading rooms of a public library. Some are sturdy, with bulging muscles like truck drivers' or wrestlers'; some are long-haired poets. Some have been lawyers in Boston and Kovno, engineers in Buffalo and

Rio de Janeiro, and so many ex-doctors and ex-Ph.D.s from central Europe have gone into chicken farming (though privately, for the most part) that if anyone shouts "Herr Doktor," a whole work crew may shout back, "Who wants me?"

The kibbutz does not level these people who have come from everywhere. They remain what they were at four and five and nine, but they are forged by the trial-by-fire intimacy of communal life.

They live a stoic, Spartan life—idealistic intellectual farmers who draw even the shirts on their backs from the community storeroom. They own almost nothing, except perhaps some books and a radio. Whatever profit their kibbutz makes in selling their products is plowed back into the kibbutz. These are people building not only for themselves, but for their children.

Yet the kibbutz (sometimes also called kvutzah) is not the basis of Israel's economy. Israel is a capitalist country with cooperative experimentation. A new farmer coming into Israel today can choose to farm as a complete capitalist or as a semiprivate farmer or as a member of a cooperative. He may even choose to try out kibbutz life and, if he dislikes it, leave. Unlike the Soviet collective farm, kibbutzniks, carefully voted on before they enter the kibbutz, are free to leave for good whenever they choose.

The young pioneer of the kibbutz, the khalutz, is the symbol of the founding father in Israel, and the khalutza, the pioneer woman, the symbol of the founding mother. They are Israel's equivalent of the pioneers who crossed the American West in covered wagons. There is no question—if there is a State of Israel today, it is not only because there were Jewish cities but because Jewish khalutzim went into the swamps, drained the malarial marshes (often dying in the process), pulled up rocks with their bare hands and their fingernails, planted trees, and built the early farm settlements.

In most pioneering countries, like the United States and Alaska, pioneers came upon fertile soil and in the first flush of pioneering cut down the trees to build their settlements. In Israel, where nearly everything is topsy-turvy, where middle-class merchants have become street cleaners and farmers, even the pattern of pioneering is being reversed. Here the pioneers come back to the land, but they have to create the land as they go along. They have to plant the trees. They have to make the arid soil fertile again.

The kibbutz has been compared with the Soviet collective farm, but the kibbutz developed at the turn of the century long before the czar was overthrown. It was founded on the democratic ideals of freedom and equality then sweeping Europe. It grew out of necessity. It was built as defense against the Arabs and offense against the land. A farmer and his family dared not go out alone into the Galilean hills or the Negev. A group working shoulder to shoulder could protect each other as they dug some of the most unpromising soil in the world. Actually they had little choice. The barren soil, the unrelenting sun, would have broken the back of the most rugged individualist. Collective living was a practical technique for taming this frontier.

The kibbutz was the Jewish state long before the State was born. It was a Jewish island in the midst of a hostile Arab sea. The khalutzim built their settlements like a necklace of pearls north of Dan and south of Beersheba. On land bought by the Jewish National Fund, from money collected in nickels and dimes in little blue boxes that hung in Jewish kitchens around the world, the pioneers built for food, for industries, and for defense. They built even better than they knew. The U.N. map of partition was essentially a map drawn, like a Sunday picture puzzle, linking the little dots that were Jewish villages and farms.

The war and the need for security and the need to house new immigrants more than doubled the need of farms. The corridor to Jerusalem is being cushioned for defense and settlement with semiprivate and collective farms. The dangerous Arab borders are being settled by young pioneers. There are still thousands of acres of land, especially in the Negev, waiting to be reclaimed.

"There is no room to swing a cat in Palestine," Sidney Webb, Britain's colonial secretary, told Dr. Weizmann in 1929. "It is full. Nobody can enter. What is the good of asking me for immigration certificates?"

"Count up the number of cats," Dr. Weizmann told the Anglo-American Committee of Inquiry on Palestine seventeen years later. "Count up the number of cats which have been swung since that time, the number of immigrants, the number of villages, the number of industries which have been created, and judge whether the country has been impoverished or just the opposite, and see whether it is so chockablock that there is no room for anybody to enter."

The young khalutzim who swung the cats taught the world a new lesson: that each new immigrant carries his own "absorptive capacity" like a pack on his back. Each immigrant clears a few inches of the wasteland. Each immigrant, by having children, by needing to eat and dress and read newspapers, gives the wheel of commerce an extra turn. For the Jews in Israel, land means life and no land means death.

The pioneers in Israel have a twofold dream—to reclaim the ancient deserted Home Land and thereby to reclaim themselves. To leave eastern Europe in the three decades before Hitler meant not only enormous courage and adventure, but often a complete break with their families. In Poland just before World War II, I met Jewish families who held funeral services for their sons and daughters emigrating to Israel. Now most of those families are ashes and the only survivors are those who left home.

Within the kibbutz, too, the young émigrés broke with the past. Eagerly, they sacrificed individual comforts for the collective good. There was to be complete social, economic, and sex equality. Women were emancipated—and in their passion for the new freedom, they sometimes swung the pendulum to absurd extremes.

Emancipation seems always to demand excesses. Just as the suffragettes in England and America spent wasteful energy in smoking cigars and wearing bloomers to show that they were the equal of men, so the khalutz girls had to prove, through excesses, that they were just as strong and free and independent as the khalutz boys. They awoke at five-thirty in the morning to go into the fields, to lift heavy rocks, or to build roads through swamps and over wadis. Consciously, they rejected the comforts of middle-class life. One room. A bed. A crude table. Sometimes, but rarely, a crude chair. These were enough. No cosmetics. Pull your hair straight back. Look like a man. Wear rough working clothes. Rush in and out of the communal dining room. Wolf down your food. Get back to important things. This is the romance. Build against time. Build for history.

The sound you heard in the kibbutz was the twentieth-century sound of old gods tumbling, of science replacing religion. There were, to be sure, a number of orthodox kibbutzim where the pioneers lived completely by the Torah while they farmed co-operatively. But in most of the kibbutzim, the farmers revolted against nearly all the traditional forms of orthodoxy—to the horror of the rabbis and the fundamentalists and the delight of the liberals and agnostics, eager to prove the separation of church and state. If need be they worked on Shabbat. They abandoned nearly all religious services. To some of the Israel bloomer girls, even the orthodox marriage ceremony seemed nothing but a hangover of medievalism.

Rumors have been spread that everything is communal in the kibbutz, even the women. But "collectivization of women" is sheer nonsense. A union made in a kibbutz, when two people, married by a visiting rabbi, go to the Committee on Housing and ask for a room together, is as holy in the kibbutz as a union made in the rabbinical court in Jerusalem or Tel Aviv.

Yet, after all, marriage in a kibbutz is different from marriage in a city. In a kibbutz a woman does not need to marry for convenience, or for economic security. She need not worry whether her fiancé has a good enough job to support her and start a family. She can marry purely for love. The kibbutz society takes care of all the family's economic needs. Since the most stable members are generally the happily married ones, the kibbutz constantly gives its young marriageable men and women long vacations to go out and find mates.

Ultimately, in America, the suffragettes grew wise and learned that they could be emancipated without rejecting their femininity; so too in Israel, the khalutza learned that she could rebuild the Jewish land and still be feminine and perhaps even a little traditional. She realized that heavy manual work was not only hard on

her body, but on her looks. She was aging more quickly than her
sister in town. The kibbutz changed its work pattern and women
their back-breaking tasks. They took softer jobs in the vineyards
and the fields; they worked in the laundry, the kitchen, the sewing room, the children's quarters, the storeroom. They hung curtains and drapes in their windows, pictures on their walls; they
put gay spreads on their single-sized beds, and outside their doors
planted little gardens with climbing roses and anemones. At first
surreptitiously, later more openly, some began to visit beauty
parlors on their trips to town. After the workday, they showered
and spent quiet, peaceful hours playing with their children on the
lawns.

On Friday nights, they put white cloths on the wooden tables
in the communal dining room and the smell of freshly baked
Shabbat bread filled the whole settlement. The children, allowed
to stay up a little longer than on week nights, sang and recited,
told stories and danced the gay, swift hora. Little synagogues were
built for the old parents who had gotten out of Europe in time
and came to live in the kibbutz in the special parents' quarters.
The nonorthodox kibbutz even celebrated the holidays that had
a national rather than a religious significance, the traditional festivals of the seasons and of Jewish history in the Bible land.

For single women, the kibbutz is a kind of paradise. Whenever
the demand is greater than the supply, women have the advantage.
In most of the kibbutzim, men outnumber women two to one;
in some kibbutzim, three to one.

It was when the khalutzim bore children that they knew that
they had found a kind of immortality. The kibbutz child helped
cement the link they had forged with the land.

Today the kibbutz seems to revolve around its children. Every
kibbutz has toddlers, with black hair, blond hair, red hair, running
around like chickens. Nurses and teachers assigned to the children's quarters take care of them; mothers come into the nursery
to nurse their infants at fixed hours. Parents play with their children after work and at night each mother tucks her own children
into bed in the dormitories in the children's quarters. The most

beautiful sight to me in a kibbutz is the sight of babies' cribs being wheeled into the sun each bright morning. All day little naked
babies laugh and coo and sleep and demand attention as they
drink the Israel sun through their skin. The kibbutz sabras are
the sweethearts of the whole settlement. When children run into
the dining room, they are stopped at nearly every table as women
laugh with them, or men toss them into the air. Shabbat is children's day in the kibbutz, and all day fathers and mothers walk and
hike and romp through the fields with their children.

Violent debates rage on whether children should sleep under
the same roof with their parents or be separated from them immediately after birth. In most kibbutzim, infants, brought back
to the kibbutz from the city hospitals, are placed in nurseries and
sleep in special children's quarters. In the discussions about that
once brave new experiment, there are those who argue that kibbutz parents see their children more often than parents do in
an average middle-class home. They see them when they are not
tired, after they are showered and rested. They see them all day on
Shabbat. The children are less likely to fall victims to an Oedipus
complex, less likely to be tormented by abnormal dependence
upon a mother who scolds bitterly one moment and caresses hysterically another. They are less likely, as they grow up, to be tormented with guilt in their mother-son relationship.

But others argue that children who are denied the intensity of
constant mother attention and mother love become colorless, in-
stitutionalized children, that in order to have genuine security,
children must sleep under the same roof as their parents. Some of
the kibbutzim, like Kfar Blum, are now experimenting. No longer
do children of the same age sleep in one room; older ones are
mixed with younger ones, as in any average family. In other kibbutzim, like Dagania A, an old and very prosperous kibbutz, the
children stay with their parents until they are six.

The arguments grow more heated each day. I must say that I
never saw any lack of mother love in the kibbutzim. And nothing
seems funnier to kibbutz mothers than the naïve questions of

tourists who ask them, in all seriousness, "Can you recognize your own children?"

As the sabra outgrows his diapers, he graduates from the kibbutz nursery into the kibbutz kindergarten, then the kibbutz elementary school, and from there to a secondary school in one of the larger kibbutzim or in town. If he shows talent, he goes to the Hebrew University or the Technion in Haifa, or to a naval school. All his expenses are paid by the kibbutz. At seventeen he comes to a three-way crossroad. He can go to the city and spend a year at the kibbutz' expense in industry or a vocational school; he can remain in the kibbutz and join it as a full-fledged member at eighteen; or he can go off with a group of youngsters and found his own kibbutz.

Just as you can pick out an American abroad, so you can nearly always pick out a kibbutz sabra. He is generally handsome. Frequently he has muscles like a circus strong man. Sometimes he sports a huge handle-bar mustache, sometimes a roguish beard; sometimes he is cleanshaven. But his face, hirsute or not, is the sunburned face of the desert and the hills and the sea. He walks with pride in his land. His parents created this soil and his roots are in it deep. He has fought for his land.

It was 1939. Sixty young people had settled down to build a home in the desert, at the gateway to the Negev. They called it "Negba," which means "Southward Ho." They built a huge water tower that looked like a stone tub on thin stilts, sunk into a concrete pillbox. Its tank stood ninety feet high on four slender legs. The water with which they were to conquer the desert was piped into the tank and from there flowed through six-inch pipes to the showers, the dining hall, and the sixty acres of land they now were cultivating.

Negba flourished. Its settlers helped feed Palestine with long seedless grapes. Their orchards were ripe with fruit. Their desert waved with wheat and rye and oats and barley. Their enclosure grew until their farm village covered four acres, with white houses and lawns and gardens, cowbarns, chicken coops, and workshops.

For Negba was industrializing its agricultural economy, producing windows, doors, tables, and even knocked-down houses for little Negbas that were being built in the Negev.

Negba, by 1947 a village of three hundred and fifty people, was like a square green island in the rolling yellow desert. Near her lay friendly Arab villages; roads linked her with other Jewish colonies in the Negev.

In New York, it was Saturday evening, November 29, 1947. In Negba, it was 2 A.M. Sunday. The settlers were sitting in their dining hall, listening to their loud-speaker. Six thousand miles away, they heard thirty-three nations of the world, assembled in the highest legal body that civilization had yet created, vote "yes" to a Jewish state.

They pushed the tables aside, locked arms with each other, and, with tears streaming down their faces, danced the hora. They awakened all but the babies, so that even the little children would remember this as a great night in history. Five days later, three of Negba's boys were ambushed by Arabs and killed.

The wheels of international machinery, which had meshed together to create the Jewish state, were suddenly clogged with intrigue, double talk, and undisguised attempts at sabotage. The Jews knew they would have to fight for their freedom. Negba, like all the other kibbutzim, began preparing.

The war was the vindication of the kibbutz in Jewish history—if the kibbutz needed vindication. Nearly every kibbutz became a front line of defense. Nearly every farmer fought with his life for every inch of his own soil.

Negba declared a state of emergency and put her people on twenty-four-hour alerts. She built underground shelters and an underground hospital. She trained her people to shoot after dark. The guns were few, but the people said, "If God is willing, even a broom can shoot." Negba knew that she had to have underground reservoirs in case her fine water tank was destroyed. She had dug a hole for a swimming pool, with funds sent from America, and she turned it into a reservoir.

The kibbutz sabra, born of the land, healthy, laughing, secure

The Iraqi Jews fled to Israel from ancient Babylon in the largest human airlift in history

Prime Minister David Ben-Gurion and Avram Biran, former District Commissioner of Jerusalem

Moshe Sharett, first foreign minister, and the author

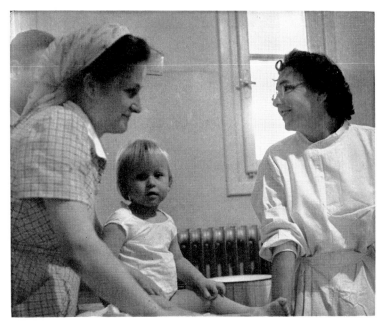

(*Top*) Dr. Pearl Ketcher examining an immigrant child in Hadassah's Nathan Straus Health Center in Jerusalem. (*Bottom*) Apprentice in the printing workshop of Hadassah's Louis D. Brandeis Vocational Center in Jerusalem

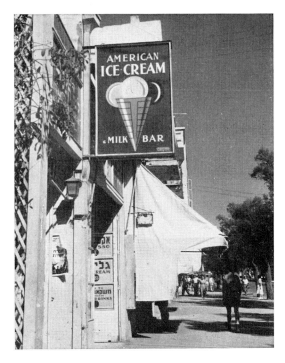

Israel has Yankee ways

Israel's children grow up learning the facts of life from Hollywood and Broadway

Negba became the military and strategic center of the Negev. West to east ran the vital Majdal-Faluja road, from Gaza to Jerusalem through Hebron. North to south ran the equally vital Julis-Kaukaba road, from Tel Aviv to the Negev. Whoever controlled that crossroad controlled the gateway to Tel Aviv, Jerusalem, Egypt, the Negev. The British, realizing as far back as 1941 how important Negba was, had built a fortress police station, called Iraq Suweidan, right on Negba's own soil, in the very middle of her wheat and rye and cornfields. Nothing had been more welcome then. Building it had given added income to Negba's people; it meant protection against Arab thieves and brigands and a fortress against a possible Nazi invasion of Palestine through Egypt.

But on the fourteenth day of May, 1948, the day that Israel was born, the Iraq Suweidan police station was taken over lock, stock, and barrel by the Moslem Brotherhood, the irregular Egyptian forces, who in turn handed it over to the Egyptian army.

The Egyptian army moved into the once friendly neighboring Arab villages of Beit Affa and Iraq Suweidan. Negba was frozen in by several thousand Arabs less than a mile away. She was cut off from the vital crossroad. She could move north only through the rear. She could no longer move southward.

In the desert, the Egyptians captured two Jewish colonies near Negba. To the beleaguered Jews, it seemed obvious that the Arabs were planning a blitzkrieg drive on Tel Aviv. If they could conquer Tel Aviv, the settlements would fall like a string of broken pearls.

In the south, there was one major obstacle on the Arab march to Rehovot and Tel Aviv. That obstacle was Negba. If Negba fell, the southern front would crumble. If Negba fell, the heart of the tiny state could be punctured. If Negba fell, the area in which Israel planned to settle new immigrants and create new industries would be lost. The Israel High Command sent orders to Big Itzkhak Dubnow, the commander: "Hold Negba until your last bullet and your last man."

At noon on the eighteenth of May, Negba, as always at noon,

stopped working. Most of the settlers dragged their feet to the sunny but abnormally quiet dining hall. They heard the roar of four British Spitfires buzzing over them.

Big Itzkhak, sitting in headquarters (a pillbox beneath the water tower), ran to help man the Bren guns. He stretched his right hand to show the planes to the five boys at the guns. A bomb dropped. Itzkhak and his companions were blown to pieces.

Five yards away was the packed dining hall. Obviously, the Arabs, who had often broken bread with the settlers, knew their noonday habits well.

The settlers ran for the trenches. For half an hour the Spitfires kept circling the village, flying low and spitting machine-gun fire. There was no answer from Negba. The first bomb had destroyed the only two Bren guns in the settlement.

The people were sure they would be surrounded now and wiped out. They knew the enemy would not content himself just with bombing and aerial machine-gunning. Kuba Wayland, who has now changed his name to Yaacov Vilan, was given full command. The village was divided into four sections with deputy commanders. In each section there were a number of posts, each with its own reservoir of water and food. The water was stored in tall milk cans. Eight or ten people were to relieve each other on twenty-four-hour duty. The khamseen, the hot desert wind, had already begun—an east wind that seems to bring mental depression in its wake.

At twilight four men, carrying the remains of Big Itzkhak and their five other neighbors, walked to a little eucalyptus grove and buried their dead. There were no speeches.

Far away in Tel Aviv, the Haganah High Command took a decision. Negba was the key to the desert. Negba must be helped. The men had just laid their leader in the hard-yielding earth when they heard four trucks approaching from the one dirt road still open, which lay under constant fire. A new detachment of Haganah troops had come to help them.

The silent Negev changed in a few hours into a blistering battlefield. Its sky was filled with birds of prey. Jackals howled around the barbed-wire fence, trying to get close to the dead cattle strewn in the fields. The sun rose over the Hebron Mountains and the desert.

At four o'clock on the afternoon of May 19, the battle for Negba began. The Jews knew the mentality of their neighbors. They suspected the Arabs believed they could take Negba without fighting, by killing it off with thirst. After shelling the water tower, the Egyptians sat back waiting for the Jews to die of thirst or surrender. The Jews did neither. The tall milk cans gave them their water. The hole for the swimming pool became their chlorinated reservoir and as long as their two wells worked water could be piped into the swimming hole directly.

A new style of life began in the desert, a life in which food and shellfire became the only things that mattered. The people moved out of their houses into the warren they had built beneath their soil. It was a life almost without water. Toilets were useless: field latrines were dug in scattered places. The only sunlight the people saw was the light that came in diagonal shafts through the sand-bagged entrances to the garrisoned village, which now lay completely submerged.

Days passed. They had no guns to start an offensive. They crouched in their hot shelters. The girls tried to make the underground life homelike. They prepared hot soup every day in the underground kitchens and ran with the pots through all the trenches under snipers' fire.

To help time pass, they began to play chess by telephone, one outpost competing against another. They even issued a mimeographed newspaper, called Kol Negba (The Voice of Negba). Kol Negba was received by the settlers and army people with joy; it was their first contact with the outside world, save for the homing pigeons, which kept bringing them letters from their children who had been evacuated.

For almost two weeks they lived under siege, expecting the Egyptians to break out of the police station at any moment and attack. They sent urgent coded messages to the High Command near Tel Aviv, asking for more reinforcements, for anything to use against tanks. All they had now were homemade Molotov cocktails —soda bottles filled with gasoline and a fuse. But the High Command was getting the same requests from the north and the center. Then one night, toward the end of May, reinforcements came. Three-inch mortars and one antitank Piat with ten shells were to hold off the enemy. Negba was prepared for a tank attack.

Having failed to thirst the village out, the Egyptians seemed determined now to burn it into surrender. On the first of June, they started a fire near the police station. The wind carried the fire across the fields. Negba realized the Arabs were clearing the fields for a major attack. At four the next morning, the underground settlers heard the earth explode. Trees were ripped apart and hung in shreds.

The barrage lasted for two long, loud hours. At six, Zev Birovnick, a young soldier standing watch on the shaking water tower, telephoned underground. "I see ten . . . no, twenty . . . wait, no . . . twenty-two armored vehicles—six of them moving from behind the police station." A shot almost drowned out his next words. ". . . fanning out. Encircling us from the west, east, south . . . infantry behind them. A lot of infantry. Looks like thousands. I can't estimate. Maybe . . ." His voice failed. Zev had been killed.

The tanks opened fire. The Arabs hit every house that Negba had built in her nine years. Every structure in the village seemed to be burning fiercely. Negba was ruptured with explosions.

Four Arab planes roared over the settlement, crackling the air with machine-gun fire. A key machine-gun crew reported they were short of ammunition. Kuba Wayland, the commander, turned to his prettiest runner, a lithe, sun-tanned, chestnut-haired dancer, Tzigane Hartman. Tzigane was eighteen. Her parents had been burned alive by the Nazis. Could he send Tzigane to certain death? She was the only one he could spare. Tzigane carried the ammunition and danced through the trenches. She crouched in the trenches, listened for Arab fire, detected its direction, and snaked her way in the opposite direction. No one saw Kuba wipe his cheek swiftly when Tzigane came back to headquarters alive.

In the middle of the morning, a message arrived at headquarters. Twenty-four Arab tanks were moving toward the settlement, toward its weakest defense point. One tank broke through the two inner barbed-wire fences and was almost on top of the trench leading to Post 5 when Tamara Weinfeld, one of Negba's first settlers, tossed a Molotov cocktail. Flames encircled the tank. The Arabs were killed.

The Egyptian infantry took positions lying on the desert, unable to advance on the village or retreat to the police station. Behind the infantry was another row of tanks, which turned tail and raced back toward the police station. The infantry was left completely unprotected. Overhead the airplanes continued to circle and machine-gun the settlement. Urek, one of the early settlers, put his light machine gun, an RK, on his shoulder and, standing near Post 5, shot three volleys at the planes. One of the planes caught fire.

At two in the afternoon, the Arabs withdrew. The first tank battle for Negba was over. A handful of some two hundred settlers had held out against more than one thousand Arabs equipped with tanks and planes and cannons.

But Negba was in ruins. Every house was shattered. The tractors and the farming tools were burned to a crisp. The factory was destroyed. The white children's home, where once more than a hundred children had played and sung and slept, was blasted open.

For miles around, the desert sky was lit up with the flames that consumed the corn and wheat and hay stored in sheds. Water was too precious to use in putting out the fire. Negba, the garden spot of the desert, smoldered in ruins for two weeks.

At this stage, the United Nations voted a month-long truce, but no one really believed that truce would lead to an armistice. They were right. Negba licked its wounds all that month. There was no time to rebuild the shattered village; every moment had to be used to dig more underground hospital space and more trenches; to store up water, food, ammunition; to prepare for the second round.

On July 9, the cease-fire ended. Negba waited underground for the next attack. It came July 12, at six in the morning—a coordinated bombing, infantry, and airplane attack that made the battle of the tanks on June 2 seem like a warming-up before the onslaught.

The Egyptians opened with a barrage of artillery, threw in a row of tanks, then artillery with a cover of Spitfires, and a screaming row of tanks and troops as a climax.

Negba's last road to Tel Aviv was cut off. The semicircle of Arabs that had surrounded the village was drawn full circle. Negba was caught in an iron ring.

Thirty-two Egyptian tanks maneuvered about, searching for a weak point in the village's defenses. But Negba had laid her own encirclement of antitank minefields. Seven Egyptian tanks were blown up. The men inside them were killed.

The Egyptian infantry surged down the road searching for soft spots. Israel's machine-gun fire mowed down the soldiers. The shrieking of the wounded and the dying on both sides roared across the high, long ping of bullets.

Egyptian artillery found the few weak arteries of life that were left. Some of their shells damaged Negba's sewerage pipes, still filled with old refuse and night soil. The sewage seeped into some of the trenches and made the runners' job a hideous one.

No food could be carried through the trenches during the day and Negba took energy from the chocolate and biscuits in emergency "iron" rations. Then the Arabs' artillery found another life artery—the aerials. Negba, encircled physically, was now cut off from the world for several hours.

Three waves of infantry had poured down on the village and been repulsed. Negba waited for the Arabs to return. At seven that evening, by radio, Kuba Wayland asked the Israel commander of the southern front to send water and ambulances to take Negba's forty wounded people to a hospital.

The commander answered that it was impossible to send anything until they had broken the iron ring that encircled Negba.

That night Israel troops from the northern desert stormed Hill 110. They were repulsed with heavy losses.

All the next day, the Arabs shelled Negba from every angle of the encirclement. At night again, the Israelis attacked Hill 110. This time they succeeded. The Arabs surrendered with all their ammunition, four Bren carriers, and two pieces of heavy artillery. The ring was broken.

Two hours later, the Jewish commander of the Egyptian front kept his word. American fire-engine trucks came with water. Three ambulances arrived. And, most welcome of all, mail came from the children.

On the night of July 13-14, Negba, still under immobilizing artillery fire from the Arabs, emerged from its trenches. The offensive had begun.

In three radial moves, Negba attacked the semicircle of the Arabs around them in the police station and the two villages of Beit Affa and Iraq Suweidan. They were thrown back. But a commando unit of jeeps rushed in from the east and overwhelmed the Arabs. Karatiya, a village lying behind the police station, surrendered swiftly to the army of jeeps and the concentrated weight on Negba was eased. The enemy went on the defensive.

"The lesson we learned," Kuba Wayland told me, "is that if you love your soil, if you never leave it, they cannot conquer you." The Jews had vindicated their return to the soil.

A year after the war, Negba was rebuilt. New houses went up. Roses blossomed. A new water tower, bigger than the old one, was erected. The old tower was kept standing as a national memorial. A new barn, a new garage and machine shop, and a new laundry were built, with equipment from America. The rolling, treeless land around the settlement was put under cultivation. Negba had come back to life.

The kibbutz sabra, fighting side by side with new immigrants and city sabras, had not only helped save the kibbutzim and the cities in the war of independence. He had fought in other wars. He helped turn back Rommel, led the ships of aliyah beth, ran up the hills to defend Jerusalem, and defeated Nasser's Sinai army.

Yet he was shaken by the wars. His is the dilemma of postwar youth with the special problems of Israel. Much of his childhood in the twenties and thirties had been interspersed with Arab riots. The one skyscraper on the skyline of his kibbutz was a watchtower; the houses in which he and his friends lived were hemmed in by barbed wire. Still, in some of the kibbutzim, he may have played with neighboring Arab children, or the children of Bedouins who wandered into the kibbutz. Perhaps they had exchanged gifts, a donkey maybe, or a dog.

The U.N. decision and the war for independence changed it all. The Arab was either an enemy trying to kill him or a refugee fleeing. A world was in upheaval and the kibbutz sabra lost some of his sure footing. It was happening all over the land. These were the dog days of the postwar period. Israel had to live with herself in the letdown. Her captains and majors became businessmen and bus drivers; her heroes were clerks in a dull office; her pretty girl sharpshooters pointed their trigger fingers at the keyboard of a typewriter, a piano, or an electric range. The days of reconstruction became days without glamour, doubled in dullness by nostalgia.

Many of the sabras have gone on the land and formed new kibbutzim. Some have gone to the city or the sea in search of a new meaning in life. Some have left the collective of the kibbutz and gone into the moshav, a cooperative farm. In the moshav, each family has its own home, its own cattle, its own chickens. Some are going into the newest kind of settlement, the moshav shitufi, the collective smallholders' settlement, a kind of halfway house between the kibbutz and the moshav. For no form in Israel is static. As youthful dreams and hard facts have clashed head on, the two cooperative forms, the kibbutz and the moshav, have undergone constant changes. The bridge between idealism on paper and the frailty of the flesh needs constantly to be crossed and recrossed. The moshav shitufi is an attempt to synthesize the collective life of the kibbutz with the individual family structure of the moshav.

Each family owns its own home and maintains it out of income from working on the collectively owned land. The children live at home, but all the social services, such as health, welfare, and schools, are maintained from the money earned cooperatively.

Inevitably, as in any big business or large trade-union, the farms closest together in their thinking joined into federations to solidify their gains and strengthen themselves. Over a period of years, beginning in 1926, the kibbutzim have developed several different federations, of which the three largest are Hakibbutz Hameukhad (United Communal Settlement Movement), the largest; Hakibbutz Haartzi (National Federation of Communal Settlements), which encompasses all the settlements whose members are affiliated with the Hashomer Hatzair, the Left Wing Socialist Party; and Ihud Hakvutzot Ve-ha-Kibbutzim (Union of Collective Settlements). The farmers of the moshavim have joined into a general federation of smallholders and prospective settlers called "Tenuat ha-Moshavim ve-ha-Irgunim."

Politically, a kibbutz is like any village or town within the framework of the government. Some of the kibbutzim have a majority of Mapai members (belonging to Ben-Gurion's party); others, like those in the Hakibbutz Haartzi Federation, are Mapam (extreme left-wing socialists); Mizrakhi members belong largely to the orthodox kibbutzim. But people of eight or ten parties may belong to any single kibbutz. They elect their own kibbutz officers and in the general federal elections vote like any citizen in the nation. A kibbutz background is one of the best qualifications for political leadership. Ben-Gurion was a kibbutznik; so was Golda Meir; and so are a number of cabinet members and diplomats, who return to the kibbutz whenever they can—and go back to the routine of washing dishes, waiting on table, or herding sheep.

The kibbutz is Israel's most exciting laboratory experiment. Here, where everything is scaled down—laid out, as it were, on a table—are not only the dreams of the new state, but its still unsolved problems and disruptive anxieties: schisms between orthodox and liberals; between Mapam and Ahdut Avodah, left-wing neutralists; between Mapam and Mapai; the paradox of individuals living cooperatively inside the kibbutz while the kibbutz itself competes in the market like the most rugged capitalist. Political differences have always made discussions and debates stimulating; now they poison friendships.

Some of the kibbutzim have almost been wrecked by the East-West war. Since 1956 some kibbutzim have actually split in half, even physically dividing their dining room with a wall separating the two factions. Other kibbutzim voted to become all Mapam, or all Ahdut Avodah, or all Mapai. The minority members, after a lifetime in the kibbutz, moved out to begin a new life elsewhere.

After a great peak of idealism and success, the kibbutz movement has reached a period of plateau and crisis. The three large federations held constant conventions to discuss this crisis. They found it basically twofold: new pioneers are not entering the kibbutz movement from abroad and members within the kibbutzim are leaving.

New immigrants are going on the land, but many recoil from joining a collective farm. People who spent long, deteriorating years in the concentration and D.P. camps are sick of communal living and tired of life without privacy. The newcomers who do go into the kibbutz are still not numerous enough to keep it growing.

The original khalutz and khalutza came out of the great youth movements of eastern Europe. They were carefully chosen, carefully trained; the idealistic elite of a country that was to be built by only the noblest and finest youth. The new immigrants come without training and without selection. They have to come. The program of hakhsharah (training) still goes on around the world, even in a few farming settlements in the United States. But only a few hundred trained pioneers come into the country each year.

Whatever happens to life in the kibbutz—even if the whole form should change—the kibbutz idea itself has already written history. There are flaws, inevitably, in the pattern—the flaws of human beings who cannot always measure up to their own ideals. For in a kibbutz, just as in a large city or small town, there are lost people and bewildered ones, people of character and people who become characters because they have no character.

But the basic idea of the kibbutz is one of sheer idealism, the idealism of brotherhood and equality. With its sense of destiny, of building for a bright future, the kibbutz is the reflection of Israel's dream.

8: The Waters of Israel

Water is the word of mystery in Israel. Water is the word of life. "Without water we cannot go on living here," the engineers tell you. "Without water we cannot farm, we cannot grow our own food. Water may be a source of conflict with the Arabs, but if we can solve our differences—then water may be the bridge to peace in the Middle East."

Water is politics. There is ample water for all in the Middle East, but it is divided neither by nations nor by geographical frontiers. There is water to spread across all the lands, and turn them green. But the Arabs prefer to keep their own lands arid and barren, to prevent Israel from turning her land green. The United Nations has offered to help all the Arab states irrigate their lands, build new farms, and set up village industries and agriculture. In 1954 the United States sent Ambassador Eric Johnston to the Middle East to create a project that would use the waters of the Jordan and the Yarmouk, the two rivers that flow in Israel, for the Arab states and Israel. Thus far the Arabs have accepted neither the U.N. nor the U.S. plan.

Israel has refused to sit idly by, twiddling her thumbs. She has diverted her own Yarkon River at Tel Aviv, cleared her swampland, and taken water from the profligate north to the thirsty south.

For endless years the land in the summer had been brown—parched and desolate. The Hills of Judea were so rocky they appeared as if some divine force had dropped all the stones of the world upon them.

Now much of the country has turned green. There are vineyards and orchards, terracing and trees. The people did it, the new immigrants did it, the hard toil and back-breaking work did it. But without water, nothing would have succeeded.

There is not only an industrial revolution in the state; there is an even greater agricultural revolution. Israel is growing industrial crops from the Galilee to the Negev—cotton, sugar cane, peanuts. Her peanuts are so delectable that she exports her own brand to England for eating, and imports a cheaper brand for making oil. Her winter tomatoes are a delicacy in London restaurants, where they are specially advertised as "Fresh tomatoes from Israel." Jaffa oranges are on breakfast tables across America.

Her over-all plan is to use American techniques for quicker food production to feed her ever growing population, and to train new immigrants in farming. As soon as the new immigrants arrive, they go on the land and earn a weekly salary working on large industrial farms while they raise their own vegetables in their own back yards. Ultimately, Israel hopes many of them will stay on the land as farmers.

Israel hopes some day to be completely self-sustaining in food. But she can do it only if she has the water. The first immigrants coming into the Holy Land in the nineteenth century searched for water and held festivals of thanksgiving when they found it. The early pioneers, willfully converting themselves from city-dwellers into men of the soil, searched for land that had a source of water. In 1946, when the British were keeping Jews out of the Holy Land, a few hundred young Jewish men and women, on Yom Kippur eve, the eve of the Day of Atonement, went down to the Negev and opened eleven new settlements. They put up watchtowers and prefabricated houses. And they searched for water. In the war of liberation, with every border under fire, the search went on for water. New immigrants keep coming, some penniless but with a wealth of skills. They need houses. They need food. They need healing. And they need water.

Without water, Israel is finished as a nation. As a precaution, she is already rationing all her ground-water sources. In the Negev, she is using a water-spreading device that Dr. Nelson Glueck, the American archaeologist, and her own Israeli archaeologists uncovered among the ancient Nabateans who lived in the Negev desert over two thousand years ago. There is not much water in that desert, but when it comes, it comes quickly. The Israelis are trying now to put dikes near the wadis, and spread the desert water slowly with thirty-inch pipes.

It is the rivers that Israel needs. Only the rivers have enough water to feed her people. Knowing that, she lives by a Ten Year Master Plan for irrigation and hydroelectric power, prepared for her by a group of well-known American engineers. This master plan attempts to use every drop of water in the country—rain water, flood water, river water, underground water. It links the whole country through irrigation canals. It stores water in reservoirs from the Galilee to the Negev for crops and food and even for breeding fish in fishponds. Jewish and Arab villages that were hungry for water in Bible days now have water flowing from taps.

The first ambitious part of the Ten Year Plan, already in operation, is the sixty-five-mile Yarkon-Negev pipeline. It was opened officially on July 19, 1955. I have never before seen a whole country celebrate a pipeline. Thousands of people came to the official opening at the springs of the Yarkon River outside Tel Aviv. All of Israel's top officials, diplomats from all over the world, came to listen to speeches and watch actors perform a pageant dedicated to the pipeline. New York's Governor Averell Harriman came and made a speech in praise of water. The water began to flow through the pipeline a week before the elections for Israel's Knesset were to be held. For that whole festive day, the newspapers and the political parties put aside all electioneering and talked only of a pipeline and a river.

Tel Aviv's own river, the Yarkon, had been harnessed and sent south in 66-inch pipelines to the thirsty Negev desert. Now it would supply the Negev with a hundred million cubic yards of water annually, increase the area of irrigable land by twenty-five per cent to some two hundred and twenty thousand acres, carry water to about two hundred new settlements in the Negev, pave the way for establishing at least thirty new villages with eight thousand agricultural units and homes for thirty-five thousand more people.

Even more dramatic than the opening of the Yarkon-Negev pipeline was the reclamation of Lake Huleh, ten miles north of the Sea of Galilee. For thousands of years, the Huleh had been a stagnant swamp of papyrus and peat. Signs were still all over the road: KEEP OUT. MALARIA. Wild boars and water buffalo roamed through the papyrus jungle. Exotic birds nested in the swamps.

Each winter the rains from the mountains swelled Lake Huleh. The Jordan River, flowing out of the lake, could not carry away the water fast enough. The waters spilled over wastefully into the marshes and evaporated.

In January, 1951, Israel's engineers began to deepen and widen the Jordan River for a distance of some three miles to catch the overflowing waters and channel them down the river bed. Construction workers drove earth-moving machines up to the Jordan River to begin the work.

The Syrians, sitting in the eastern hills overlooking the work, opened fire. They killed some of the workmen. Then they brought the question of widening the Jordan to the United Nations, saying that some of the work was being done on privately owned Arab land.

U.S. General William E. Riley, then chief of the United Nations staff in the Middle East, ruled that the work on the Jordan River bed was vital to the life of Israel. He recommended to the United Nations that Israel continue its work, provided the Arab owners would give their consent. The Arabs never gave their consent, though barely seven acres were involved. So the Israelis, with a green light from the U.N., revised the project and continued their work on the western bank of the Jordan. Dredgers moved mountains of earth and mud from the river bed until the river, catching the wasteful waters, could flow freely.

Now work began on the Huleh swamp itself. An American Jewish engineer, Jacob R. Sensibar, came to Israel during his vacation in late summer of 1951. Sensibar, a short, soft-spoken, creative industrialist, had been born in 1890 in a small Russian village called Aswia. His family fled from oppression to Palestine; from there his father, a landscape artist, took the family to Chicago. When Jake was seventeen years old, he began to push wheelbarrows of sand to fill in the land that was to become the steel city of Gary, Indiana. He has been pushing sand ever since. He pushed the sand in Chicago to fill in the land beneath the Field Museum and solved the problem of a foundation for the museum that had nearly licked the architects. He pushed Lake Michigan so far that nearly three-quarters of Chicago's beautiful lake front is on the land that Jake Sensibar filled in. He pushed back land for the East River Drive in New York, and the ocean front at Los Angeles. He pushed back the waters of Steep Rock Lake in Canada to get at a rich deposit of iron ore.

Now Jake began to push back the Huleh swamp. He brought young American engineers from his Chicago company, the Construction Aggregates Corporation. Working through the Jewish National Fund, he brought in two dredges to dredge out the swampy lake. He brought hoists and rubber hose lines. His workmen were unskilled Israelis: old and new immigrants whom he trained.

By 1955, Jake had cleaned up the Huleh swamp. Twenty-one miles of canals and ditches drained the lake into the River Jordan and irrigated the land. A small wild-life preserve was kept for the exotic birds and fish. For the rest, the little circle on the maps marked Lake Huleh has now disappeared.

In place of that circle, in place of the papyrus and malarial jungle, you now see beautiful geometrical patterns, as if drawn with a giant ruler, of green cotton, sugar cane, peanuts, rice, and garden vegetables. Fifteen thousand acres of the richest soil in the world have been cleared for large-scale farming. Israel hopes that this once stagnant marsh land will provide food and homes and a livelihood for some hundred thousand people.

The search for water goes on. It was the search for water that led the United States to send Eric Johnston to the Middle East to divide up the waters of the Jordan and the Yarmouk Rivers among the Israelis and the Arabs. By far the greater part of the water was to go to the Arab states. In the summer of 1956, Johnston traveled through the Middle East and won the approval of the engineers and technicians of all the countries involved. That fall, Johnston appeared before the New York *Herald Tribune* Forum and spoke with moving eloquence of how the water experts in the Arab countries and Israel had already approved the project. He was waiting now only for political approval, which he expected at almost any moment.

Success seemed imminent. For this was a plan that would benefit everyone. It would bring water and electric power to thirsty land; it would raise the standard of living of even the most poverty-stricken, disease-infested Arab villages. Everyone had everything to gain from the plan, and the United States was offering to underwrite most of the cost.

Johnston drew a picture that captured the imagination of every peace-loving citizen in the Middle East: the Biblical Jordan River once more flowing through lands of milk and honey. Where diplomats in the United Nations had failed for years to find a way to get the Arabs and Jews to sit down together to talk peace, Johnston seemed to have found the magic formula. Water itself would become the highway to peace.

Then the Arab League met in Cairo in 1956 to consider the plan. Syria, through which not one ounce of Jordan water flows, vetoed the plan. But Colonel Nasser, aspiring to rule all the Arab states, promised Eric Johnston that he would get the Syrians to change their veto in a few months. Johnston took him at his word and kept all action in abeyance, waiting for Nasser to deliver.

Nasser never did. After a few months, he washed his hands of the whole deal. He was now getting war equipment from the Soviet Union. He no longer needed Johnston or the United States. He could obviously achieve his ambitions faster as a war leader with Russian arms than as a messenger of peace supporting the Johnston Plan. According to Israeli intelligence, he seemed delighted to flaunt the failure of the Johnston Plan as part of the decline and fall of Western civilization in the Middle East.

Meanwhile, the Israelis decided to go ahead with the Jordan River projects of their own Ten Year Master Plan, projects that can be linked into the Johnston Plan at any time. The major scheme is a giant Jordan-Negev pipeline, to carry water from the Jordan in the north to the Negev in a 108-inch pipeline, the largest water pipe in the world.

All of this project, of course, is in Israel territory. But a mile-and-a-half canal goes through the demilitarized zone between Israel and Syria at the Benot Yaakov (The Daughters of Jacob) bridge. Once again Syria rushed to the United Nations, and in 1955, with the help of a Soviet veto in the Security Council, succeeded temporarily in halting work on the canal and on a projected hydroelectric power station.

Syria knows that unless Israel can build this tiny section of the canal, the entire Jordan-Negev pipeline project will collapse. She knows that water is life in Israel. Thus she threatens Israel's entire future, her agriculture, her economy, and the lives of her people.

Late one Friday afternoon in July of 1956, I dropped in at the police station in the sleepy town of Rosh Pina, overlooking the Sea of Galilee. First Inspector Shlomo Colman, looking freshly shaved and dressed for his Shabbat rest, left his apartment in the police compound and joined us in the police station. He told us he would be happy to give us a police escort to see the Jordan canal just south of the Benot Yaakov bridge. But would we mind waiting until the next morning? There was a little trouble on the Sea of Galilee. An Israel fishing boat had just been shot at by the Syrians.

We returned the next day. During the night, Inspector Colman told us, an Israeli police boat had gone out under fire to bring the fishermen back safely. The Syrians had fired on the police boat. The police boat had returned the fire. The two sides had brought up reinforcements and these were now facing each other.

We left for the canal with a police escort, Mordecai Waknin, a handsome young man with a huge black mustache, who had come to Israel from Morocco in 1948 with Youth Aliyah, the children's rescue organization set up by Hadassah.

We drove toward the Jordan River, through fields of unreclaimed land and tall, yellow, parched weeds. There were no trees, no grass, none of the signs of life and farming.

Just south of the demilitarized zone, we stopped on top of a hill that was bare and covered with stones. Facing us was an equally bare hill, where the border of Syria began. We could see two Syrian military camps on the hill. We could see the Syrians walking around. Our policeman, Mordecai, kept close watch, his gun poised, while we stood taking pictures of the canal. At the foot of our hill, inside Israel territory, the Jordan River flowed, like a sudden gash in the bare cliff.

The famous white canal, dug into the slope, and lined with reinforced concrete, glistened eloquently in the hot morning sun.

Standing there, looking at this extraordinary feat of engineering, of carving a pipeline through the mountains, the valleys, and the yawning desert, I realized that this Jordan River Project was Israel's lifeline. The new settlements in the Negev, brand new towns like Dimona and Arad, were dependent for their very lives on water.

General Yigael Yadin, archaeologist and former Chief of Staff, summed up Israel's attitude toward water:

My country has to face the alternative of starving in the next ten years or meeting an invasion from Syria. Obviously our working on the Jordan is no act of aggression. Israel has promised to take out of the Jordan not one ounce of water more than the Johnston Plan agreed to give her. If the plain facts were told, the world would soon realize that the Arabs are biting off their noses to spite their faces. Under the Johnston Plan, Jordan would get much more water than Israel. Yet she allows herself to be dictated to by the Arab League. Lebanon has water. Egypt has the Nile. And Syria has far more water than she can use for centuries."

General Yadin quoted a wonderful passage from the Bible to prove that even in Biblical days, Syria had boasted that she had far more water than the little Jordan River in the Holy Land. "If you will read Kings II, Chapter 5, you'll find that twenty-eight hundred years ago, when the commander of the Syrian army was stricken with leprosy, he went to Israel to the Prophet Elisha to be cured. Elisha told him, 'Go wash in Jordan seven times, and thy flesh shall come again to thee, and thou shalt be clean.' But the Syrian was furious. 'Are not Abana and Pharpar, rivers of Damascus, better than all the waters of Israel?' "

A week later, on a warm Saturday afternoon in Jerusalem, peacefully drinking homemade ice cream soda in the home of Israel's prime minister, I asked David Ben-Gurion what would happen if Syria carried out her threat to declare the Jordan project an act of war.

Ben-Gurion leaned forward. His soft white hair, which frames his face like that of a Biblical prophet, seemed to stand up around his head. His cheeks grew flushed. "By what right does Syria say that the peaceful use of water is an act of war? The Arabs cannot reach any agreement on water because they are the victims of their own propaganda.

"The world is feeding Arab refugees. But there are some four hundred thousand Jewish refugees in Israel now who fled from Arab lands in this population exchange. And we've taken in another four hundred thousand refugees from terror in Europe. The United Nations does not feed them. It is only Israel, with the help of Jews abroad through the United Jewish Appeal and other organizations, that feeds them. Without water, they cannot live.

"Our strongest argument," he said to me, "is a moral one. Is it not a crime against humanity to allow Jordan River water, which we need for life, to flow wastefully into the Dead Sea?"

9: Sam's Farm

In 1956, the cotton crop of Israel, vital to its hard-pressed economy, was in mortal danger. The boll weevil seemed to have become immune to insecticide and millions of dollars' worth of cotton, fully grown, was being destroyed. In this emergency, a cable was sent to Sam Hamburg, the California millionaire desert farmer who introduced cotton into Israel in 1952. It reached him in the morning. In the afternoon Sam was on a plane heading for Israel.

Two million dollars' worth of cotton was hopelessly eaten up, but under Sam's direction a great salvaging operation was soon under way. By prompt action at least six million dollars' worth was saved.

Much of Israel's agricultural revolution stems from this one American's skills and faith. A play that I wrote for the Eternal Light radio program in 1958 tells the story of Sam Hamburg's contribution to Israel.

SAM'S FARM

CANTOR: SIGNATURE AND DOWN "SCHMA YISROEL"

VOICE: (echo) And the Lord spake unto Moses, saying, Command the children of Israel that they bring unto thee pure oil olive beaten for the light, to cause the lamps to burn continually in the tabernacle of the congregation, and it shall be a statute forever in your generations.

CANTOR: UP WITH ORCHESTRA AND FINISH

MUSIC: THEME AND DOWN

NARRATOR: (cold) You're Sam. You're Sam Hamburg. You're six feet tall, but you're stooped from thirty years of smelling and

77

turning the good earth. You're fifty-seven. But sometimes you look seventy, with furrows in your face like the furrows in your land.

MUSIC: NARRATIVE THEME—IN AND UNDER

You're Sam Hamburg who conquered the desert in California and out of the agony and loneliness and torment of your life, you did good and noble things. You were always a lonely man, Sam Hamburg. A dreamer who was drawn to the land. From the days you landed on these shores in 1920, a penniless immigrant of twenty, you were drawn to the desert.

UNCLE SAUL: Sam. Sam. (music out) Stay here in New York. You are my sister's son. We will help you.

SAM: (at twenty) No, Uncle Saul. New York is not for me. I'm going out to California to study farming.

UNCLE SAUL: What kind of nonsense is this—farming? A bright young boy like you—a farmer. Stay in New York. You belong here. You're a writer—a poet. Shmulek, I remember how you translated Hauptmann's "Weavers" into Hebrew when you were twelve years old. You'll work in my printing plant a while—then you can write. You love music. You can go to concerts. This is a world for you to conquer.

SAM: I don't belong here. I belong on the land.

MUSIC: IN AND DOWN

NARRATOR: Penniless, Sam Hamburg went to California to study farming at the University in Berkeley. His professors recognized his talents and offered him a job as a teacher. But the land was in his blood. Desert land. Sam heard that desert land was being given away for practically nothing to any brave man who would dare to tame it. With two dollars in his pocket, Sam put up a tent and took on the land that had licked hundreds of men before him.

MUSIC: FADING AND CROSSFADE PICKAX AND SHOVEL

For thirty years, he fought a desperate, nearly suicidal fight against everything the desert could throw at him. His cotton crop was wiped out by early frost. His wheat crop was wiped out by rust. His wells ran dry. He brought a river forty miles away to his ranch and lifted it three hundred feet to water his land. He married. (*accent sound*) He had three children. (*accent sound*) But his life was the desert. (*accent sound*) By 1952 he was the master of a ranch the size of the island of Manhattan. He was a millionaire farmer. (*crossfade sound of farm machinery, tractors, combines, etc., one at a time*) He had conquered the desert. But the desert also conquered him. (*all sound out*) His desert was blooming—but he had all but destroyed himself. At fifty-two, he was a lonely, restless, almost broken man. He left his desert and went to the mountains to search his soul. High in the Rockies at Aspen, Colorado, he heard Dr. Albert Schweitzer play Bach at the Goethe Festival. He was playing the 130th Psalm, "Out of the Depths Have I Cried unto Thee, O Lord."

MUSIC: ORGAN PLAYING PSALM

NARRATOR: Sam sat there in the vast hall listening to Schweitzer, and a conversation took place in his mind. But because it took place in his mind, did it not actually take place?

SAM: Dr. Schweitzer, my name is Sam Hamburg.

SCHWEITZER: Sit down, please. (*organ continuing under*)

SAM: Dr. Schweitzer, I want to tell you something. I listen to you play and I say to myself—such peace, such peace I have never seen in any man's face. How does one achieve such peace? Dr. Schweitzer, I'm a rich, successful farmer—as we reckon these things in America. But I'm finished.

MUSIC: OUT

I'm broken. I don't know where to go from here. I live alone on my desert in agony and the torture of solitude.

SCHWEITZER: Mr. Hamburg, you are not alone in agony. Everyone has a burden of pain.

SAM: Tell me.

SCHWEITZER: It is good to know pain. Those who have learned what physical pain and bodily anguish mean, belong together.

SAM: You've been in Africa a long time. Have you missed thirty years of culture?

SCHWEITZER: A man doesn't miss anything if he loves what he's doing.

SAM: I shouldn't be bothering you.

SCHWEITZER: Man belongs to man. Man has claims on man. Does anyone have a claim on you?

SAM: What do you mean?

SCHWEITZER: I thought the people in Africa had a claim on me. Does anyone anywhere have a claim on you?

SAM: Yes. There are people who have a claim on me. Six million people have a claim on me.

SCHWEITZER: There is a living remnant, is there not?

SAM: Yes. There is a living remnant—in Israel. I know who has a claim on me.

SCHWEITZER: Why don't you go to Israel and teach your people? (pause) There are deserts in Israel.

MUSIC: BACH DOWN UNDER SEGUE* TO ISRAELI MUSIC

NARRATOR: A rich and broken man returned to his people in search of himself. And the desert was in Israel, and Sam Hamburg raged with anger, and went to David Ben-Gurion.

SAM: Your farms are ridiculous.

BEN-GURION: (tongue in cheek) We still eat.

SAM: Your people are afraid of this land.

BEN-GURION: We came here.

SAM: Sure it's no jungle. You've been farming for fifty years—barnyard farming.

BEN-GURION: (angry) Our people ripped up these rocks with their fingernails.

SAM: So what?

BEN-GURION: They love this land.

* Radio term for modulate or fade.

SAM: (shouting) Love isn't enough. What are you talking about love? Love with apologies. Love with fear. Love without horizons. That's not love.

BEN-GURION: Horizons. Our whole vision is of one great horizon.

SAM: Your farms have no horizon. Your farmers know only how to plant tiny fields with tiny plants.

BEN-GURION: What do you want?

SAM: Little fields mean little production. Little production means poverty. Big fields mean good living.

BEN-GURION: We found a wasteland. . . .

SAM: I know. It's still a wasteland. But the wasteland is not only in the desert. It's in the heart of the people. You're all afraid. You have vision, Mr. Prime Minister. But you—you too are still afraid.

BEN-GURION: Afraid of what?

SAM: Of your land. Of your capacity to produce. You don't know what you got here—the best soil in the world. The most uniform climate.

BEN-GURION: Mr. Hamburg, what do you know of our desert?

SAM: I'm a desert farmer. You can raise the finest cotton in the world.

BEN-GURION: (pause) Come to the Negev with me tomorrow and pick out the places for cotton.

SAM: Not tomorrow. I got to fly to California tomorrow to get in my crop. I'll come back in thirty days.

MUSIC: SEGUE TO SOUND OF A CAR

NARRATOR: On the morning of the thirtieth day, on the fifteenth of March, on the eighteenth day of the month of Adar, a safari of some fifty experts set out for the Negev. In the lead car sat two men, two dreamers whose life work was to repair the desert—the human desert.

SAM: Driver, stop the car. (sound out) I want to take a look.

NARRATOR: Sam lay down on the ground and smelled the soil.

SAM: (disappointment in his voice) Dead land.

BEN-GURION: How do you know?

SAM: The way you know history—that's the way I know soil.

BEN-GURION: If we brought water . . .

SAM: I tell you, this land is a corpse. Nature has discarded it. You find corpses like this all over the world. Let's not waste time. Driver, go on.

MUSIC: SOUND OF CAR ON GRAVEL ROAD. REGISTER AND DOWN

SAM: Stop here. (*sound out*)

BEN-GURION: This is Ibim. Is this good land?

SAM: Yes, Master. This land is good.

BEN-GURION: Not a blade of grass here.

SAM: It will raise crops.

BEN-GURION: How do you know?

SAM: I feel it.

BEN-GURION: How do you feel things like this? The experts tell me this land won't take water.

SAM: (*with scorn*) Experts. (*exploding*) Bookkeepers. You don't know what you got here. I'm selling you real estate. This land is your salvation. (*pause*) Give me a piece of desolation, and I'll build you a farm. I'll send you my machines and my men from California. I'll bring you my seeds. I'll teach your farmers to look up from their tiny fields and their tiny barnyard crops. I'll teach them to plant straight furrows.

BEN-GURION: Your price?

SAM: Master, I don't need money. I need you. (*pause*) I need to help you.

MUSIC: SOUND OF CAR. REGISTER AND DOWN

NARRATOR: Sam Hamburg looking for a piece of desolation. (*Sound up and down*) Drought-ridden land. Yellow. Parched. For years no one had touched it. Fifty years. Yet the River Jordan lay below, two hundred feet below. Driving with Chaim Gvati, Israel's Director of Agriculture, Sam found a piece of desolation.

GVATI: Sam. This is abandoned land.

SAM: It's rich.

GVATI: Look at those weeds and thorns.
SAM: We're going to farm it.
GVATI: Why?
SAM: If it can grow thorns, it can grow crops.

MUSIC: AND SEGUE TO SOUND OF CRACKLING FIRE

NARRATOR: They made a fire. They burned weeds. They burned thorns. Wild pigs ran out of the suddenly naked hills. Sam bent down and smelled the soil.

SAM: This is the richest land I've ever seen. We're going to farm good here.

MUSIC: BIBLICAL THEME

NARRATOR: This was the land which the pioneers had rejected. It is written: "The stone which the builders refused, is become the head stone of the corner. This is the Lord's doing. It is marvelous in our eyes."

SAM: First thing we'll do—we're going to bring the river upstairs. That river! Ah! I have a love affair with rivers. I love to see a river kiss the mountaintop. God and me . . . we're partners in this deal.

GVATI: We can have a lot of settlements here, with families.

SAM: We're going to keep this land just for crops.

GVATI: Six hundred acres—just for crops?

SAM: You're still afraid of big fields.

GVATI: O.K., Sam. This is your farm. Chavat Shmuel, we'll call it—Sam's Farm.

MUSIC: IN AND DOWN

NARRATOR: Because Israel is a small country, everyone is digging deep. Everyone is going down, digging deeper into history, deeper into the mind, deeper into the subsoil of what it is that makes a man a partner with God.

Sam Hamburg flew back to the United States. Soon he was back in Israel with an American water engineer—Eugene Wooley.

WOOLEY: Sam, I always thought you were a character. I change my mind. You're a madman.

SAM: O.K. But lift the water to the mountain.

MUSIC: IN AND DOWN

NARRATOR: Engineers from America! Equipment Sam had designed! Sent from his ranch in California! They built lifts, ditches, canals! They raised the River Jordan two hundred and twenty feet high. Sam had the water now . . . to kiss his land. He taught men and women how to plant long straight furrows of cotton, hybrid corn, peanuts, sugar beets, tobacco, winter tomatoes! They worked on Chavat Shmuel, on Sam's farm, by day and went home to their immigrant camps at night. Shoemakers from Tunisia, merchants from Bagdad, silversmiths from Yemen, beggars from the mellahs of Casablanca, planting furrows to the horizon. And when the water came up out of the Jordan and flowed across the straight furrows, the men and women from all the ingathering stopped their work to watch the miracle!

MUSIC: SOUND OF WATER FLOWING

CHILD: We read it in the Book of Isaiah: "And the parched land shall become a pool, and the thirsty land springs of water."

SAM: (gruffly, trying to hold back emotion) Isaiah said it, and he was right. But it's going to be rough work. We got to fix the desert. We got to fix the people too.

FOREMAN: You're ruining this cotton.

WOMAN: I'm doing what you taught me.

FOREMAN: Pick up your check. You're through.

WOMAN: I have a sick husband, little children. What will I do?

FOREMAN: See the Welfare Department.

SAM: (coming on) What's all the fighting about?

FOREMAN: She spoils every boll of cotton she touches. How can we raise cotton with such people? They were never on the land.

SAM: You can't fire her. This is her land. Lady, what's your name?

WOMAN: Sarah.

SAM: A good name. A mother in Israel. You never saw cotton grow before?

SARAH: Never.

SAM: I'll teach you. You'll be the best cotton picker in the desert. Watch.

NARRATOR: (cold) Sam Hamburg, millionaire, repairer of deserts, working in the fields with a woman who had never seen cotton . . . Sam Hamburg, repairer of deserts and men, walking to the foreman at the end of the day.

SAM: It's not the cotton pickers who should be fired. They're not afraid. They just need to be taught. It's you, the people at the top, who need to be fired. (shouting) We fire no one on these fields for not knowing. You hear me. We fire for laziness, for stupidity, for fear. Watch out I don't fire you.

MUSIC: IN AND DOWN

NARRATOR: You're Sam. Tormented dreamer, who can serve only through service. Some rich men find happiness in giving money. You can find happiness only in giving yourself. Sam Hamburg, serving God by giving Sam Hamburg.

AVRAM: Sam, look at these tomatoes. Winter tomatoes. I never dreamed you could raise so much on half an acre. I never knew how big half an acre is.

SAM: How big is half an acre, Avram? As big as your imagination.

MUSIC: IN AND DOWN

NARRATOR: How big is Israel? How big is man? Measure it in height and depth and heart. How big is Israel? As big as the capacity of your land to produce. As big as the desire of your people to suffer and survive and win. Sam was learning to measure Israel. He flew back and forth—California to Israel, Israel to California, five, six times a year. Sam, Sam, Sam, the repair man—repairing the desert, repairing the people, repairing Sam. The loneliness still there. The agony still there. That other lonely man, David

Ben-Gurion, still there. (*organ sneaks in "Out of the Depths Have I Cried unto Thee."*) The two lonely men met one night and talked of the great vision of loneliness.

BEN-GURION: Why do you love your California desert, Sam?

SAM: Master, why do you go to Sde Boker in the desert?

BEN-GURION: There's a tremendous sense of achievement when you're developing a desert. The desert is our future. The Negev is the future of Israel. We're moving south in the desert the way your Americans moved westward in the prairies.

SAM: The whole world is one desert.

BEN-GURION: Every man must go to the desert to find himself —to get away from people for a while—and become part of the stars. That's when you can see things clearly. That's when you know what road you should take.

SAM: To me the desert is loneliness. Loneliness is a clean thing. Loneliness is atonement. Loneliness is dedication. Loneliness is the power to take scorn, defeat, nightmares. Loneliness is strength —the strength for tomorrow. There are no friends in the desert. We desert people—you and I—we don't know how to have friends. But there's a brotherhood of anguish there in that loneliness.

BEN-GURION: You know, Sam, in Jewish history, the people who wanted to do something for other people had to find themselves first. Remember our prophets had to go to the desert to purify themselves. That was standard training for prophets. To be a prophet you didn't go to college and get a Ph.D. You had to suffer. You had to know hunger. You had to know pain. You learned it in the desert. Sam, what are you looking for in the desert?

SAM: I'm looking for God.

BEN-GURION: And . . . ?

SAM: Master, I don't know nothing about theology or philosophy or history. But I learned in that California desert that you develop a desert forever. It's not like you're building a bridge or a factory. It's eternity. You're moving into eternity. You're moving into the mystery of the universe. Everything has a rhythm—day follows night, night follows day, summer follows the spring, the earth moves around the sun, the moon rises and sets, a woman gives birth in nine months. The universe is working for you. When you learn the direction of life, then you've learned what the desert can teach you.

BEN-GURION: Why were you so long in coming to us?

SAM: I wasn't ready. Thirty years on the desert purified me. Now I go to Israel clean.

MUSIC: "OUT OF THE DEPTHS HAVE I CRIED UNTO THEE" IN AND
          DOWN

NARRATOR: It is written that "he who begins a good deal is asked to complete it." Sam Hamburg had begun his mitzvah, his good deed. Now his days and nights were spent completing it.

He drove around the country. He came to a transit camp in Beer Tuvya. He saw new immigrants, unemployed, doing makework jobs, weeding trees.

SAM: (yelling) I see two hundred thousand dollars lying on that soil. And you've got people wasting their time weeding trees.

MUSIC: FADING

GVATI: What would you do?
SAM: Teach them to raise carrots.

MUSIC: IN AND DOWN

NARRATOR: He brought carrot seeds from America, and the new immigrants raised fine carrots. He taught them to put the carrots into cellophane bags, and they sold the bags of fine carrots to the American troops in Germany. Immigrants no longer unemployed. And they moved out of their tents into pretty white stucco houses.

MUSIC: OUT

SAM: Hey you, how you doing?
SHALOM: Fine.
SAM: What's your name?

SHALOM: Shalom Gamliel.

SAM: You ever raise carrots before?

SHALOM: I never saw a carrot before. In Yemen, we believe in miracles. There's an American. His name is Sam. He flies down here like a bird. When Sam comes, the land is empty. He works the land. When he is gone, there is a farm, and there is food, and there is joy in the hearts of the people. Before he came, we were hungry. Now we can eat.

SAM: Did you ever see this man?

SHALOM: No. I never see him. No one sees him. He comes fast. He goes fast. . . . But I tell you, we are an old people. When we pray in the *Schachrit* service every morning, we thank Sam. He gives us shoes. He gives us food. He gives us work again. (pause) You are Sam.

SAM: How do you know?

SHALOM: I see it in your eyes.

MUSIC: IN AND DOWN

NARRATOR: You're Sam. And the agony and the terror of the years on your desert are softening a little. But still an angry man— shouting at everyone with a voice like a truck going over gravel.

SAM: (furious) You're supposed to be idealists. You're supposed to be great ideologists. I don't know nothing about your ideology. But your cotton is burning. I know about cotton. If you don't irrigate that cotton, I'll take it away from you.

NARRATOR: Sam returned the next day. The cotton field was irrigated.

SAM: (voice a little relaxed) Look, you don't owe me nothing. Why is everybody afraid of me? Why?

MANAGER: Because you care.

SAM: The main thing in life is to care. Take care of your crops.

MUSIC: IN AND DOWN

NARRATOR: Nothing ever came easy to Israel or to Sam Hamburg.

Golda Meir, former schoolteacher from Milwaukee, now the only woman foreign minister in the world

Abba Hushi, mayor of Haifa

Moshe Castel, well-known painter, at home in Safad

In the war of independence, the water tower became the badge of Negba's courage

Negba was in ruins; every house was shattered

Sabras and new immigrants
dance the hora

The most helpful and
blessed migration to Israel
is the Migration of the
Children, the Youth Aliyah

The Yemenites have come out of such barbarism that anything in Israel is almost too good to be true

"It is all written in the Bible: 'But they that wait upon the Lord . . . shall mount up with wings as eagles' "

One morning a cable reached him in the desert in California.

SAM: (*tearing open cable: reading*) The cotton bug has learned to live with the insecticide. Spreading like wildfire. May lose entire cotton crop. Please come.

MUSIC: SEGUE TO SOUND OF AIRPLANE

POLICEMAN: (*bustle and noise of airport*) Shalom, Sam Hamburg. You going to save our cotton?

CLERK: Welcome back. We hope you'll save our cotton.

BROADCASTER: This is Kol Israel. Attention! Sam Hamburg has just arrived.

MUSIC: MONTAGE OF VOICES

SARAH: Sam is back.

SHALOM GAMLIEL: That's Sam—flies in—like a bird.

MUSIC: CAR REGISTER AND DOWN

SAM: (*screaming with fury*) I warned you farmers if you leave an inch of cotton unsprayed, you're in trouble. What were you doing? Drinking tea? You can't lick the desert with committee meetings. Anyway, here's new insecticide.

MUSIC: FADING AND CROSSFADE TURNING WRENCHES AND SPRAY-
          ING

NARRATOR: Sam spent nineteen hours without rest, fixing the nozzles of sprays so that not an inch of cotton would escape the coating of the new insecticide.

MUSIC: BROADCAST SOUNDS

BROADCASTER: This is Kol Israel. We have asked Sam Hamburg, the father of Israel's cotton, to speak to you tonight on the cotton crisis.

SAM: My friends. When I got the cable, I was mortally afraid. I have never been so frightened in my life. I thought the whole thing we had built together was falling apart. But these are the pangs of birth. Now I'm glad it happened. I know the love and devotion you've brought to the planting of cotton. Now you'll be more careful. This is precision work. You can't outsmart nature. She never lets you get careless. We learn by our mistakes. Expensive mistakes. But the cotton is saved.

MUSIC: NARRATIVE THEME IN AND UNDER

NARRATOR: And the cotton grew tall at Chavat Shmuel, Sam's Farm, the land that the builders themselves had rejected. From all over Israel, farmers came to look and to carry home with them the picture they saw. Desert land blooming. Desert land made fertile. Rows of green cotton and corn marching like proud soldiers straight to the horizon. A desert that sang. The sun was setting in pink shadows on the bareback mountains of Jordan when Sam looked at the fertile land and the River Jordan flowing through it. And he remembered the weeds and thorns and the wild pigs that had lived there, and tears streamed down his face and he fell down and kissed the soil of Eretz Yisrael.

SAM: The loneliness in the desert is the price you pay. You marry the desert. Never leave your desert. As long as you work to conquer your desert, no one can destroy you.

MUSIC: CODA

END

Sam Hamburg has become a one-man Point Four program. He is a kind of farming missionary, dedicated to the idea that successful American farmers should teach backward peoples how to fight poverty by farming their land more efficiently.

"Let our successful men take a year out of their lives and teach others what they have learned," Sam says. "I tell you there's no greater satisfaction in the world. It's not just giving of your money, it's giving of yourself.

"I look upon my work in Israel merely as a starter. I hope to go to Burma soon. I'd like to go to Iran. And more than anything else I'd like to teach the millions of hungry Arabs how to conquer the deserts east of the Jordan and west of Sinai. This is the constructive way to win over the Arab world to democracy."

10: "Sing My Songs to the Stringed Instruments"— Isaiah

IN THE FIRST week of 1958, as Israel began her tenth year of independence, I took a kind of Gallup poll of some of the artists I knew who had performed in Israel.

"Tell me what you think of Israel as a country of music and of the people of Israel as an audience," I asked. These were their answers:

ISAAC STERN, *violinist:* "The basic fact of life in Israel is that the people live with music as a necessary part of their lives. The concert audiences in the cities and in many of the kibbutzim would sooner go without meals than without music.

"It's one of the warmest audiences in the world. Young people especially are very appreciative. In every concert you see a tremendous cross section of the whole population—the people of the land, of the army, the white-collar workers in the cities. In the hotel there was not one maid, one porter, one desk clerk, who didn't ask me to get him a ticket to a concert. When I played for the opening of the Frederick R. Mann Auditorium in Tel Aviv in October, 1957, I came back to the hotel at four in the morning from an all-night party. One of the bartenders in the hotel said to me, 'Mr. Stern, why don't you play the Spring Sonata of Beethoven? You played the Second and the Seventh four years ago, but you've never played the Spring.' I had forgotten what I had played four years ago. But I checked and he was right.

"The first time I played in Israel was in June, 1949, a year after independence. The audiences were so enormous that I had to play two concerts at 5 P.M. and three more at 9.

"Someone asked me before the evening concerts if I would like to meet Ben-Gurion. I said I would be deeply honored. We went in a taxi to his modest house in Tel Aviv. I started to pay off the driver who turned to me and said, 'Thank you, Mr. Stern. But look, don't stay too long with Mr. Ben-Gurion. Remember you have another concert tonight.'

"At Ein-Gev, a kibbutz on the Sea of Galilee, a kind of Tanglewood in Israel, we gave a concert in the shedlike concert hall for three thousand people. People came from the kibbutzim all over the north, from the Lebanese border, the Syrian border, and the Jordan border. Playing for such people is something rare. But the important thing is that every artist who goes there has this kind of experience."

JENNIE TOUREL, singer: "The audiences are marvelous. They are very warm, very discriminating. No matter what language I sang in, and I sing songs in many languages, they understood.

"I was the last artist to sing in the old hall in Tel Aviv, the Ohel Shem. It was June, 1957, and I sang with the Israel Philharmonic Orchestra. For all of us, it was a memorable farewell. I have been to Israel four times and each time I become more enthusiastic because the audiences grow more enthusiastic and more discriminating."

MILTON KATIMS, conductor Seattle Symphony Orchestra: "After making music in Israel, I felt that my emotional batteries had been recharged.

"The audience in Israel is fantastic. Especially the audiences in the kibbutzim. They are like a sponge—ready to drink in all the music which you can pour out, making you feel that you can never give them enough. If I had acceded to their wishes when I made out my program, I would have played all night, every night.

"But it was a two-way street. Their reaction to the music was a tremendous experience for me. I conducted six weeks in 1952 and six weeks in 1953. Those were difficult years. There was constant trouble on the borders. Yet they went on filling the concert halls."

LENA HORNE, *Broadway star:* "Israel gave me a spiritual rejuvenation. I've never gotten over it. It's not only the music and art. It's the tremendous spiritual excitement of the country. Their kind of full living meant so much to me, that I still live on it.

"There were those beautiful Yemenite children in a children's village. The girls looked like my daughter Gail. The teacher told me how lovely and old-fashioned they were when they first came. Then right away how modern they become. Instead of the old-fashioned things rubbing off, it was they who became sabras right away.

"We traveled on the S.S. *Artza* and we took in ninety-six children from North Africa. They had been in Youth Aliyah camps for three months. They ran around the deck blowing little penny whistles, and every evening they sang and danced with me before they were put to bed. That was our entrance into Israel—coming in with those kids.

"When you see those people coming in—Poles, Moroccans, all of them—you never forget it. No matter how hard it is, everybody's working together. And the way they welcome you. Even when I didn't sing, they would welcome me just as a person. And those children—they thrilled me. I don't want anything to happen to them. I'm praying for them. If anybody touches them, I'm ready to go to war and fight for them."

EDDIE CANTOR, LEONARD BERNSTEIN, EARTHA KITT, ZINO FRANCESCATTI, IZLER SOLOMON—scores of artists have gone to Israel and are now carrying on a love affair with the people of Israel.

Tel Aviv, with some three hundred and ninety thousand people, supports more legitimate theatres than Los Angeles and has more subscribers to its Philharmonic Orchestra than New York, Philadelphia, or Chicago. Israel's two great exports today are oranges and pianists. It is a country of music. Walking down a residential street, you hear eager musicians practicing the violin, drums, oboe, saxophone, even the harmonica through almost every apartment window.

Music is encouraged by scholarships to any children who show promise. Two seven-year-old twins, both violinists, were recently given awards by the America-Israel Cultural Foundation. Singers, drummers, cellists, composers seem to spring up from the soil. One of Israel's leading composers is Oedoen Partos, who is perhaps best known for his "Yizkor for Viola and Strings" and his "Song of Praise" for viola and orchestra, first performed in the U.S. in 1951 by the Israel Philharmonic Orchestra.

Tel Aviv has now built a fantastic cultural center, spread over sixty acres, with the Habimah Theatre for drama, the Helena Rubinstein Pavilion for Contemporary Art, the House of Tchernikowsky (the Hebrew Writers' Association), Beth Sokolov (the journalists' house), and the Frederick R. Mann Auditorium for music—all of them erected with Israel government funds and money raised by the America-Israel Cultural Foundation.

In a gala première the Frederick R. Mann Auditorium was opened on October 2, 1957, with Leonard Bernstein conducting the Israel Philharmonic Orchestra. Top government officials, from David Ben-Gurion, who spoke at the opening, to the diplomatic corps in white tie and tails, and Israelis who could pay the unheard of price of thirty-seven dollars a seat, filled the twenty-eight hundred seats. Actually, over a million people listened free. The concert was broadcast, and in every city and farm and border settlement, life came to a standstill as Israel listened to Isaac Stern play Mendelssohn's Violin Concerto, Artur Rubinstein in Beethoven's Emperor Piano Concerto, and Paul Tortelier in Bloch's "Schelomo," a Hebrew rhapsody for cello.

Israel's theatergoers are as enthusiastic as the music lovers. Habimah is still the ranking theater in Israel, but there are also Ohel, Chamber, Matatey, and a light opera company called Do-Re-Mi. Its star is the lovely Yemenite singer Shoshana Damari.

Habimah, started in Russia under Stanislavsky, traveled through Europe and the United States from 1926 to 1928, then settled permanently in Palestine in 1928 as a cooperative society and, after great successes, began building its own home in Tel Aviv in 1935. Its leading lady, Hannah Rovina, is the Sarah Bernhardt of the Israel stage.

Habimah's greatest success was Ansky's "The Dybbuk," which mirrored ghetto life in Poland and Russia with khassidic lore. " 'The Dybbuk' is Habimah's success and signature," Brooks Atkinson wrote in the New York Times. But the success of "The Dybbuk" became a Frankenstein monster; the Stanislavsky technique characterized everything Habimah did and blocked any efforts to understand and portray modern Israel. After World War II, when a new generation of theatergoers who knew nothing of ghetto life arose, Habimah was forced to break with its "Dybbuk" repertoire and past. It produced a popular play about the Arab-Jewish war called "In the Wastes of the Negev," by an Israel playwright, Yigal Mossenson. It brought over Harold Clurman, of Group Theatre fame, to direct "Hostages" or "Montserrat" (its original name), by Emanuel Robles, later adapted for the American stage by Lillian Hellman.

The Ohel (which means tent), begun as a workers' theater by the Histadrut, the Federation of Labor, was a splinter group of the Habimah. It set itself up as a cooperative society, paid all its actors Histadrut wages, built its own 720-seat theater in Tel Aviv, and differed from the Habimah only slightly, in trying to choose plays that had a workers' angle. Its acting was the stylized acting of "The Dybbuk." Ohel, too, read the handwriting on the wall and began doing modern plays like "The Incubator on the Rock," a comedy of kibbutz life, played by its great comedian, Margalith. It put on an interesting play about the siege of Jerusalem by a promising young playwright, Yoshua bar Yosef, and in honor of the reburial of Herzl's bones on the highest hill of Jerusalem produced a play by Herzl himself called "Solon in Lydia."

The revolt against Habimah and Ohel, brewing for some time, took shape when a group of young actors and actresses, in Group Theatre fashion, created a new theater called The Chamber Theater (Theatron Kammeri) during World War II. Most of their material was locally written and at the beginning was largely vaudeville humor. The leading man was Yossi Yadin, the dark, curly-haired son of the famous archaeologist Dr. Elazar Sukenik who first identified the Dead Sea Scrolls, and the brother of General Yigael Yadin.

The group started with nothing. For two years they had no salaries and almost no training. They acted in an old movie house. They were experimental and fearless. Yossi told me one night, "When we broke with Habimah it was because the Habimah was closed for years to young people. That became the main reason for their failure. Like the other theaters, we are a cooperative society in general, but we differ from them in a number of ways. Before the crisis in the Habimah and Ohel, the whole company sat together, read a play, and voted whether to use it. We are the first theater to use a new system. We appoint a special committee responsible just for the repertoire and give the director the last word."

The most original and successful play in the country is about life in the kibbutz, the most original facet of life in Israel. It is a Chamber Theater play, "He Walks through the Fields," by Moshe Shamir. It was performed in Paris in 1956 in Hebrew, with a French narrator explaining some of the action, and it was as successful in France as in Israel.

On a summer night in the fields of Ein Kharod, a kibbutz in the valley of Jezrael, I watched "He Walks through the Fields" performed. Some six thousand farmers from Ein Kharod and from the neighboring villages paid two kilos of potatoes or the equivalent (since kibbutz people have no money) to see a play written by a kibbutznik. Some of the people sat on chairs, some on the grass; some, who had driven there, stood on top of their armored cars, buses, trucks, automobiles, and horse-drawn hay wagons. I sat on the floor of a big open truck with a group of former Canadian and American kibbutz members. The sky was a rich Mediterranean blue. The air was cool after the heat of the day and the smell of the fields sweet and fragrant.

On a simple home-built stage, whose props were stone stairs, symbolizing a kibbutz, and an impressionistic tree, representing the great outdoors, the actors brought the kibbutz to the kibbutz and the kibbutz loved it.

The play told the story of Mika, a kibbutz girl, in love with Uri, a kibbutz boy who joined the army and was ultimately killed while blowing up a bridge. When Mika, wearing kibbutz blue shorts rolled to the top of her shapely thighs, complained, "I have been told to go and harvest. I hate it, but I hate kitchen work more," the audience roared with laughter. The farmers grew hysterical when one of the actors, trying to shave his face, said, "The treasurer should shave with these razor blades." They nearly fell off the trucks when Uri went to the man in charge of housing in the kibbutz, told him he wanted to get married, and asked for a room for that very night. The housing man said, "I owe you congratulations, but you owe me prior notice. It's very easy to find a life companion, but to find a room . . ." But they wept when Uri died and Mika, discovering she was pregnant, decided to stay in the kibbutz and have her baby.

After the play I went backstage, where Yossi Yadin was taking off his make-up, one of the women was taking off her crepe hair, and others were cold-creaming their faces. The actors hurried into their street clothes. Tel Yoseph, the neighboring kibbutz, was giving a party for them. We drove over in the darkness and though it was past midnight found most of Tel Yoseph waiting excitedly in the huge dining room.

Unlike banquets in America, where people eat first and make speeches afterward, Israel makes its speeches first and then eats. They say that otherwise people would rush out the moment the food is eaten and the talking begins.

A tractor-driver kibbutznik, with a beautiful black Theodor Herzl beard and black-rimmed glasses, opened the banquet in the kibbutz dining hall by saying, "Now that we have learned what a kibbutz is like, we can discuss the play."

A kibbutz intellectual talked for about twenty minutes, giving a critical appraisal. He declared that the play was important because it presented the kibbutz as an accomplished fact; nobody could question now whether the kibbutz had a place in Israel's society.

At last the speeches were over. We were served huge trays of cheese, a variety of fruits grown in the kibbutz, cakes, coffee, and tea. The food disappeared rapidly. Then Yossi stood up.

"You bored us with speeches," he said, with the brutal frankness of a sabra. "Now we'll bore you with recitations." The actors and actresses recited long poems with gestures and histrionics. Yossi and the leading lady sang a duet.

At about two in the morning, the party broke up. The actors were given rooms in the kibbutz, while kibbutz members doubled up with friends. The guests who had come in armored cars and trucks drove off. The kibbutz, which had seen its life seriously mirrored on the stage, went to sleep.

These are a people to whom music and painting, folk-dancing and drama, are as important as bread and water. Art is part of the fabric of the people and their state.

The children grow up not only speaking the Hebrew of the Psalms, but speaking familiarly of Beethoven and Bach, of Michelangelo and Picasso, of Shakespeare and Goethe and Eugene O'Neill. In the schools, which are compulsory, art and music are compulsory, as essential as the three R's.

In all lands people create art. In Israel, people create art but art also re-creates people. In a country where healing is of first importance, art is therapy. In every mental hospital, there is an art therapist who is often a practicing and successful artist.

Israelis are people who seem to have antennae sticking out in every artistic direction. Recently, Shimon Oppenheimer, head of Israel's Cattle Breeding Association, went to Texas to buy breeding bulls for Israel and to New York to raise money for his magnificent Museum of Oriental Antiquities in Kibbutz Hazorea, where he lives.

Art galleries spring up all over the nation. Jerusalem, Tel Aviv, Haifa, and many of the small towns have their own galleries. The Bezalel Museum in Jerusalem is world famous. Some of the kibbutzim have galleries that draw visitors from all over the land.

Israel has one whole village of art. It is Ein-Hod, which means Source of Glory. Ein-Hod is Provincetown and Montparnasse rolled into white houses and lush gardens that face Mount Carmel on one side and the Mediterranean, just south of Haifa, on the other. Ein-Hod was an old Crusaders' village on the main highway. During the war of independence, the Arabs had used it as a military vantage point to snipe at Jewish convoys. When the war ended, the houses and roofs, made of a mixture of mud and tree branches, fell into almost complete collapse.

Marcel Janco, one of Tel Aviv's leading artists, who had been one of the founders of Dada in France in the 1920's, discovered the ruined village on the hill. He induced the Custodian of Alien Property to allow Israel's artists to rebuild the village. In May, 1952, a group of painters, sculptors, and dancers, armed with easels, clay, shovels, and trowels, cut their way through the brush and rubble and began to rebuild. They put up roofs, cut doors into walls, put in windows, laid floors, and then planted trees and gardens whose flowers soon covered the landscape. They kept the character of the village intact. The stone arches, built in the style of the Crusaders, were cleaned up and became the landmark of the village.

The first building you see in the piazza as you drive up to the village is a boldly painted café that reminds you vaguely of coffee shops in Greenwich Village. The bar was originally run by a young Yemenite who fought in the battle of Jerusalem and lived awhile in Paris, his claim to art. His constant companion was a big shaggy dog who became the mascot of the colony.

Here is Bohemianism in Crusader style. In preparation for a mad Purim ball in 1955, some of Israel's most famous artists, like Moshe Mokady, painted the outside and inside walls of the café and the houses with gay scenes from the story of Queen Esther. The most spectacular are in the house where Gertrude Kraus, the famous ballet dancer, now lives, sculpts figurines, and entertains her artist friends with music from her baby organ.

Since nothing is done in Israel without thinking of children, the artists spend their summers, as part of their payment for the houses, teaching Israel's most talented youngsters. Competitions are held in all the high schools. The final judges are Janco, who is the mayor or mukhtar, as he is called in good Arabic fashion, Mokady, and a few others. The students come for a month's course of free training under some of the country's best painters, lithographers, sculptors, potters, and dancers.

It is a madly wonderful village in which everyone lives as he likes, paints as he likes, sculpts as he likes, and hopes that someone will come along and buy his work.

In Safad, the second holiest city in Israel, there is another art colony. Ein-Hod is a Crusaders' village; Safad is a Cabbalists' village. Here the mystic Cabbala movement of the Middle Ages had started and lives on today. Bearded patriarchs with fur hats walk up and down the ancient stone steps and through the narrow streets, whose houses are jumbled together like those of a medieval woodcut. There are small, beautiful synagogues in the labyrinth of alleys, and the arch of an old Byzantine church.

At the end of the village is the Street of the Artists, with brilliant red and blue and yellow signs pointing to the artists' homes. These houses, too, had lain in rubble as an aftermath of the war of independence. The artists turned them into breath-taking studios with lush gardens and filled with their own works of art.

Moshe Castel, one of Israel's most successful painters, lives here. Castel is a sabra. His family, he told me, has been in Israel since 1492 when they were expelled from Spain. His pretty young wife, Bilka, a sabra from Tel Aviv, whose family came from Poland, acts both as his business manager and guide through his gallery. His whitewashed walls are hung with paintings from his earliest romantic, almost Chagall-like period, to his present abstractions.

Sonya Sachs, a former American, lives next door to Castel. She built her house from ruins and planted her garden herself, filling it with her own stone sculpture, until now it looks like a Roman garden. Her small house, filled with her oils, gouaches, ceramics, wood carvings, and stone sculpture, is a gathering center for the coffee-drinking, tea-drinking, wine-drinking artists of Safad.

Many of the artists paint for their supper. The Herzlia Hotel,

run by two art patrons, Moshe and Sarah Perl, is not only a tourist
hotel in the cool hills but an enormous art gallery. The Perls, who
are discriminating collectors, call their paintings affectionately
Fress-bilder (eating pictures)—barter for a summer of suppers.

Israel is now exporting some of its artists. Yossi Yadin of the
Chamber Theater came to the United States in late 1957 and
became a successful television actor while he studied American
techniques. Habimah took Euripedes' "Medea" and Ansky's "The
Dybbuk" to Paris for the International Festival, in July, 1957, and
scored a roaring success. The tour was a great personal triumph for
Habimah's leading lady, Hannah Rovina. Shai K. Ophir, a mime,
who first became famous with the Chizbatron, the Israel U.S.O.,
appeared with great success in night clubs and in television with
Steve Allen, and in 1958 with Shirley Temple as the dwarf in
"Rumpelstiltskin." Theodore Bikel, who came out of the Chamber
Theater, appeared on Broadway in Morton Wishengrad's "The
Rope Dancers," with critical acclaim.

In 1958 Israel sent her Yemenite dance troupe, Inbal (which
means the Tongue of the Bell), to the United States. They were a
company of nineteen young Yemenite boys and girls, all in their
twenties. The boys, all bearded, short, and powerful, were mostly
drivers of jeeps and official cars; the girls were teachers or former
sergeants; all of the troupe had served in the Israel army. Some
of them were born in Israel, most had come from Yemen and
Aden on Operation Magic Carpet. Their leading dancer, a young
beauty named Margalith Oved, with enormous green eyes, olive
skin, and a body that seemed to dance even when she just sat
quietly on the floor, had come to Israel just in time to see the state
born. The troupe had been put together by a Yemenite woman,
Sara Levi-Tanai, in 1949. One day as I sat watching the dress re-
hearsal of the Yemenite Wedding Dance, Mrs. Levi-Tanai told
me that all of their movements, physical and musical, were Yemenite in origin. "In our dance," she said, "you can see our landscape.
In our movement you can feel the camels. In the flexibility of our
feet, you can feel the sand."

The Inbal dancers not only dance, but sing and act and mime

just as they did in Yemen. When Jerome Robbins, the great American choreographer, first saw them in Israel, he became so excited that he began to work with them. Then Anna Sokolow went over to help them prepare for their tour through Europe and America. The two Americans gave the troupe technical discipline—teaching the youngsters how to jump and dance in chorus but leaving untouched their creative art and ecstatic dance and exuberant vitality.

"We try to base our dances on ancient Yemenite dances while we look for a vocabulary of artistic expression," Sara Levi-Tanai told me. "Our dance group has developed in these years since 1949, so that now our vocabulary is quite rich. But always you can see the connections with our sources.

"We work in three directions. First, we perform from Yemenite folklore—like the Yemenite Wedding Dance. We perform it in authentic form, with dancing, singing, and ritual. The second direction is the Biblical subjects—Deborah, and the Queen of Sheba. The third direction is the Israeli subjects. This is the new life for Yemenites. All of us came to Israel. Now as a nation in Israel, we want to express our life in the new land. It is a modern expression, but it is based on our Yemenite sources. The movement, physically and musically, is Yemenite. But you will see that our Yemenite origin, too, has many sources—Arabian, African, Indian, and all of the Mediterranean."

Inbal opened in New York on January 6, 1958. "It is superb contemporary theatre" Walter Terry wrote in the *Herald Tribune*. "A rich and rare treat," John Martin wrote in the *New York Times*. "Nothing remotely like it has been seen in these parts before."

All the critics singled out young Margalith Oved, who was a schoolteacher in Israel as well as the star of Inbal. Everyone took joy in her art and her grace. But nobody was more excited than the American women of the Women's League for Israel. The League built a number of beautiful homes for immigrant girls in Israel's larger cities. Margalith lived in one of their homes when she arrived in Israel, and when they asked her what she would like to study, she said she wanted to be a teacher of little children and a dancer. The League gave her a scholarship for each. Now she does both, equally well. "A superior artist," Walter Terry wrote of the lithe, dark, beautiful girl, "who can communicate the pitch of intense passion as Deborah, enchant the viewer with her commentary for 'Yemenite Wedding' or play the coquette as Sheba."

~ After the première, Abba Eban, then ambassador of Israel, gave a reception for the cast and the United Nations diplomatic corps. The ambassadors of a number of countries in the Asian-African bloc reacted with greatest enthusiasm to the dancers. The ambassador from Liberia told me, "We are friends of Israel. We have the same kind of attitude that they have toward life and the world and toward mystic things."

The ambassador from Ceylon said something that to me was the most significant comment of the evening. "I cannot understand how the Arabs and the Jews can fight. There is so much of the Arab in the Jew, and so much of the Jew in the Arab. There must be peace."

Through Inbal in particular, and through the Yemenites as a whole, Israel may well find a bridge to the Asian-African world. The Yemenites have the characteristics needed to make them Israel's interpreters in Asia and Africa.

The dance performance was a revelation to other nationals too. The German consul-general said, "I have known many of the Jewish community in Cologne. Yet I never knew that the Jewish people include not only Europeans but representatives of the Arab and Oriental world. What impressed me terribly much, during the 'Yemenite Wedding' was that the bridegroom sings, 'If I forget thee, O Jerusalem, may my right hand lose its cunning.' Now I realize how deep this religious national feeling is among Jews— that they carried it for thousands of years even in this lost corner of the Arabian peninsula."

Others among Abba Eban's guests noted with amazement the similarities between the movements and costumes of the Yemenites and the dances of their own people. The Mexican delegate to the U.N. saw it; some of the movements reminded him of the dancers in villages in the outlying hills. I detected suggestions of Eskimo hoods and Eskimo dances, and amazing similarities in the

"Wedding Dance" with the wedding ritual of the Jews of Djerba.

The country is flourishing with art, performing and visual. Jacques Lipchitz bequeathed to Israel three hundred original plasters, from which all his bronze sculptures were cast. Lady Epstein, the widow of Sir Jacob Epstein, gave two hundred of his original clay models to Israel. Billy Rose has given some of his world famous Rodins, Maillols, Daumiers, and Lehmbruchs—all to be housed in a new Museum of Art in Jerusalem on a thirty-acre hill, a complex of forty-eight galleries built of Jerusalem stone and glass.

Each year the International Music Festival has brought some of the world's great musicians to perform not only in concert halls but in a kibbutz, Ein Gev, on the Sea of Galilee, and in the magnificent Roman amphitheatre recently excavated at Caesarea. Pablo Casals came to play at the Music Festival and to be chief judge at the Pablo Casals International Violoncello Competition. Later, at a dinner in his honor, he said, "I have heard your hearts beating and this is why you are a great people: because you hear what your heart dictates to you."

Israeli artists and musicians toured America: the Israel Philharmonic, the Ramat Gan Chamber Orchestra, the Rinat Choir. Twenty-one-year-old Shmuel Ashkenasi won second prize in the Tschaikowsky International Violin Competition held in Moscow. Samuel Rubin, President of the American-Israel Cultural Foundation, established the third Rubin Academy of Music in Haifa; the others are in Jerusalem and Tel Aviv. Cultural centers were set up for the new immigrants to learn the new art and to conserve their old art forms in new settlements in the Negev desert and the hills of Galilee. The Palinsky Arab-Jewish Cultural Community and Youth Center was established in Haifa to bring Arab and Jewish youth together.

In February of 1962, Marc Chagall dedicated his greatest work, his twelve stained glass windows symbolizing the twelve tribes of Israel, in the synagogue of the Hadassah-Hebrew University Medical School. "How is it," he asked, "that the air and earth of Vitebsk, my birthplace, and of thousands of years of exile, find themselves mingled in the air and earth of Jerusalem?"

11:   A Village of Children

SUPREME COURT JUSTICE William O. Douglas flew into Tel Aviv in the summer of 1949. He had been traveling through most of the Arab countries; he had gone horseback riding with sheikhs and shahs; he had journeyed with Arab tribesmen across the desert. Now he was in Israel to see the newest experiment in democracy in the Middle East.

He traveled up and down the country, talked to the leaders, visited the cities and the villages, and then went to a children's village to see the most hopeful and blessed migration to Israel—the Migration of the Children—the Youth Aliyah. It was the ascendancy of children who needed parents, a home, security, and, most of all, love.

The Youth Aliyah was started in 1934 by a great and simple American woman from Baltimore, Henrietta Szold. From 1934 until ten years after the creation of the state, over eighty-five thousand children from seventy-two lands were rescued.

"If we cannot save the parents, at least let us save the children," Miss Szold had said. Thousands of children whose parents were later burned in gas chambers were thus rescued.

It was early in the morning when Justice Douglas, his son, a few officials and I visited Onim (Inner Strength), a Youth Aliyah village for emotionally disturbed children. Onim had a swimming pool, charming white-stucco houses, terraced lawns. It had been built by the Histadrut as a workers' rest home, but when emotionally disturbed children were brought into Israel the government decided the children's need for beauty was greater than the workers'.

Justice Douglas walked around the grounds with his son, talking with the children, who made up a small United Nations. They were from thirty-seven different countries. Now they talked Hebrew to each other, and some of them, especially those who had come from Shanghai and Bombay, talked English with the judge. He wanted to know whether Israel was better than the countries they had come from. "Oh, yes, sir," a black-eyed Indian boy answered. "This is our home."

One of the teachers was a tall, strong Lithuanian, a Buchenwald concentration camp graduate, whom the children called "David Hagadol" (Big David). Big David walked with us, patting the children on the head with unashamed affection. He led us into a shady classroom where children were studying arithmetic, into the large kitchen where other children were preparing lunch, then into the dormitories, where the children's beds were all neatly made.

As we walked on the grounds toward the swimming pool, he told us of their ape child. The ape child walked with his hands hanging almost to his knees. He didn't talk. He acted as if he understood nothing more than an animal.

One of the things some children lose under shock, Big David said, is the power of communication, the magic of words. In Onim, the teachers search for the "point of confidence," the point at which the child regains security and begins to talk.

"One day," Big David said, "we reached the point of confidence with the ape child. He spoke. He said, 'I came from Czechoslovakia.'

"We knew that. We had rescued him.

"He said, 'Just before my parents were burned in a concentration camp, they turned me over to foster parents. My foster parents had no food. So they took me into a forest and all day, while they searched for food, they tied me to a tree, with my hands tied around it—this way.' "

Big David extended his arms and clasped his fingers tightly, like a little boy's hands tied around a tree trunk.

" 'When they came back at night, they untied me. Sometimes they had food. Most of the time they didn't. In the morning, before they left, they tied me up again.' "

Big David paused. Then he went on. "He was tied up for a year and a half. He had no one to talk to. His arms grew long; he began to act like an ape, to walk like an ape. Now that we have reached the point of his confidence, we can see that his hands and arms have stopped growing and the rest of his little body is catching up with the hands and the arms. He is a child again."

He told us about the boy who had been found wandering about in the woods of Yugoslavia and who had been brought with hundreds of other orphaned and homeless children to Israel. They had reached the point of his confidence just a few days before we came to Onim. A woman arrived. For four years she had wandered through Yugoslavia, the D.P. camps of Germany, Austria, and Italy. She knew her son was alive. He had to be alive. Then she came to Onim and saw him. She flung her arms around him, weeping. That day they reached the boy's point of confidence. Now he could become normal again. He sat under a tree with his mother, talking. The other children, seeing their friend with his mother, seeing him talking, took fresh hope.

For Youth Aliyah children, coming to Israel or not coming, often meant life or death. Lonely, bewildered, sick children, spitting blood, half blind, streamed in to be healed physically and mentally.

A children's village is a settlement run just for children. Each children's village has its own story, its own heroism in the war, its own way of finding the point of confidence. There is Raanana, the beautiful Mizrakhi village, where the older children become teachers for the younger ones. There is Nizanim, a farm colony that was captured by the Egyptians, then recaptured and turned into a new Youth Aliyah village with children from Turkey and one hundred children from an orphanage in Antwerp.

Of all the children's villages, the most famous was Ben Shemen, near the Lydda airport. It was the village that the United Nations Special Committee on Palestine (UNSCOP) visited in 1947. It looked then like an idyl out of Pestalozzi's notebook. Beautiful little boys and girls were tending ducks. Children were swimming happily in a large outdoor swimming pool. In a sun-filled room little girls, wearing bright white blouses, with hand-embroidered collars and guimpes of kibbutz blue, sat at looms.

Dr. Siegfried Lehmann, the head of Ben Shemen, his face aglow with love, his voice a little breathless as he showed us around, said, "I think children who live this way do not love the city."

"The symbol of our education," Dr. Lehmann said, "is back-to-the-soil. Our children do their own weaving, stitching, spinning, sheep raising, welding. We are even trying to develop a Jewish peasant art."

Dr. Enrique Fabregat, the UNSCOP delegate from Uruguay, asked Dr. Lehmann about the morale of the children who had come out of the trauma of the concentration and D.P. camps.

Dr. Lehmann rubbed his hand through his thinning hair. He answered slowly, "It is not easy. They have no trust in anyone. Sometimes it takes us three months, sometimes six months, sometimes a year, before they begin to have faith in us. Sometimes we find them stealing bread; they cannot yet believe that if there is bread today there will be bread tomorrow. Under Hitler they learned that to live you must steal and lie. They learned that to work means to die, because work exhausted you. Tired people were no longer useful to the Nazi war machine, so they were burned. We have to teach them that work has dignity. Through work and play we try to heal them.

"We teach them agriculture, languages, trades," Dr. Lehmann said. "When they leave, they are able to take their place as healthy citizens. Thousands of children from our school are now building farm settlements all over the country."

In the large gymnasium, the children's orchestra, led by a tiny conductor in short pants, played the Overture to Coriolanus and parts of Beethoven's Ninth Symphony. The overflow children, who could not squeeze into the gymnasium, stuck their heads through the windows and listened with joy.

A few months later, the idyl was blasted. Immediately after Palestine was partitioned, on November 29, 1947, the Arabs cut off the road to the children's village. Soon there was no food. On December 14, 1947, fourteen Haganah boys decided to brave the

Arab blockade and bring in two truckloads of food. They were shot down by a unit of the Arab Legion under the command of British officers. The five or six who survived finally forced the reluctant British to give them safe escort and food came through.

All around Ben Shemen the war raged, but the village itself was never attacked. Dr. Lehmann, who had lived all these years by the Bible precept of "love thy neighbor as thyself," had made warm friends of the neighboring Arabs. The golden rule paid off. Most of Ben Shemen's small children were safely evacuated. A hundred and forty older boys and girls and the forty staff members remained throughout the war. They were often hungry but were never fired upon.

This little Jewish village that lay in a sea of Arabs became a kind of symbol of peace to both Arabs and Jews. Prisoners of war were exchanged at Ben Shemen, and when Youth Aliyah boys and girls from neighboring villages and farms were captured by the Arab Legion, the boys were confined to a temporary prison camp, but the girls were brought to Ben Shemen in an Arab armored car flying a white flag.

During the first truce in the summer of 1948, Dr. Lehmann moved Ben Shemen away from the front lines to an old army camp at Kfar Vitkin. The children's village was to be kept alive in its new temporary home, and the children healed and trained to help build Israel.

"Kfar Vitkin then," Dr. Lehmann described it to me, "was a desolate, neglected, barren military camp, with mostly black barracks, without a tree and without a touch of green to relieve the desolation. We had a hard winter."

A year later, I visited Kfar Vitkin. The military bleakness had been wiped out. Dr. Lehmann's quiet pastoral touch was everywhere. The Quonset huts and barracks were painted white and yellow. Flowers were growing. Once again the children were spinning and weaving and learning trades.

All over Israel, there were miniatures that told the country's whole story. Ben Shemen was the children's miniature. Here was the Herzl dream of rescue and reconstruction, the building of a Pestalozzi village, the healing of shocked children from Hitler's Europe, the U.N. vote, the independence won in blood, the Arab invasion, the rebuilding on barren soil of a home for more waves of children.

It was typical, too, of the ironies in which Israel was rich that each day these immigrant children played and sang and ran up and down the sand dunes in the shadow of a gray police station that the British had built to keep immigrants out of the Holy Land.

On a warm August night, the Ben Shemen children danced in a moonlight festival beneath the police station. They were celebrating the laying of a cornerstone for a "New England village," to be built as part of Ben Shemen by New England Hadassah women. Two hundred and forty orphans were to be brought from the immigrant camps the moment the model village was completed.

We drove out of Tel Aviv by bus. In an hour we were suddenly back in the pioneer days of the Land of Israel. The children danced folk dances on the sand dunes in a cove of the Mediterranean. We could almost see the sand filling up with houses, workshops, nurseries, flower gardens.

While a huge round ball of red sun sank into the Mediterranean and a huge round ball of red moon rose opposite it, like a mirror over the wasteland, the children read a passage from the Prophets describing "Kibbutz Galuyot," the ingathering of the exiles. Sitting on a wooden platform, built on the barren sand, the children's orchestra played music by Mozart. The stars were shining as adolescent girls, wearing red and gold robes and carrying ears of corn, danced a symbolic harvest dance accompanied by the orchestra and the washing of the waves. Suddenly the sand dunes all around us were lit by torches carried by running children. For Ben Shemen's children, the point of confidence had been reached.

Each year I revisited Ben Shemen and Kfar Vitkin, now called Neurim. Ben Shemen remained my favorite Youth Aliyah village in the country. Neurim became a teen-ager's paradise. The lovely pink houses of the "New England village," built by funds from New England Hadassah, were finished. The village was green and fertile. There was a beautiful football field, a huge modern dining room, and even a romantic fish pond to catch the moonlight. Neurim was now a rural Vocational Center run by Hadassah and the Youth Aliyah Department of the Jewish Agency.

Teen-agers came for six weeks of vocational study and recreation. Even Arab farm boys came for six weeks to study modern farming, living in the same dormitories with Jewish boys. It was a lesson in "togetherness" for Arabs and Jews.

Meanwhile the Ben Shemen Youth Aliyah children were returned to their original village near the Lydda airport. New children came to Ben Shemen from new lands of terror. A beautiful boy with dark hair, a sensitive mouth, and huge soft brown eyes sat at a desk in one of Ben Shemen's schoolrooms one cold January morning in 1952. In the midst of the neat rows of happy children, he seemed to sit apart. His hands were folded tightly, in an almost anguished quiet. There was little indication that once, long, long ago, when his young teacher had asked a question, he too had waved his arms enthusiastically, flashed a sudden smile, and perhaps jumped up and down in his seat as the other ten-year-olds were now doing. Now, in Israel, among immigrant children who spoke some seventy-two languages and who had known all varieties of terror, his memories were of Arab pogroms. He had recently come from Bagdad in ancient Babylon. His father had been hanged for the great crime of hiding an Israel emissary in his house.

On the floor below, in another classroom, a child bent low over his notebook, writing square and rounded Hebrew letters with the symmetry of an illuminated manuscript. I asked Dr. Lehmann why the child bent so low. Did he perhaps need glasses?

Dr. Lehmann shook his head. "He was in a Nazi concentration camp. His father was killed before his eyes. He does not need glasses. He needs love."

This was the problem of Ben Shemen as it was the problem of other Youth Aliyah villages and in fact of the whole nation.

From the East and the West, from Arab terror and totalitarian terror, the children, like the adults, had come here to be healed.

In this children's population of about five hundred, most of the newcomers were from Oriental and Arab lands. Ben Shemen was a small, intact Western civilization, a children's democracy, to which these hundreds of illiterate, frightened, and desperately lonely youngsters from Iraq, Iran, Yemen, and the troubled lands of North Africa had been transplanted.

At first many of these new children didn't know what a fork, knife, or spoon looked like. They didn't know what a pen or a notebook was for.

Dr. Lehmann searched for a common framework in which the children of two alien worlds, the Oriental and the Western, could live together. "Sometimes," he told me, "there were real fights between the two groups. They hit each other with towels, sticks, and shoes. They didn't want to sit together, eat together, sleep under the same roof. The abyss between the groups seemed almost hopelessly wide. But gradually the very process of living itself narrowed the misunderstandings. Though not forced, assimilation was swift.

"We've found," Dr. Lehmann continued, "that the Iraqi and Oriental children learn very quickly. And they have a real contribution to make to the other children. The Yemenites, who were segregated in ghettos in the Yemen, continued to develop their own culture, their own songs and dances. Now they teach us their culture.

"The Oriental children had much more discipline than the European children, a greater recognition of the authority of the parent, grandparent, and teacher. So it is easier to instill discipline in them in school. The Oriental girls are very interesting. They had almost no education in their native countries, and often lived in separate quarters of the house. Now they share their rooms with girls who had been strangers to them and worry more about the opinion of their roommates than they do about that of their teachers."

The immigration of children from the Arab world, caused Ben Shemen—as it caused all of Israel—to re-examine its old theories and revise them to suit the needs of the newcomers. Hadassah and the Youth Aliyah Department of the Jewish Agency soon discovered that one of their first tasks was to give the Oriental children a basis for understanding Israel's Western culture. The children's villages had to be made so attractive and friendly that, despite their fantastic strangeness to the newcomers, these children could really feel "at home."

It was not easy. It required patience and enormous understanding on the part of the teachers; it required the orientation of the whole school; and, most important of all, it required a love for all children from all lands of the world.

Dr. Lehmann was singularly equipped to take the children to his heart. It was the core of his philosophy that children are entitled to both patience and loving care. "With all the children, whether from East or West," he said, "our problem is first to win their confidence. When they first come to us, most of the children believe the world of adults is a bad world. They begin with a wall of distrust. It takes extreme patience and love to win a child's faith. But unless you have patience and an abiding love for children, you cannot work with them at all.

"In the last twenty-five years," he continued, "we have had thousands of children in Ben Shemen. With most, we have had good results, but not with all of course. Some have become judges, diplomats, soldiers, teachers, farmers; our graduates are all over the country."

Walking across the grounds, where the familiar buildings were being repainted and repaired and the foliage had grown green and rich, we saw a charming little boy, dressed in a sweater and short pants, leading a tiny dog.

"Orphans must have someone to love. And they must be loved themselves," Dr. Lehmann said. "So we give the children dogs and other animals to play with."

Somehow the whole meaning of Ben Shemen, its beauty and

the power and healing of love, seemed to have been caught in the scene of the little boy with his tiny dog. The idyl, though scarred by war and fraught with new difficulties in the aftermath, was being reborn. The face of Ben Shemen was once again the face of Israel at peace.

12: From Darkest Yemen

THE MOST JOYOUS migration—after the children's—was the migration out of the Yemen. It was a flight into Israel such as the world had not seen since the flight out of Egypt. The whole Jewish population poured out of the Yemen, out of the mountains and the desert of darkest Arabia where the Red Sea flowed into the Gulf of Aden and on into the Indian Ocean.

The oldest Jews in the world were fleeing into the youngest land of Jews. It was hunger, simple hunger—hunger for food, hunger for a home, hunger multiplied fifty thousand times for fifty thousand people fleeing.

And of all the nations pouring into the pressure cooker, none came with more joy than these small, gentle, dark-eyed Jews. None came out of greater darkness into the blinding light of the Home Land.

Immigrant camps? the Yemenites said. Tents, overcrowding? No matter, it is our soil. Misery? You do not know what misery means if you have not seen the Yemen. Did you not know that a Jew in the Yemen could not build a house more than two stories high, because then he could look down on a Moslem? Did you not know that in the Yemen a Jew could not leave the ghetto at night, or have lights in the ghetto streets, or wear shoes? That out of every thousand children who were born about eight hundred died? That every orphan became the property of the state and was forced to convert to Islam? The camps are hard, but here at least our children can live and be Jews.

They have come out of such hunger, and such earlier-than-Dark-Ages barbarism, that they expect almost nothing. They have been rescued from such humiliation that anything in Israel is too good to be true. They are simple, honest, happy, exotic, and lovely to look at. They are exquisite craftsmen. In the Yemen they were not

116

allowed to work at any but secondary trades. They could become itinerant blacksmiths for the Arab farmers, silversmiths, makers of plows and nails and goatskin waterbuckets. Yet within those restrictions they became artists. Their silver jewelry is famous throughout the Middle East. Their embroidery is the loveliest in the whole Arab world. Their artisans were paid only in food, after the harvest. If there was a good year, they ate. If there was a famine, they starved.

For years the Jews trickled out of the country illegally and under the threat of capital punishment. In 1949 they were permitted to leave. If they had any property they had to abandon it or sell it for almost nothing. They had to pay a human head tax for themselves and their treasured Bible scrolls. They crawled out of the Yemen on foot and found their way hundreds of miles down from the ' mountains to the British Protectorate of Aden. The American Joint Distribution Committee (J.D.C.), through the United Jewish Appeal, was flying them on giant silver-winged C-54 Skymasters, piloted by American boys who wore cowboy boots from Texas, who had flown freight over the Hump during the war, and who now were flying Bible Jews along the Red Sea Bible route to the Bible Land.

When Magic Carpet Operation was at its height, in the summer and fall of 1949, I flew down to Aden in one of the Skymasters with three Israeli doctors and Joan Comay, whose husband, Michael, later became Israel's ambassador to the U.N. We left Lydda at midnight. Eight hours later, at the tip of the Red Sea in Aden, we had flown back into history. On the hot desert wasteland, stretching into the horizon, ten thousand people were making a temporary halt in their long flight. Bearded patriarchs, with traditional prayer shawls hanging over their shoulders, stood in slow-moving queues to get the day's issue of food for their families. A few carried white bleached umbrellas. Some carried babies, whose arms showed ugly blisters from the sun.

A few families, searching for shade, had built wigwams from their straw mats. Some of the women washed their children with water from little pots. The sand lapped up the water thirstily before it trickled off.

All over the desert camp, people were talking, shouting, running, cooking, eating, laughing, singing, praying, worrying. Hundreds were crowded in a little wooden lean-to where they were getting vaccinations; the sick ranged in and out of the little J.D.C. hospital; others pushed fearfully around a shed where a photographer was taking their pictures for identity cards.

The heat hung suspended until a sandstorm came up swift and unannounced and blackened the camp with gray, blinding clouds of sand. The people covered their nostrils and eyes with their clothes. Everyone ran for shelter, but there was no shelter, there was protection only in the family. Mothers ran screaming for their children. Fathers peered anxiously through the sand clouds, but they could see nothing. Infants were smothered inside their mother's robes.

About an hour later, the wind died as suddenly as it had been born. The children began to run about again. The long, patient queues re-formed. In the wigwams the men took long draughts of their water pipes.

Most of the people still wore all or part of the clothing they had worn for centuries. The women wore narrow striped trousers, elaborately embroidered, that showed beneath their flowing robes or one-piece dresses. In the Yemen, one of the women told me later, if you wanted to say a man was effeminate, you said, "He wears the pants."

Days later, I was able to discern the variations in the costumes of the people from different parts of the Yemen. You could always tell the women who had come from Sana, the capital, because of the lovely hood or gargush that they wore, Eskimo fashion, framing their faces, with gold and silver fringe across the forehead. Women from other parts of the Yemen wore shawls wound gracefully around their heads and chins and falling onto their shoulders. Yemenite women wore no veils, but they frequently drew their large head shawls modestly across their faces. Most of them wore heavy necklaces, dangling earrings, and bracelets.

We walked through the hot, blazing camp to a little warehouse shed, where three Yemenite girls were distributing new clothing to a long queue of new arrivals. One man was issued a pair of pale pink silk pajamas, which he promptly put on top of all his other clothes. The women put colorful calico dresses from the West over their Eastern robes, with the legs of their embroidered trousers showing. Some kept their gargushes; others tied bandanas around their heads. Shimon Salem Chaim from Djuban, a tall, handsome boy of twenty, was still a bachelor, he told me, because he had never been able to earn forty-five riyals (about fifteen dollars; there are about three riyals to every dollar) to pay a bride's father. Shimon, who served as a shomer (local guard), had the fanciest outfit in the camp, a British army cap, a South African wool vest, a soft sport shirt buttoned to the collar, and khaki shorts. His long black earlocks dangled on his cheeks and fell to the top of his shirt from beneath the general's cap.

One man lay on the sand with his legs in the air, trying to negotiate a pair of khaki pants. An Israeli doctor helped him stand up and showed him how to put one leg into the trousers at a time. He finally got the pants buttoned up and then put the khaki shirt on. The shirt seemed far too beautiful to hide, so he let it hang outside the pants, with his prayer shawl over his shoulders. The doctor shook his head and said the shirt had to go inside the trousers. The man reluctantly raised the shirt and revealed an enormous belt around his waist. The doctor made him take off the belt, which was a craftsman's masterpiece, and wear it outside.

Suleiman Moosa Tenami was typical of the tens of thousands who were fleeing from Yemen into Aden. Suleiman was about fifty. Like the patriarchs of the Bible, he was barefoot. His hair was white; his earlocks were white; he wore a striped black and white robe and a black and white gypsy-like bandana tied around his head. His light gray eyes still carried the terror of the long flight out of Yemen. His voice was low and dignified.

We were sitting inside the camp late one night talking. Our interpreter was Joseph Doar, a dark-eyed second-generation Yemenite boy from Jerusalem.

"Only a few years ago, it meant death if we tried to leave Yemen and go to Eretz Israel," Suleiman said. "But this year the Imam announced that we could all go if we left everything we owned. We all decided to leave. We learned that the Land of Israel had been reborn. We learned that there was a new Jewish state that had been prophesied in the Bible.

"I owned a few things in Lidan. I left everything and, with my wife and our baby—he is six months old—walked on foot for fourteen days. We walked with thirty people, so we would have protection against Arabs who might rob us and kill us. On the way, some Arabs beat us and robbed us and insulted us. They took whatever they could find of our hidden money, and whatever we owned.

"In the ghetto outside Sana, we were taken in by the good Jews. We waited there another two weeks until more people came, so we would have even more protection together. Then, when there were about a hundred people, we went on foot again for eight days to Sayani."

"Why on foot? Were there no donkeys or camels in the Yemen?"

"We had to leave all our animals with the Imam. For food, we took honey, dates, and samni [a creamy butter]. In Sayani, we rented motor trucks. It cost us forty riyals for each person. That was for the truck driver. Then we paid a special ransom, a head tax of three riyals, to the sheikh. At every customhouse we paid a ransom for everyone and for the scrolls and the holy books.

"The rich paid for the poor. I had a little money, but I borrowed fifty riyals from someone to help pay the way. I will pay it back when we get to Israel and I find work.

"We traveled two days by truck from Sayani to Lahej." (He pronounced the name of the sheikhdom as if it were "Lochedge.") "We had to pay the Sultan of Lahej another head tax of three riyals for each person, and for every piece of our belongings, especially the books and the scrolls. I had to pay ten riyals for my holy scroll; it's more than a hundred years old. We stayed at Lahej one day and then came here."

Forty-five thousand Yemenites like Suleiman, I thought, would add a new and exotic seasoning to the pressure cooker. Israel was beginning to study Yemenite history, to rediscover the origins of these people, to choose between barely recorded fact and centuries of embroidered legends.

The Yemenites are said to be the oldest Jewish community in the world. Some of the legends say that they left the Holy Land in King Solomon's time. Some historians say that they went into voluntary exile in 628 B.C., to escape from Nebuchadnezzar; that seventy-five thousand Jews of all professions—military men, merchants, political leaders—crossed the Jordan and traveled down the desert and through the mountains of Arabia to the Yemen. They soon made themselves felt among the native population for their intelligence and ability. They built palaces; they planted gardens and orchards. When Cyrus, King of Persia, conquered the Babylonian Empire, he sent word to the Yemen through Ezra, his scribe, inviting them to return out of exile.

"Thus saith Cyrus, King of Persia," the proclamation read. "The Lord God of heaven hath given me all the kingdoms of the earth and he hath charged me to build him an house at Jerusalem, which is in Judea. Who is there among you of all his people? His God be with him, and let him go up to Jerusalem, which is in Judea, and build the house of the Lord God which is in Israel (he is the God) which is in Jerusalem"—Ezra: 2-3.

The legends say that the Jews of the Yemen refused Cyrus' invitation to return. According to Joseph Schechtman, they excommunicated Ezra and forbade their children to bear his name. They continued to prosper, and one of the kings of the Yemen became a Jew. Mohammed's march across Asia ended their power. In a war between the Moslems and the Jewish tribes, the Jews were defeated at the battle of Wa'th. By the beginning of the seventh century, the Jews were destroyed as a political force in the Yemen; soon they ceased to be an economic force. They became second-class citizens, whose status was defined in the Islamic "Covenant of the Prophet." They became dwellers of the ghetto. Oppressed and humiliated, they turned to the wellsprings of the Jewish faith. They accepted the Talmud and, though they were thousands of miles from Jews in the Holy City and in the lands of exile, they lived by the same Bible.

The world lost sight of them until the Middle Ages. In the twelfth century they were rediscovered by Maimonides, who wrote "Iggeret Teiman" (Epistle to the Yemenites), offering them consolation for their misery in Yemen. With a profound yearning to return to the Home Land, they developed authors and lively scholars who, in the fashion of the Middle Ages, wrote commentaries on the Bible. Their cabbalistic writings prepared them for the greatest of all the false Messiahs, Shabtai Zvi, who shocked his followers when he left them to be converted to Islam in 1666.

The Jews continued to search in poetry and scholarship for an outlet for their oppression. Once again, they turned inward and lost contact with the world, until the middle of the last century, when some Jewish travelers risked their lives to enter Yemen. In 1858 a Jerusalem Jew, Yaakov Sapir Halevy, traveled to the Yemen to search for the lost ten tribes, who were believed to be somewhere in Arabia. Rabbi Sapir published a report saying that "The Jews in Yemen are in a position of inferiority, and are oppressed by a people which declares itself to be holy and pious, but which is very brutal, barbarous, and hard-hearted."

Sapir's journey had wide repercussions. The people began to emigrate in small numbers. In 1911, the Jews of Palestine sent S. Yavnieli to Yemen to invite the landless people to help colonize a peopleless land. Hundreds of Yemenites migrated from Sharab to the farms and villages of Palestine.

On his accession to power in 1906, the Imam Yahya issued a proclamation ordering every adult Jew to pay an annual poll tax in return for the protection he received.

The Jews [the proclamation read] must annually pay a fifth of the value of their property. They must not band together against a Muslim. They must not build higher than the houses of Muslims, disturb Muslims at rest, encroach upon the boundaries of Muslims, cast obloquy upon their religion of Islam, curse any Muslim prophet, or vex any Muslim on matters of religion. They must ride only sidesaddle. They must not witness the discomfiture of a Muslim, display their religious books outside their synagogues, raise their voices in prayer, or sound ram horns. They must pray in a subdued voice. They must not dissuade Jews from seeking to be judged according to the laws of Mohammed. They must show honor and respect to Muslims.

The Jews were the property of the Imam. They lived in city ghettos or in ghetto-like areas on the fringes of towns. Though their houses in the Qu'ul-Yahud, the Jewish quarter outside Sana, were low mud-baked huts, built in a dark labyrinth of streets, the few people allowed to visit them were astonished by their cleanliness, dignity, and sheer artistry.

The Arabs were largely illiterate, but not the Jews. Inside the ghetto, they formed their own society, with synagogues and even a few schools. The language they spoke was Arabic, but the boys all studied Hebrew. Most of the schools were too poor to have more than one book. The teacher held the book in front of him while the children, sitting in a semicircle, learned to read from every angle.

The book they read was the Bible. For they were the people of the Book. It was the Bible that had kept them intact. The Bible was their lifeline. They sang its psalms when the sun rose and when the sun set. They knew the Bible in Hebrew and Aramaic, as few people in the West. Their scribes copied the Old Testament in beautiful scrolls, as the scribes had copied the Dead Sea scrolls in the Holy Land.

They printed the square Hebrew letters like artists, with a piece of wood sharpened to a fine pen point. They wrote on scrolls of natural sheep leather and for ink they used the juice of boiled-down fruit. Some of the scrolls were four and five hundred years old; some belonged to Jewish congregations in the Yemen; some had been handed down from father to son. Now, with the whole Jewish community uprooting itself, they were rescuing the scrolls, guarding them like children, wrapping them in cloth, then in odd-shaped boxes. Some of the boxes were long and octagonal-shaped, brightly painted in red, brown, and blue juice colors. Some were Socony Vacuum tin cylinders.

The scrolls were so precious to them that when, in Aden, I took a picture of Suleiman Moosa Tenami holding the Torah he immediately began to sing. This was the word of God and you had to praise it.

In all their poverty, they kept the Shabbat as carefully and as beautifully as the most prosperous and devout Jews in the Western world. Shabbat was the Lord's Day and the Jews, oppressed from without, reached within themselves to find beauty and faith.

The Jewish women of the Yemen, though they received no education, still held a high position in the home. Yemenite men could marry several women, provided they paid the proper dowry. Children married at twelve and thirteen, I was told, so that if they were orphaned, they could pose as heads of families and not be converted to Mohammedanism. The women rarely left their houses; the men had to do even the marketing. Except for those who were itinerant craftsmen, most of the men worked at home. Fathers taught their sons, mothers their daughters.

By law, they were second-class citizens, but between World Wars I and II even their second-class position deteriorated. The Imam introduced cheap products from Germany and Japan. The Arabs lost their taste for the fine craftsmanship of the Jews. According to Professor S. D. Goitein of the Hebrew University, the Imam forced the Jews to teach the Arabs their trades and then ousted the Jews from these industries. The Jews were faced with economic ruin. In 1934 the notorious Mufti of Jerusalem visited the Yemen. He left new ruin in his wake. The Imam clamped a ban on all immigration to Palestine, but after a few years he relaxed the ban a little and once again the river began to flow. A cemetery at Qataba, on the border between Yemen and Aden, held the hundreds of emaciated, sick, hungry Yemenite Jews who, like Moses, began the long trek but never reached the Land.

While European Jews were fighting their way on aliyah beth to Palestine, Yemenite Jews were fighting their way out of Yemen into Aden, their escape route to Palestine. Since millions of Jews were trapped in Hitler's fortress, a percentage of Britain's White Paper certificates was made available for the Yemenites in Aden. From November, 1943, to October, 1945, about seventy-three hun-

dred Yemenite Jews entered the country legally. The overflow remained in Aden. They lived in poverty and constant terror of the
Arabs. Their homes were the streets and hovels of the Jewish
ghetto in the Crater, a town built inside an actual crater of rocks.
The British finally put them in a desert camp at El Hashid.

In 1946, a small, motherly Jewish doctor, Olga Feinberg from
Chicago, arrived in Aden. Dr. Feinberg had operated a sanatorium
in Jericho and had countless Arab friends and patients. In 1938,
during the Arab riots, her sanatorium was destroyed by fire, but
Dr. Feinberg managed to escape, disguised as a Moslem woman.
She went to India, where she served during World War II in a
British military hospital. On her way back to the United States,
she stopped off in Aden and was appalled by the condition of the
Yemenite Jews. She sent a cable to the late Dr. Judah L. Magnes,
President of the Hebrew University, who was chairman of the
J.D.C.'s Middle East Advisory Committee. She offered to stay in
Aden and take care of the refugees. The J.D.C. cabled her a free
hand. She ran the camp singlehanded; she became its doctor, di-
rector, teacher, mother, counselor, judge, jury, and protector.

She trained young Yemenite women to act as nurses. Two young
Yemenites from Israel helped her run the camp, teaching the
children the Hebrew language and the songs of Israel and preparing
them for the Promised Land. In about two years, the camp's
population grew to nearly four thousand.

Disaster struck Aden on December 2, 1947, a few days after the
United Nations voted to partition the Holy Land. The Aden
Arabs went on a wild rampage through the Jewish quarter in the
Crater and killed seventy-six Jews, wounded seventy-eight others,
and for a whole month burned and looted Jewish homes and businesses. The Jewish boys' and girls' schools were gutted, their windows turned into gaping holes through which you could see the
sky. At the Hashid camp, Dr. Feinberg kept a twenty-four-hour-a-
day vigil against Arab attacks. Fortunately they never came.

By the spring of 1948, the Jews were running out of the Yemen
in such hordes that the British governor of Aden, Sir Reginald
Champion, tried to dam the flow. He strengthened the British

border patrols. Local sheikhs and sultans were warned to allow no
Jews to enter their kingdoms. J.D.C. representatives were told to
harbor no new refugees in the Aden camp. Sir Reginald appealed
to the Imam himself to prevent the Jews from leaving Yemen.
The Imam agreed.

Until the Arab war in 1948, the Yemenite Jews had sailed from
Aden up the Red Sea and through the Suez Canal to Palestine.
Now the Egyptian government closed the Canal. The Yemenite
Jews were sealed off from Israel. The J.D.C. decided in December,
1948, to use a kind of Berlin air lift, whose freight was people, not
coal or food. Operation Magic Carpet, one of the most spectacular
air lifts in history, was begun. The Alaska Airlines, which had been
flying passengers and freight in subarctic Alaska, began to fly passengers out of one of the hot spots of the world. The Arab-Jewish
war was still on. The planes were fired on a number of times. Fuel
was one of their greatest problems. They established a fueling station in Asmara, in Eritrea, some five hundred miles from Aden.
They pumped extra gasoline in the tanks at Asmara, then flew to
Aden and, with a hundred-foot garden hose, drained the gasoline
into other planes to take the people to Israel. Within two months,
some forty-five hundred refugees arrived in Israel, most of them
women, children, and old and sick men.

In April of 1949, the American consul in Aden heard strange
news through an informant. The Imam had announced that all
Jews could leave the Yemen. The dam broke. The Jews began
their mass flight. They dared not wait a day for fear the Imam
would once again change his mind.

Meanwhile, in America, the government clamped down on the
Alaska Airlines for wandering overseas and hunting for foreign
business illegally. A new company was formed in August, 1949,
called N.E.A.T. (Near East Air Transport Company) and headed
by two Americans, James Wooten and Robert Maguire. Five and
six planeloads of people began to leave Aden each day.

Down from the mountains, across the sparse roads, over track-
less desert wastes, the people continued to pour out of Yemen,
paying a ransom for their bodies and their Bibles to each sultan

as they fled, until, outside the Crown Colony of Aden, they came to the last Arab kingdom, owned by the Sultan of Lahej. Lahej was the last stage of the passion, the last Arab customhouse, the last border of head tax and terror. Beyond Lahej lay the J.D.C. camp in the Hashid Desert. Beyond the camp lay Israel.

13: On Eagles' Wings

I DECIDED to get to the Sultan of Lahej's kingdom, if I could. I had to see the payment of the head tax, the human ransom in our time for every Yemenite man, every newborn baby, every holy scroll and Bible.

The J.D.C. people in Aden warned me against Lahej. "You're mad to go. It's barbaric country. They might kill you."

"How can they? I have an American passport."

The British agent in charge of the West Aden Protectorate was J. W. T. Allen, a tall thin Englishman who wore white shorts, long socks, and a monocle. I called on him one morning in the Crater, the city built within the natural crater of rocks.

I asked Mr. Allen if he could give me a pass through the Protectorate to the Sultan of Lahej's kingdom. He telephoned the Sultan, who said he had no objection. Mr. Allen's secretary filled in the pass.

I hired a car and, with a young Arab interpreter, drove through the Crater. Camels, cars, children, police brushed against each other; screaming Arab vendors yelled into the taxi, trying to sell trinkets. Indian merchants stood quietly in their shops, displaying silk saris and Scotch plaid cotton, which Arab men wear as loincloths. Somali women glided noiselessly down the noisy streets. Despite the heat, they wore heavy cotton skirts that reached the ground. Long cotton shawls encircled their heads, flowed the length of their bodies, and fell to their ankles.

If patterns of culture are shown in clothing, Aden was at the crossroads of two worlds. In its clothes, as in its commerce and politics, it lay between Arabia and India. For almost a hundred years, it had been ruled from India, in effect the colony of a colony. When the British captured this Arab land from the Turks in 1839, they made it part of the Indian Empire. Finally, in 1937, with India in the ferment of its movement for independence, they took Aden away and put it under the Colonial Office.

For the British, Aden's importance is its position on the map. At the tip of southern Arabia, it lies on the Gulf of Aden, between the Red Sea and the Indian Ocean. On the far-flung route between Egypt and India, Aden is England's Red Sea Gibraltar, her naval base, fueling station, and harbor for trade with the Arab Peninsula.

We drove out of the Crater and through the Main Pass, an archway of barren, solid rocks, the overland road to the rest of Arabia. We passed Maala, the shipbuilding and dhour-building harbor, where beautiful old Portuguese dhours floated in the sea like illustrations from a schoolbook on ancient history. We drove on along a good highway to Khormaksar, the R.A.F. airfield from which the Yemenite Jews took off for Israel. The heat bore down on us like a lead curtain. We rode past salt pans—Aden's main industry is salt—with Dutch windmills lifting water from one salt pan to another until the salt was crystallized. It would then be dried and crushed for export.

Just up the road from the Hashid camp where the Jews were waiting, some ten miles from the Crater, we drove through a colorful Arab town of some twenty thousand people. It was Sheikh Othman, the terminal point for most of the camel caravans from the interior. Its sun-glazed streets were lined with Arab shops and little mud houses, in front of which a dozen or more wooden cots lay, stacked on top of each other.

Sheikh Othman was known as the red-light district of Aden. For Jews, it was a village of terror; during the 1947 riots, some thirty people were said to have been killed there.

Two miles beyond, we came to the first customs post, Dar Elamir. Half-naked Arabs, with long hair hanging down their backs, turbans, loincloths, and big guns, halted the car. One of them took my pass and went into the customs shed. Another kept his gun trained on us in the car. While I watched, the gun began to grow until it looked like a cannon.

After an interminable ten minutes, with the sun boiling through the car, the guard returned, jotted down the number of the taxi,

charged an auto tax of ten annas (about twenty cents), and allowed
us to proceed. We drove on past crude, primitive huts where Arab
women with head shawls rushed out to stare curiously. Arab men,
naked to the waist, yelled after us, as if it were a dirty word, or a
joke, "Taxi, taxi." The road became narrow and wild and gutted.
We left it to drive on the desert floor itself.

The ruined walls of an American landing base, Bar Nasr—used
in the war—rose up in the desert. Three huge buzzards, each as
big as a ten-year-old child, walked around a dead camel like under-
takers. Camel caravans eyed us with interest. Here and there in
the desert were a few signs of life—straw huts in front of which sat
almost motionless half-naked men.

About an hour and a half out of the Crater, we approached a few
rows of scrawny palm trees rising out of the desert, some white
water buffaloes, and herds of goats. In the distance lay Lahej.

The first building we passed was the palace of the twenty-eight-
year-old sultan, Fadhl Abdul Karim. It was a gray and white stone
three-story modern house, completely surrounded by a tall, pro-
tecting wall of stone and steel. We drove into the crowded village
to the sultan's customhouse. My interpreter went into the building
with my pass. I sat alone in the taxi while a mob of Arabs encircled the car, shouting, leering. At last the interpreter came out.
He led the way silently into the customhouse.

We entered a small, dark alley. A crowd of Yemenite people
huddled together; an Arab squatted on the ground counting little
piles of riyals. The Bible Jews were paying their ransom.

Towering on a high platform about six feet over them (is there
not some added terror in height?), a barefoot Arab with a black
mustache, wearing a wilted European shirt and a plaid loincloth
that came like a short skirt just above his knees, sat on his haunches.
He had a sheaf of papers on which he noted in huge Arabic numerals the money the sultan was collecting.

I walked through the narrow alley into a huge, open courtyard.
A hundred or more people squeezed against each other in fright.

I fingered my passport. How did fleeing people feel, with no
passports, no papers at all?

When the people learned that I was not an Arab, they crowded around me, talking rapidly. My Arab interpreter translated: "Sick, sick. Help us." A woman pointed to a young girl lying on the hot stones trembling. The heat felt like 150° to me, but she was shivering as though we were in an Arctic blizzard, as though the journey to the Promised Land would end for her that day.

Children pulled at my skirt. "Water. Water. We have no water."

"Have patience," I said. I don't know how I dared to use the word. "This is the end of the journey. Tonight we'll send the trucks for you. Tonight you'll be in the camp. There are doctors there, and food. Tonight you'll be safe."

We drove back to the J.D.C. camp in Aden. The trucks traveled only at night; the recent pogrom was still too fresh to risk upsetting the Arabs.

Long after midnight, the lights of the trucks moved down the desert road like the eyes of jungle cats. We rushed out of the barbed-wire camp. We didn't use big lights; we turned flashlights and hurricane lamps onto the trucks. The Yemenites sat on the truck floors terrified, still not believing they were safe.

"Safe, safe. Come down now," we said. "No more danger. No more Arabs. Only Jews. Israelis, Americans."

Little by little, they seemed to understand. They climbed down from the trucks. An old man carried a shriveled woman on his humped back. Had he carried her this way along most of that flight?

A tall man jumped down, then turned to the truck again to help his wife. She sat seemingly unable to move, paralyzed with fear. A pretty little girl jumped down alone. She looked at us swiftly; then, stricken with terror, she ran off screaming into the darkness of the Hashid camp. Women clutched babies. Men held a child in one arm, a holy scroll in the other.

The J.D.C. people gave them bread and water and milk and dates. Then the people lay down on the dark sand exhausted, but comforted and safe.

I could not sleep that night. I walked through the camp, picking my way through a labyrinth of tired, safe people. Two bodies were covered with shrouds. They would be buried in the morning. Two women lay on the sand giving birth to babies.

In the morning, one of the mothers carried the newborn infant in her skirt to the hospital, where the nurse helped her finish the birth. That baby lived. They didn't always live. Each day there were seven or eight deaths described on the death certificates as due to natural causes. Natural because of the long trek; natural because of the heat by day and the cold by night, because there was no food and no water, because of the terror along the route.

One midnight I was sitting in the staff compound when a man rushed in breathlessly. The gestures of his hands told his story. "The Arabs caught our group. They tried to strangle us." He put both hands to his throat. "They searched us for our money." His hands moved restlessly across his robe. His head shook. "We had nothing. They tried to kill us." He clapped his hands swiftly and slapped one hand down from the other. "We ran and ran. All the way we ran!"

After he left I lay down on a cot in the sand. Though I had hardly been able to breathe in the heat of the camp by day, I was freezing now. Blinding sandstorms kept whipping through the camp. I must have dozed off, but about three I was awakened by a soft, beautiful murmuring that came from every part of the enclosure. I walked quietly through the camp. Men were praying before the rising of the sun, keeping themselves pure and holy, as they prepared for the journey home.

The people stayed in the camp for a week or longer. The J.D.C. doctors and nurses vaccinated them and began the long uphill climb against malaria. Many of the people had contracted the disease in a swamp at the border, where the British kept the overflow, to limit the size of the camp.

The Jewish Agency took pictures of the people and gave them identity cards. For the first time after hundreds of years they were first-class citizens.

They rested, ate, read their precious holy scrolls, and prayed as once the children of Israel had prayed, as Moses led them out of the wilderness. Each day they sang "Next year in Jerusalem." And each day for some five hundred the prayer was coming true.

I flew back to Israel in an American Skymaster with a hundred and forty Yemenite Jews, yet the payload was no greater than that of fifty passengers in America. Some of the men weighed seventy or eighty pounds; some of the children of twelve weighed what an American child of four weighs. Some of the children were so ill they had to be taken right from the plane to a hospital in Israel.

In the plane, I asked an old man, "Have you ever seen a plane before?"

He shook his head.

"Are you frightened?"

"Frightened? Why should I be frightened? It is all written in the Bible." He quoted the beautiful passage from Isaiah:

"But they that wait upon the Lord shall renew their strength; they shall mount up with wings as eagles; they shall run, and not be weary; and they shall walk, and not faint.

"For all these years, we waited upon the Lord and He kept renewing our strength. Now we're mounting up with wings as eagles. Only the Bible didn't say they would be American eagles' wings."

All the way up the length of the Red Sea, we kept remembering that other great exodus. To the west lay Somaliland, Eritrea, Ethiopia, Egypt; to the east lay Yemen and the vast desert land of Saudi Arabia, over whose holy cities no plane was permitted to fly. A forced landing in any of these Arab countries would have meant death. Yet somehow we knew that nothing could happen. It had all been written in the Bible.

Soon after sunset we flew over Elath, King Solomon's port at the southern tip of Israel. Here the soldiers of Egypt, Jordan, and Israel eyed each other suspiciously. At nine o'clock, eight hours after we had left Aden, our plane came down at Lydda. The people hurried out of the plane and touched the holy soil. It was as if the glory of Zion shone on their faces.

I asked the old man who had quoted Isaiah, "How does it feel now in Israel?"

He threw his arms out and said, "Thank God, we are home and we are safe!"

They were taken inside a shelter and then driven to a reception camp. It was Rosh Haayin (Head of the Eye), the British Ras el Ein Royal Air Force camp, taken by the Iraqi irregulars and won back by the Israelis. The hangars, now converted into dormitories, had the marks of their former inhabitants; Arab soldiers had left their names on the pillars—Ibrahim, Mohamed.

Reconstruction was a slow process; but as soon as it was feasible the people were resettled by the Jewish Agency in villages, on farms, and in cities. They were working in the orange groves and on public-works projects. From the Galilee in the north to the Negev in the south, you saw these gentle, sweet-faced Bible Jews building roads. The wits called them "Golda's roads," because Golda Meir had started road-building projects all over the land. In the new farm settlements in the Huleh Valley you saw happy Yemenites walking together, smiling.

Many have found homes in former Arab villages. Akir, about forty-five minutes from Tel Aviv on the Jerusalem Road, was a village whose Arabs, sniping at travelers, had made the road there impassable. When the fortunes of war turned against them, the Arabs fled. In 1948, Akir's mud houses fell into swift decay. A year later, 1,320 Jewish families were moved in, most of them Yemenites and Bulgarians. The whole village was like a Chagall painting, with little crooked houses with crooked doors and crooked hand-cut windows perched at the side of a winding crooked road. The houses and shops were freshly whitewashed; there were neat signs in Hebrew, Bulgarian, and English, saying BARBER, PHARMACY. There was a school, and a hospital with a warmhearted woman physician, Dr. Erica Ferber.

I went to visit Avram Gamliel, a thin, slight, handsome Yemenite, who had flown to Israel in 1949, a few months after his wife, their two sons, his mother, and his sister. It was Purim time when he came, a lovely season in Israel. But Avram had contracted tuberculosis during the long trek. He could not be a worker in Israel. Yet sitting in their little garden, he looked completely adjusted to the new land. He wore Western clothing. His gentle face lit up, almost saintlike, when he smiled. His little eight-year-old son Shalom wore a tattered hat on his soft brown hair. Shalom ran back and forth around the tiny garden. He played with the chickens and darted through the courtyard, where we sat in the shadow of a gnarled tree.

Avram's wife and seventeen-year-old son earned the family's food by picking oranges and grapes in season. They each earned about twenty-eight dollars a month, supplemented by fifty dollars which Avram, an indigent, received from the Jewish Agency and the Department of Social Welfare.

It was Sa'ida, the old mother, who kept the family intact. She had a lined and leathery face and a look of ancient wisdom. She wore a dark blue cotton scarf woven helmetlike around her head and throat. A calico dress reached to her knees. She cooked the food in the outdoor kitchen that Avram had built for her. She washed the figs at the well in the courtyard and when she finished her cooking chores, she sat barefoot on the floor weaving a basket from straw that the W.I.Z.O., the Women's International Zionist Organization, one of the finest nonprofit enterprises in Israel, gave her, buying the finished basket from her for resale.

A breath-takingly beautiful girl came into the garden. She was Avram's eighteen-year-old sister Miriam. She had the wan beauty of a person in the last stages of tuberculosis. Dr. Ferber had told me that tuberculosis was the worst disease in the village. "Yet Akir is a happy village," she said, "because the people want to be healthy."

Now it was Rosh Hashanah, the Jewish New Year, and I asked Avram, "Did you imagine last Rosh Hashanah that you would be spending this New Year in Israel?"

He shook his head. "I had been hoping it for so many years and it never came true. I didn't dare believe it would come true. It's very good to be here. Next Rosh Hashanah you must come back. It will be even better."

"It will be even better," I thought, as I took leave of the Gamliels and began to walk back through the village. To be sure, there were grave problems—not enough work, not always enough food, mud houses that might crumble in the winter's rains, the tragic doom of tuberculosis—but there was a solid feeling of hope, of having come from bondage into freedom.

You could almost see them taking their place in the new land, adding their gentleness and beauty to the rich mixture of nations building the new Israel—Jews from everywhere, Arabs, giant Circassians from old Russia, and handsome Druses from the mountains.

As I started to leave the village I asked Mika Vikal, an old Bulgarian, and his wife, who were eking out a living in a tiny shop, making tin dustbins and sand pails for children, "How is it here in Israel?"

"It is good," the old woman said. "If you can just eat bread here, it is already good."

14: The Jews of Djerba

ONE OF the largest migrations into Israel in the early 1950's was that from North Africa, and of all the newcomers the most exotic were the North African Jews from the island of Djerba. They lived on the coast of Tunisia, just west of Tripoli and some three hundred miles from the site of the ancient city of Carthage. Here, on an island of rare beauty, dark superstition, and a miracle-working Jewish shrine, some forty-five hundred Jews lived in an unbroken mirror of history.

Djerba is said to be the enchanted island whose perfumed lotus flowers made Ulysses forget his wife and his home. For the Lotus Eaters that Homer sang of, time stood still on the island. For Djerba's Jews, time has, until recently, stood still too. Ancient Jewish history and folklore are written here in the present tense.

In Europe, much of the Jewish past now lies buried under the gray dust of rubble; Djerba is one of the few places where a phase of that past still lives. The scholar, seeking to reconstruct medieval Jews from books and legends, finds them walking down the sun-drenched streets of this African island.

Lovely, massive women, with soft skins, silky black hair and huge eyes, glide through the ancient courtyards wrapped in red and gold and striped robes, wearing gold earrings, bracelets, great hooped anklets, their bare feet intricately tattooed with henna dye.

The witch doctors still heal, the keffeers still cure, the children still wear amulets, the hand of Fatma is still painted on the houses to ward off the Evil Eye; the blind, the lame, the sick, the sterile women begging, like Rachel, to have their wombs opened, all journey each year in a huge pilgrimage to the Holy Synagogue of the Ghriba, a "Jewish Lourdes," to be healed by magic and faith.

Living off the beaten paths of scholarship, these Jews of Djerba may help to fill in some gaps in the knowledge of the Jewish past.

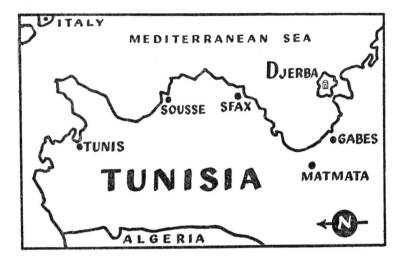

Their roots are deep in Africa and the Orient, far deeper than many of us suspect. Here is no erudite intellectualism, here are no modern revolutionary movements. Here are African folkways and cultural patterns entwined with Talmudic lore.

Those of us who grew up in Western traditions, and who have only now, since Israel's great ingathering, come to know the Yemenite, Iraqi, Irani, and other Oriental and African Jews, are beginning to realize how vital a role they play in the new state. Israel partakes of the richness and the sufferings of their way of life. The African Jews now living in Djerba are a symbol, a lesson and a warning—the past is manifold, and the question of what is to be allowed to disappear, and what encouraged to flourish and develop into new forms, is a complicated one with which Israel will be struggling for many years.

These are Jews with a kind of regal splendor in their poverty. They are proud. They are enormously attractive. They live on their own terms. Though theirs is the whole history of North Africa—of its golden age and its vandalization, of its invasion by Moslems, Spaniards, Turks, French, the anti-Semitic Vichy regime, and the Nazis—they were able to remain intact: two Jewish villages engulfed in Judaism, living it with dignity and sensitivity, as well as with medieval superstition and mysticism.

For more than a year, my friends Sylvia and Lou Horwitz—he was the country director of the Joint Distribution Committee in Tunisia and was later the director of J.D.C.'s operations in Israel —had been writing to me about North Africa. There were people here, they said, such as I would find nowhere else in the world. I must come to Tunis and they would drive me down the whole Tunisian desert, around its mountains and oases, to see Jews who were among the most primitive in the world.

I was eager to see North Africa again. During the war, in 1944, I had seen its western coast on my way to Italy to help bring back the thousand refugees whom President Roosevelt had invited to Oswego, New York. The Jews living in the *mellahs*, the ghettos of Casablanca and Algiers, were poverty-stricken, disease-ridden, and almost crushed. Since then, Israel had been reborn, and I wondered if that dynamic revolution in Jewish life had wrought any changes in the face of North Africa.

In the spring of 1951 I was able to accept the Horwitz' invitation, for I had returned to Israel on my honeymoon. It was, to be sure, a kind of busman's honeymoon, since we were both busily taking pictures and I was gathering material for the New York *Herald Tribune*. From Israel we flew to Rome, then across the Mediterranean to Tunis, and then set out by car south across the Tunisian desert. There were five of us: Lou Horwitz, my husband Phil Michaels, our chauffeur Raphael, a European Jew who had settled in Tunis and spoke Arabic, and Moshe Barbout, a former Tunisian wine merchant who had gone to Israel as a khalutz, become a shepherd in the kibbutz at Regavim, near Pardess Hanna, and now had returned to his native Africa as an emissary. Moshe, who has changed his second name to Hababou and today is one of the most important North African leaders in Israel, was built like a peasant, strong, earthy, with an irresistible sense of humor and a vast knowledge of the folklore of Tunisian Jews. He was in charge of J.D.C. and Jewish Agency educational work for the whole area. He was setting up classes, teaching the people the language, music, and history of the Israel in whose war of independence he had fought.

We drove about three hundred miles to a mountain village, called Matmata, where both Jews and Arabs live like troglodytes in wonderfully concealed caves dug into the sides of hills. About a mile from the village, the gasoline line of our car became clogged. We left Raphael to fix it, and climbed up to the village, which lay camouflaged in yellow sand and stone. Little domes rising in the hills marked the underground rooms built around an underground courtyard. Only the souk, the market place, was above ground. We went to the souk in search of a Jewish merchant whom Lou Horwitz knew, and were immediately taken into custody by two long-robed and barefooted Arabs. One of them, carrying a kind of policeman's nightstick and a knife, had a bad eye which he kept closed most of the time, opening it grudgingly on occasion.

He finally opened it fully when he told us that we would have to get out of the village—under his escort. He was taking us to the French military post about two miles up in the mountains. Phil and Moshe went down to get the car, while Lou Horwitz and I were held as hostages. The sun sank. All through the hills, Arab men suddenly emerged from their caves, stood on the little platforms that led into their homes, bowed silently to the East and then in loud chants sang their evening prayers. The hills caught and echoed the music. The world that had been all yellow sand and barren hills suddenly became pink and mauve, with little islands of green. The domes that marked the cave dwellings seemed to swirl. The palms stood breathless.

The chanting was over. The men returned inside the caves. For three or four interminable minutes there was a deathly silence. Then suddenly every donkey brayed, every camel complained, every baby in the village screamed.

In about half an hour, our men drove up. The two Arabs watched us get in, climbed in after us, and directed us around the winding roads of the village farther up the mountain. We drove through the high white-walled entrance of the French military outpost. The commander came into the courtyard, looking as if he had stepped out of a Hollywood movie about the French Foreign

Legion, young, handsome, slim-waisted, dashing in his full pantaloons. He listened to the Arabs, apologized profusely for "discom-
moding" us, invited us into his office, and set us free.

The velvet sky and the soft hills of the African night stretched
tenderly around us, as if at this hour there could be no hostility in
the world. We were the only travelers on the dark road curving
down the mountains, heading straight for Djorf, the embarkation
point for Djerba. All that remained was to drive our car onto a
ferry and journey to the Island of Lotus Eaters.

But we were wrong. Djorf lay in Stygian silence. There was only
one house in the whole port, a square two-story building, completely shuttered and blacked out. Raphael shouted, "Hallo,
hallo."

A head appeared at the window. A man asked sleepily, "*Esh
biddak?*" (What do you want?)

"*Awseen el babor mishan Djerba!*" (We want the boat to
Djerba) Raphael yelled.

"It's too late."

"What do you mean? They're waiting for us at the Grand
Hotel."

"It's too late," the man shouted. "The ferry is in Djerba. I can't
use the telephone to Djerba after midnight."

He slammed the window shut and disappeared.

We prepared to settle down for the night. The day had been
blistering but the night was cold. We buttoned our coats tightly
around our throats. Djorf encircled us like a Dali painting of a
wasteland. The road seemed to curve off into endlessness. The
sand hills rose over us like mysterious fortress walls.

Down the road, moving silently in the dark night, came a small
caravan of two camels, an ass, and three Arabs in the flowing robes
of the desert. They settled themselves for the night a little distance
from our car. We watched the Arabs unload the camels and the
ass. They made a fire from the dry straw they carried with them, fed
their animals, rocked the camels slowly like boats until the camels
went down on their knees and then lay on the ground. Their

chores finished, the men squatted around the fire eating their dinner of dried dates.

We rolled up the windows of the car and locked the doors securely. Our neighbors smoked their after-dinner cigarettes, then wrapped themselves in blankets to sleep. We grew wider awake than ever.

What to do? Obviously, throw a stone at the watchman's shuttered window. Raphael hurled the biggest he could find. The Arab watchman called down angrily. This time he suggested that we signal the ferrymen on the island with our car lights. We blinked the lights on and off like sailors in a shipwreck, flashing S.O.S., S.O.S. into the night. Even while we were flashing, the Djerba ferry appeared. We jumped out of the car. Our three neighbors slowly stood up, rocked the camels to their feet, and silently moved toward the water's edge.

I had seen primitive ferries in Asia, but the Djerba ferry was unique. Some crude planks had been laid across the center of a small fishing smack. Our car straddled the boat, with the Arabs, their camels, and donkey fitted around it.

The ferry chugged across the shallow waters of the sea of Bou Ghara to the little port of Adjim, about a mile from the mainland, the southern gateway to Djerba. We left our Arab neighbors to sway their camels to sleep again and drove across an excellent road, twenty-two kilometers straight across the island to its northern capital, Houmt Souk. The two Jewish villages, Hara Kebira (The Big Ghetto or The Big Jewish Village) with some twenty-seven hundred Jews and Hara Srira (The Small Jewish Village) with seventeen hundred, lay in the desert outside Houmt Souk.

The next morning, Clementin Cohen came into our lives. He was a prosperous importer of foodstuffs, and the volunteer J.D.C. representative for the island. We found him in his shop in Houmt Souk's market place, a large dark loft with a tiny office and desk. Clementin Cohen—his name was a typical Djerban mixture—was slim, serious-faced, in his early forties, with brown eyes and sensitive, delicate features. He spoke French in a soft voice; his manner was modest but self-assured. He wore a gray striped Western suit, a blue French beret, and, despite the heat, a gray and maroon woolen sweater. He introduced us to his brothers in the shop, and then took us to see our first Djerban Jews in the Houmt Souk market.

They were at work in a narrow labyrinth of arcades and alleys. Each street marked a separate Jewish trade—a street of silver- and goldsmiths, a street of tailors all sewing on old Singer machines, a street of carpenters, a street of Jewish cafés where both Jews and Arabs eat.

This medieval Jewish quarter was embedded in a typical Tunisian Arab village. Though it was hardly eight o'clock, the huge outdoor market arena was as crowded and animated as Coney Island on the Fourth of July. It seemed to us as if most of the island's fifty-seven thousand Arabs, Berbers, Jews, Maltese, and French colonial officials had come to buy and sell and enjoy the carnival air of market day.

The smell of fish and coffee and the tumultuous cries of eager vendors filled the souk. The hot sun beat down on the people, their camels and sheep and goats. Men wrapped in burnooses sat on the sand eating fish and dates. Others, wearing white robes, the traditional clothes of the Moslems of Djerba, walked with sticks as though they had journeyed a long distance to come here. Enterprising merchants were hawking their wares—fruits, wheat, skeins of wool, fish, sponges, olives, and steaming black coffee. Camels kneeled on the ground, still sleeping. Little Arab boys and girls, with beautiful dark eyes, led blind beggars to all the prospective customers.

Shepherded by Clementin Cohen, we left Houmt Souk and drove about five miles through a hot white world of sand, waving date palms, and some fruit trees to the all-Jewish village of Hara Srira. It lay white and parched and empty of people in the morning sun. Low white adobe walls enclosed the courtyards in which the people lived. Small domes, like mosques, formed the low skyline. A few palm trees lifted the eye from the flat dazzling whiteness.

Mystic symbols—fish, trees, hands, and lettering—were painted in Tunisian blue on several of the outer walls. Clementin Cohen explained that most of the paintings were outside the homes of

newly married couples, to prevent the *Ein Hara*, the Evil Eye, from
marring their happiness. The most common symbol was a tree,
with *menorah*-like branches, two pointing up and two pointing
down. On some of the trees a fish, painted on each side of the
trunk, separated the upper and lower branches. The symbols have
varied meanings, but the most common interpretation seems to be
light and fertility—the *menorah*, or candelabra to illuminate the
lives of the people, the fish to make them fertile. For in Hebrew
lore fish symbolize fertility. The Prophet Habakkuk extolled the
Lord who "makest men as the fishes of the sea, as the creeping
things, that have no ruler over them"—Habakkuk 1:14. Even the
general Jewish custom of eating fish on Friday night is thought by
some to be part of the symbolism of fertility on the Sabbath eve.

Throughout North Africa, Hara Srira is famous for its miracle-
working synagogue, the Ghriba, the Lonely or Miraculous One. The
origins of the synagogue, unrecorded and richly embroidered with
legend, are popularly believed to go back to Moses' time. There is a
story that I heard on the island for the first time, that when Moses
took the children of Israel out of Egypt, some refused to go east
with him to the Promised Land and went west to Djerba. A more
popular legend (wherever you turn in Djerba, there are legends!)
is that after the first Temple was destroyed, some of the people left
Jerusalem, carried one of Solomon's doors with them, and erected
it on the spot where the Ghriba now stands. The most romantic
legend is that a young Jewish girl of great beauty came to the island
from an unknown land, lived on this spot in virgin solitude, praying constantly and performing miracles. There is even a legend
that Maimonidies founded the Ghriba, and wrote four of its scrolls
in his own hand.

Today it is the center of a great pilgrimage. Students, rabbis, the
sick, the well, the crippled, mothers of sick children, barren women,
conscience-stricken sinners, and the pure in heart converge from all
over North Africa in a pilgrimage each spring on the Festival of
Lag B'Omer. The quiet village suddenly becomes a boom town.
Cars roar down the narrow roads frightening the horses, camels,
and donkeys. Street vendors do a land-office business. The pilgrims

stay on for days, praying and worshiping. The great event is the Procession of the Holy Candelabrum, when hundreds of devout march down the road from the synagogue-shrine to the village of Hara Srira, about three kilometers away, carrying an ornate silver candelabrum.

The shrine consists of the white wood synagogue, rebuilt in the nineteenth century on the site of the old Ghriba, with grilled windows and a heavily ornamented door, the ancient cemetery next to it, and, across the road, the pilgrims' house. Encircling it on all sides are scrawny palms and bleached sand. At any moment the hot African desert seems ready to claim not only the land but the last trace of the shrine.

The treasures and beauty of the Ghriba, built entirely by Djerban Jews, are inside the synagogue: magnificent tiled walls in rich mosaics of rhomboids, circles, and squares, a carved wooden pulpit, Sephardic style, in the center, and Byzantine columns. A door leads to the inner sanctuary, which they call the Holy of Holies, whose eastern wall forms the *Aron Kodesh*, containing the holy scrolls. It is dimly lit. On its walls hang ornate silver ornaments for the dead, some in the magic form of Fatma's hand, some representing the same mystic trees that we had seen painted on the courtyard walls.

The beadle of the Ghriba asked us to take off our shoes before we entered the Holy of Holies. He was the adolescent son of one of the wealthiest families on the island, the Trabelsine family. His father, a merchant like Clementin Cohen, owned a general store filled mostly with foodstuffs and blankets. Young Trabelsine was fat and tall. He wore a skullcap, light Turkish pantaloons bordered at the knee with a dark stripe, leather sandals, a Western shirt buttoned to the throat, but no tie, a fine woolen sweater, and a long jacket that was obviously growing tight for him. He pulled it together with one button that stretched the cloth in folds across his soft chest. His face was young and pleasant. He was eager to give us a good impression of the village and the shrine.

In the synagogue, five old men, with generous white beards, turbans, heavy coats, and robes, sat on a wall bench, their bare feet crossed under them, their slippers lined neatly on the stone floor. The face of one of the men was illuminated by the sun pouring through the grilled window—and by joy in the old parchment manuscript that he was reading aloud to his fellow scholars. Tacked on the wall behind the scholars was a large proclamation in Hebrew: "Call to the People of Israel."

Near the old scholars, in a wooden enclosure, sat two youngish looking men with black beards. They made no pretense of reading or studying. One was bony and lost in thought, as though he had come here to search his soul. The other, with heavy black brows, large shrewd eyes, a luxuriant beard and a turban of red tablecloth plaid, looked like a canny merchant. The thin man was oblivious of us; the stout one never took his eyes away.

We crossed the road to the caravansary, the large pilgrims' hostel. Six old men huddled against its wall on a straw mat, in the postures and clothing of beggars. They wore ancient tattered robes wound around their torn Turkish pants and turbans. Despite the heat, some of them wore heavy woolen overcoats—the clothing of charity. They were African beggars, with knotty hands, parchment-skinned faces framed with small white beards, the canes and sticks of wanderers, the look of having lived a thousand years in the desert. Around them the desert spread hot, parched, biding its time.

We walked past the old men into the hostel. It was a vast white stone courtyard around whose edges were the rooms, in a two-storied arcade of white Byzantine columns. Three generations of women were guarding the caravansary as we entered. They too looked poverty-stricken. On the concrete floor, barefoot and gnarled, sat the ancient grandmother wrapped completely in a striped robe. She was spinning some coarse wool on a long frame, using her hand as the shuttle. It was a technique that, like the old woman herself, seemed to have come down from Biblical times. A younger woman, covered too in a striped robe, barefoot, but wearing earrings and bracelets, swept the courtyard while holding a baby—the third generation—in one arm. Her two little daughters clutched her robe, one of them poised like a dancer with her hand beneath her chin.

The women were guarding the cells in which, during the great festival, each family of pilgrims lives austerely, in poverty and faith. Here in the courtyard the pilgrims cook their food during the day, and in the evening, sing sacred music.

Here the miracles of the rabbis of the Ghriba are retold. They are not unlike tales of wonder-working rabbis found in other parts of the world. There is one story that the local Arab fishermen raised the price of fish, so that the poor Djerban Jews could no longer afford to buy it. Fish is a mainstay on the island. The miracle-working rabbi threw a stone in the river and all the fish promptly disappeared. The Arabs rushed to their ruler, who called the rabbi to him. When the ruler heard about his subjects' unfair tactics, he ordered them to lower their prices. The rabbi went back to the river, threw in another stone, and the fish promptly reappeared.

Another story is about an Arab who, understanding the theory of heightened demand at holiday time, raised the price of foliage at Succoth, the harvest festival. The miracle-working rabbi said nothing until the Arab had climbed on a ladder to the top of the Succah, the traditional booth, and was laying out his foliage. The rabbi invoked his magic, and the Arab found himself off the ladder swinging in mid-air. He begged the rabbi to remove the spell—he would lower the price immediately. The rabbi performed more magic, immediately the Arab was back on the ladder, and the price of foliage at Succoth time dropped to its normal level.

With young Trabelsine, we left the shrine, drove to the village, and entered some of the courtyards where the women were cooking, washing, and sweeping. All activity centered in the enclosed courtyards, around which were the tiny cubbyhole bedrooms. Almost all of these latter were bare—no bed, no table, no chair, no rug. A few had a small wooden cupboard built against the wall, sometimes holding a small, neatly folded piece of cloth.

The women sat on the floor of their tiny rooms, escaping the burning assault of the African sun. Most of them were plump, for in Djerba, the fatter a woman is, the more desirable she is. Even the poor girls, whose fathers have little money for food, are fattened up for weeks before their wedding. The stoutest women, whose bodies seem to be great mounds of fat, are the ones everyone looks at with joy and envy. An American beauty would have a slim chance of getting a husband in Djerba.

Trabelsine insisted on being our host and taking us to his parents' home. His mother greeted us as we entered their courtyard. There was no question that she was one of the wealthiest women on the island. She must have weighed over two hundred pounds. She was warm and friendly and, like most fat women, pretty. She wore the usual robe of the island women, but her jewelry was the most opulent and finest we had seen there. Her hooped gold earrings were at least four inches long, with an extra gold ornament hanging inside them. I had seen far simpler earrings at the souk that would have cost a hundred dollars.

Of the homes we visited in Hara Srira the Trabelsines' was the only one with furniture. Mr. Trabelsine had apparently brought the trappings of culture and Western civilization from Tunis. They had a wooden kitchen table covered with oilcloth and next to the table, a bed.

Other female relatives and friends gathered in the house to welcome us. Mrs. Trabelsine brought out plates of dried fish, roasted peanuts, and sunflower seeds. While we ate the delicacies, we discussed life on the island.

A dominant note on Djerba is still timelessness. Here is a rhythm of life unbroken. There is no plumbing and no electricity; no movies teach the islanders the odd ways of the outside world. The age of anxiety and confusion has not yet reached across the shallow waters of the Sea of Bou Ghara.

This is a medieval patriarchal society, with the Grand Rabbi serving as the leader, the judge, the head of the Hebrew schools, the man who officiates at all births, deaths, marriages, and divorces. With the same type of self-government that existed in European Jewish communities, the Jews of Hara Srira and of Hara Kebira organize their separate *Kehillah*, their community government.

Their clothes are a wonderful blend of the African and Hebrew cultures in which they live. Their women dress like those whom David described in his song to Saul: "who clothed you in scarlet, with other delights, who put ornaments of gold upon your apparel." On their wedding day, they become queens, placing the Djerban diadem on their hair. It is a stiffened headdress of red cloth, fitting snugly like a cap, embroidered with silver and gold threads and hung with pieces of silver and gold. Beneath it, their hair hangs luxuriously, braided or loose. Eastern monarchs wore the diadem as a mark of their regal splendor; in Djerba, it is the mark of the proudly married woman.

Some of the men now affect Western clothes, but most of them still wear gay Turkish pantaloons that come to their knees, shirts of fine cloth, and an outer garment that is sometimes a burnoose, sometimes a loose and handsomely embroidered cape with sleeves, and sometimes a poncho that they wear draped fully over their bodies leaving free motion for their arms. They rarely go without scuffs or shoes. On their heads they wind large turbans that frame their bearded or mustached faces. Sometimes they wear small berets or skullcaps, and sometimes a red Arab cap called a chechiya, an abbreviated fez.

The woman's sole purpose here is to bear children, and she usually bears at least ten or twelve. Polygamy is permitted; two wives are common and a rich man may have three or four. The lives of the women are circumscribed by tribal superstitions. During menstruation, a wife is forbidden even to touch her husband's hand. She places his food and spoon before him, but she may not touch him, nor he her.

Divorce, called a get in Djerba, is simple. If a husband does not love his wife, or if she bears him no son, he need only go to the Grand Rabbi to obtain his get. But divorces are infrequent, since any man who is dissatisfied with one wife can take another. And in a small isolated community there is too much scandal attached to divorce to make it popular. Adultery too is almost unknown. If a married woman commits it, she is thrown out of the house and regarded as a pariah. Society may shut one eye at a man's indiscretions. But with several wives, temptation is perhaps diminished.

Marriages are generally arranged by the parents soon after birth.

Sometimes this ancient custom works real hardships. Two men may vow that their children, if they have them, will be married to each other. This vow is always kept even though the girl may be born several years before the boy whom she must ultimately marry.

The marriage ceremony on Djerba is by all odds the most exotic custom on the whole island. The festivities begin a week before the wedding with the festival of The Henna, named after the dye, a symbol of fertility. In the morning the engaged girl goes to the *hammam*, the public bathhouse. She washes herself thoroughly in the bathhouse and then approaches the *mikvah*, the ceremonial bath. To insure a sweet marriage she is given hard candy to suck as she enters the pool. While the women watch with great joy, an older woman holds her by her long hair and dunks her seven times.

The gaiety begins about seven in the evening. In a huge procession, the groom, accompanied by most of the village, marches toward the courtyard of the bride's home. At the head of the procession are musicians playing the flute and drum as loudly and joyously as they can. They are followed by two men carrying a huge basket. The handle of the basket is brilliant with small colored bulbs. Inside the basket are shoes. If the bride is rich the basket, or baskets, may hold twenty pairs. If she is poor the basket holds only one pair. Beneath the shoes are jewels: beautiful headdresses, bracelets, necklaces, and earrings. If she is rich, there are many and they are of gold; if she is poor, there are a few of silver— for the gifts are all bought with the bride's dowry. The groom usually spends 10 per cent of the money his prospective father-in-law gives him; if the dowry is a million francs, the basket contains gifts worth a hundred thousand francs. Even the poorest dowry is rarely less than forty-five dollars.

The groom, accompanied by his mother, father, ten or twelve sisters, brothers, dozens of cousins, and scores of friends, now enters the bridal courtyard. In a room with windows through which she can see everything, the veiled bride sits in a big chair surrounded by her mother, the groom's mother, and the women of both families. Her robe is of red or yellow, embroidered with gold and silver.

The courtyard is the men's province. All night long they feast, sing, and dance. Servants keep replenishing their food. They drink their favorite *bukha*, the whisky of North Africa, made of fig juice. The music never stops. Sometimes a professional male dancer does an Oriental belly dance. If someone in the family is a good dancer, he entertains. But the women of the family never dance.

For the girls, the Henna festivities reach a high climax when an old woman carrying gold jewelry and a ball of henna paste about as large as a silver dollar, places the gold in the bride's left hand, and the henna in her right. The henna is the symbol of happiness through fertility, and the gold the symbol of wealth.

The bride squeezes the paste in her right hand for about ten minutes. She presses hard. The redder her palm is, the happier her life will be. Then all the unmarried girls surround her. Each girl dips the forefinger of her left hand in the bride's palm, scoops up a little of the henna paste, and rubs it on her own right palm to insure a quick and happy marriage.

About nine o'clock the bride retires, leaving the field entirely to the men. They go on drinking, eating, dancing, and singing until two or three in the morning, or even until dawn, depending on how much food and bukha the father of the bride supplies.

Henna night is invariably on a Wednesday. On Thursday everyone rests. Friday night they attend synagogue, and on Saturday morning, after services, the men go off to the groom's house to eat and drink, while the bride throws a little party for the women and her girl friends.

The wedding is held the following Wednesday, usually ten days or so after the bride's menstruation, in the belief (only fairly recently confirmed by modern science) that this is her period of greatest fertility. The ceremony takes place in her courtyard with all her family and friends present. Again she wears a red and yellow gown and a veil covering her face. If she is wealthy, it is a different gown from the one she wore at the Henna. If she is poor, she wears the same dress. The groom wears full white pantaloons, a white silk shirt, a bolero of blue or gray, and leather slippers.

The Grand Rabbi himself performs the traditional ceremony under the *khupah*, the canopy. The groom breaks a wine glass, places the wedding ring on the bride's left finger with the usual statement of sanctification. Following the ceremony the father of the groom explains the facts of life to his son. The mother of the bride explains them to her blushing daughter. The young man then takes his bride to the bedroom that her father has designated for them off the courtyard of his house.

We left Hara Srira and drove to Hara Kebira, which lay only a mile from Houmt Souk. Though the two villages are both all-Jewish, with the same architecture of chalk-white walls, the same white domes and mystic symbols painted in Tunisian blue, the same customs and history, they are fiercely antagonistic to each other. Each village has its own rabbinical council, *Beth Midrash*, Hebrew schools, ritual baths, and other institutions. Even the American J.D.C. must deal with each village separately.

The "Joint," as the J.D.C. is sometimes known, came to Djerba a few years ago, but it has already affected the lives and even the culture of the island. It provides not only medical and child care, operating through O.S.E., the French public health agency, but it has a complete educational program. Working through the French *Alliance Israelite Universelle*, it is now modernizing the schools, providing books and supplies, offering classes in Hebrew and Jewish history, and guiding the activities of young people and cultural groups. It feeds some six hundred children with a hot meal each day. In the milk station run by O.S.E. with J.D.C. funds, local nurses distribute safe milk for infants. Infant mortality on the island is staggering; diarrhea is a fatal disease for most of the babies. Now mothers are being taught baby care and cleanliness. Trachoma, the dread disease of the eyes, has affected 30 per cent of the Jewish islanders. Yet when the J.D.C. started its trachoma program, it was held up for months because the only person on the island who was able to put penicillin drops in the eyes was a man, and he was forbidden to touch the women and girls.

In the last few years, there have been more changes in the lives of Djerba's women than in the previous three centuries. For the first time, young girls are going to school. One hundred and fifty of them, wearing the costumes of the past and incredibly beautiful, sit on wooden benches in front of crude tables, writing fine He-

A crowd of Yemenite people huddled together in the last
Arab customhouse, the last border of head tax and terror

The scrolls were so precious to the fleeing Yemenites that Suleiman Moosa Tenami sang as he held the Torah

The girls from Sana, the capital of Yemen, wore lovely hoods

Yemenite mother and child landing in Israel: "We are home and we are safe"

A barefoot Arab wrote in huge numerals the ransom the Sultan of Lahej was collecting from the fleeing Yemenites

Street market in Nazareth, with the Dames de Nazareth Convent in the background

An Arab member of the Knesset (Parliament), one of the delegates elected by the 200,000 Arab citizens of Israel

brew script in their notebooks. There is of course no coeducation, and even their teacher is a female, a charming local girl of about sixteen. She asked her class to sing for us. Without any embarrassment, they dropped the cloths with which a few of them had hidden their faces, and with high clear voices, sang the new Hebrew songs of the land, hundreds of miles away, whose birth was changing their lives.

Schooling for Djerba's boys had always been intense, but it was religious schooling only. We learned that when the French tried to establish a school in Hara Srira a generation ago, the Grand Rabbi refused to allow it. Now he has permitted not only the old *Kouttabi* or *Talmud Torah*, but also a school for modern Hebrew. The language of the schools is Hebrew and Arabic. In one of the courtyard rooms of the Kouttabi, we watched the teacher, potbellied, in pantaloons, scolding the little boys while they chanted their lessons. Most of the three hundred boys in the school, giggling like the girls and just as beautiful, wore blue berets and cast-off American clothes that were mostly rags.

The Kouttabi is the heart of Hara Kebira's life, for the making of rabbis is still Djerba's chief industry, and the export of rabbis its chief trade. There are some eighteen synagogues, each with a Yeshiva or school attached. They have a large printing shop, since Djerba is the religious capital of eastern North African Jewry, where they print the works of their great scholars, the "Responsa," Halachic works, poetry, history, prayer books, and even the stories of the miracles performed by their rabbis.

Poverty is the norm. There are a few wealthy merchants, but most of the people live in an almost hopeless economic cycle of large families, small incomes, and all the diseases caused by malnutrition. Of the hundred thousand Jews in Tunisia, some half are Europeanized in the French tradition. In Djerba, where there is no Europeanization, and where the two villages are completely Jewish, there is no anti-Semitism. Yet I discovered that about 80 per cent of the people want to go to Israel. There is no question of life-and-death urgency on the island, as there was in neighboring Tripoli, which became the Arab kingdom of Libya on January 1, 1952. Yet Djerba's Jews point out that in the encroaching anti-Semitism of the Arab world, they may soon be trapped too. The birth of Israel increased the tension with the Arabs, but Israel's open door has provided the only solution they can see to their political and economic problems.

About half of Djerba's Jews have already left the island and gone to Israel. Most of them have settled on the Negev desert, especially in the Lachish area. In Israel they are said to be the best Tunisians in the Promised Land. They have adapted themselves readily to the new life. They are still Orthodox observers, but they have already dropped many of the customs of life on the island.

Even in Djerba itself, the pattern centuries old, is now beginning to change under the impact of the outside world. An anecdote that Moshe Hababou told us pointed up the speed with which the changes now take place, so that in a few years Djerba may be as obsolete as the Berditchev or Kasrielevky of eastern European Jewry.

"Rabbi Shamus Soussi," he said, "came to see me one day in my office in Tunis to borrow some books for his Hebrew class. He had come right from Djerba. He had a fine beard, he wore big pantaloons and the typical costume of a Djerban rabbi.

"Two weeks later there was a knock on my door. A man came in wearing a fine beret, striped trousers, a white shirt, with a clean-shaven face. 'Who are you?' I asked him.

" 'I am Shamus Soussi of Djerba.'

" 'From Djerba! Perhaps you are Shamus Soussi from another village.'

" 'No, no.' He took out his identity card. He was indeed Shamus Soussi of Djerba. He explained: 'I was in Marseille for two days. It's not nice to walk around there the way I did on Djerba.' "

Moshe explained that when a Tunisian visits Djerba he looks around and says, "How can anyone live like this?" But when a Djerban goes to Tunis he is like a bird. "He hops all around," Moshe's big black eyes lit up. "He goes out."

"And when he goes home to Djerba?" I asked.

Moshe put his two hands together like a book, shook his head and body, and began to pray.

15: Tell It in Gath

IN THE SUMMER of 1955, I went to the Lachish area in the Negev to see what was happening to the Jews of Djerba. Since the time when I had visited the Djerbans at home, North Africa had exploded. The Jews, especially in the remote villages and islands, were no longer safe. They began to flee. And the country they fled to was Israel.

Israel decided to settle them in the northern Negev. It was part of the prophecy Ben-Gurion had made to me that afternoon during the war. "There will be no more sand in the desert. . . ."

The desert sand where the people of North Africa were now coming was the land around Biblical Gath, where David, lamenting the death of Saul and Jonathan, his son, had cried, "Tell it not in Gath, publish it not in the streets of Ashkelon."

Gath, once a Biblical memory, and Lachish, where the ancient Jews had fought the ancient Philistines, began to breathe again. Lachish became the center of the largest and most dramatic regional scheme in the country, a T.V.A. project that stretched from the Gaza Strip in Egypt to the Hebron Hills of Jordan. It was desert, two hundred thousand acres of desert, inside the explosive borders between Egypt and Jordan.

Here the refugees from North Africa were brought directly from Haifa, in Operation Ship to Village, the plan that was almost completely financed by Americans through the United Jewish Appeal.

On a warm late summer morning, we drove from Jerusalem south to Lachish on a fine road, passing Beit Guvrin, formerly called Jebrin. The terrain, at first fertile and green, became bony with bare-backed mountains that looked like parts of Texas and Arizona. The Arab frontier closed in upon us everywhere.

The Hebron Hills, in Jordan's hands, a hotbed for Arab infiltration, lay at our left. Gaza, in Egypt's hands, lay at our right. The road itself was called the "Security Road," euphemistically perhaps, since it was far from secure and there were constant forays upon it from both Arab frontiers.

We drove to a village that was just being born—the village of Eytan. There was not a blade of grass. On the bony hills and yellow sand, little yellow wooden houses stood in a security-planned arc. Here were the people of Djerba and Casablanca and Marrakesh, walking around, a little bewildered, a little frightened. A young woman had been to the commissary and was now carrying a long white bread home to her family. It was Friday morning, and a young man in Djerban pantaloons, the *schochet* (kosher butcher), was slaughtering a chicken in the one-room hut of a young mother. One of the first buildings put up was the schoolhouse, and the children—exquisite-looking children with blond hair, black hair, dark eyes or blue eyes—were singing "David Says," the Hebrew version of "Simon Says," putting their hands in the air, on their eyes, laughing hysterically when they were caught.

A whole team of young people, old-timers in the country, was helping the newcomers adjust to their life in the desert. The head of the village was a young man from a neighboring settlement, Josef Pardress, whose father was a rabbi in Ramat Gan. A young girl of eighteen, Esther Cohen, a Youth Aliyah graduate from Morocco, was the social worker teaching the women how to cook Israeli food, how to use the little one-burner Primus (Israel's kerosene stove), and how to use diapers for their babies.

Hamush Cohen, from Djerba, took us around the village. Hamush was a plumber, working on the pipeline that was to bring water from the big Yarkon-Negev pipeline into the village. We found the house of one of the women we had met in Djerba—Tita Hadad. Tita was a full-blown queen out of Solomon's days. She was a regal, fat mother, wrapped in a striped robe, her long braided black hair hanging down from her red and gold cap. Tita invited us shyly into her little hut. Her four young daughters and her little son were in school, she said. Her husband was working the land.

Tita showed us the food with which the United Jewish Appeal had filled her house, like those of all the other refugees, to last for ten days, so that the new families would not go hungry while they were making their first difficult adjustment.

Tita showed us the things that she, just as others, had been given by the U.J.A.—a few pots and pans, some cutlery that she set in immaculate rows on a napkin on the floor beside the Primus, a tea-kettle, beds for the family, mattresses, blankets, a table, and four stools.

In front of her house, and in front of all the little houses in Eytan, lay the concrete blocks to build new large permanent homes. Each new immigrant knew that within three months, he would be living in a good, permanent, white concrete house.

"Our life is not easy, as you can see," Hamush Cohen said, "but we are satisfied. It is good to be in Israel—and to be safe."

Eytan was only one of the villages in the vast Lachish scheme. The whole area was to be filled up with people and farms. Half the region was to be used for large-scale industrial farming with cotton, peanuts, and sugar beets. The other half was to be used for grazing cattle and sheep.

To prevent the villages from being little isolated islands in a hostile borderland of Arabs, the planners in Jerusalem had divided the area into several parts, each with five or six villages clustered together around a rural center. A huge regional center was to be built near Gath. The cotton gin was to be built in Gath, the high school, the factories to process the crops. Gath was to be the Chicago of Lachish.

For here in Lachish, Israel was bringing together the tested wisdoms of her earlier experiences and mistakes. The emergency housing of earlier years that quickly turned into slums, the months of human deterioration in the maabaroth (the transit villages) that turned the hope of some of the newcomers into disillusionment, had now been replaced by careful social and psychological planning. It was symbolic of the ingenuity and breath-taking scope of the whole project that its leaders were people in their thirties or younger. A number of them were young men who led the daring aliyah beth of Jewish refugees running the British blockade into Palestine.

The director was Arie Eliav, young, blond, soft-spoken, who was one of the leaders of the Wedgewood, a famous ship of "illegals."

"I know we will make many mistakes in this Lachish plan," Eliav told us simply in his home in Ashkelon while he bounced his infant on his knee. "But we feel it is just like the mistakes you make in raising a child. A few years ago, this kind of mass planning and settlement would have been impossible. We didn't have the know-how and the means. Now we have both, and we have wonderful human material. These refugees from Morocco and Tunisia, the people from the towns and from Djerba, are excellent workers. They just need to be taught."

It was less than a year later, in the early summer of 1956, that I returned to Lachish. The changes were unbelievable. Over seven thousand people were now living in twenty-seven new villages in the once arid desert, working the land, sending their young children to school, marrying off their older children, worshiping in little synagogues as they had worshiped in North Africa, coming to terms with a brave new life in a land encircled by enemies, a world that was neither at peace nor at full-fledged war.

The changes were on every level—physical, spiritual, psychological. The year before, the newcomers, fleeing Arab pogroms and terror, had lived in tiny one-room wooden huts. Now they lived in permanent houses with green Israeli-made Venetian blinds and red gabled roofs. Their huts had become their tool sheds.

A year before, the fields were yellow sand, like the desert of Colorado, with a thirst that was centuries old. Water was the crying need. A year before I had watched the famous 66-inch Yarkon-Negev pipeline being laid from Tel Aviv to Lachish. This year Tel Aviv's Yarkon River was irrigating thousands of acres of land in Lachish and the Negev. The yellow sand had all but disappeared. From the main road to the very horizon, there were fields of tall green corn, as much liked by Israelis as by Americans. Tomatoes were abundant. Cotton—green, tall, waving cotton—was everywhere.

In some eight months, a whole new city had been built in the Lachish desert. The city of Gath had risen on the site of ancient

Gath. The cotton gin was here, the administrative offices were here, the local industries for the whole area were here. The railroad, with fine new equipment from German indemnification, stopped here six times a day. And hundreds of immigrant families were living in permanent houses in town.

But buildings and land—important as they are—were far less significant than the human changes. What had happened, I wondered, to the people who had escaped from Morocco and Tunisia —and especially what had happened to the Jews of Djerba?

I returned to Eytan, the village in which I had spent most time the year before. Like everything else in Lachish, it was just celebrating its first birthday.

Standing in front of one of the new white houses was Tita Hadad, smiling, still looking like a full-blown queen. She was wrapped in her striped robe with her red and gold cap on her shining black hair. She stood on the terrace of her house, rolling little macaronis into a huge bowl. Beside her were baskets of tomatoes, ripening in the warm sun.

Tita was in her ancient costume. But her four young daughters and little son were all in Israeli clothes, planting little peppers in her back yard. Mr. Hadad, wearing the white pantaloons of the Island of Djerba, with a black band around the bottom to remind the Djerbans of the destruction of Solomon's Temple, walked like an Oriental lord around his garden, waving his most precious possession, a water hose.

The year before, the U.J.A. had filled Tita's house with food for ten days. This year, as Tita invited us into her spotless kitchen, it was she who was offering food and soft drinks to us.

She was now so well established that she had placed a little blue and white box on her wall, marked "For the Old People's Home in Beersheba." In the tradition of all her matriarchal ancestors, Tita was teaching her children the meaning of charity. There were always people poorer than you, somewhere in the world, who needed your help.

Once again, we were visiting Lachish with Arie Eliav, the youth-

ful-looking idealist who had helped thousands of D.P.'s run the
British blockade into Palestine.

"Are the people satisfied and happy?" I asked him.

"I can't say completely yes or no," he said frankly. "They are
more satisfied than before. But they are still in the process of ad-
justing to a new environment, a new country, new people. The
picture is dark and light. The people have grievances, and they're
not afraid to voice them. Some quarrel among themselves. There
are cultural differences between the Moroccans and Tunisians,
and they often blow up at each other. Some want to leave the farms
and go to the big cities. They are free to go, of course. But then
they get no help from us in finding houses in the cities.

"That's the dark side. On the bright side is the fact that a rela-
tively small number have left the area. Perhaps ten per cent of
the seven thousand people have rotated. The reason they stay is
that they have good housing here and there is plenty of work for
everyone."

The push in the Negev is on, full steam. The lessons learned
from the Lachish experiment are now being applied to development towns in other areas of the Negev and the Dead Sea. Bull-
dozers are leveling the dunes; modernistic apartment houses are
bursting out of a primitive waste of sand where once only Bedouins
camped in black tents. Dimona is already a thriving town whose
people work in the Dead Sea potash plant; Arad, just started with
sixty pioneers from cities and farms and 160 new immigrants, is
expected to become a desert city of forty thousand people.

Near the Gaza Strip, the B'sor area is being turned into another
regional development with the city of B'sor itself to house fifty
thousand people, and a network of small farming and industrial
towns radiating around it. Farmers are ploughing the land; young
people are moving southward; the dangerous borders are being se-
cured. With money from Israel's Development Program and investments from Israel Bonds, the new towns are taking shape over
night. Roads are being built to take the crops to Elath to be
shipped to Africa and Asia. The newest port at Ashdod, near
Ashkelon, is to carry the products of B'sor and Arad to the western
world. This is the decade of the Negev.

16: From Beersheba to Elath

THE DESERT is a word of mystery in all lands. The desert is at the core of the story of Israel.

In Bible days, the prophets went into the desert to find themselves. The desert was the proving ground, where you learned to know hunger and pain, where you cleansed yourself so that you were pure in the face of God.

The Negev desert was the home of the patriarchs. Abraham dwelt at Beersheba. He traveled through the desert with his beloved, Sara. Ishmael, Abraham's son by Hagar, went into the desert with his mother. Isaac lived here, and Jacob. Here, and in the adjoining Sinai desert, Moses kept the children of Israel for forty years until the generation of those who remembered Pharaoh and the life of bondage was dead.

Now, Ben-Gurion, steeped in the Bible, is exhorting all of Israel to go to the desert to find itself, to cleanse itself, to build for the future. His vision of the Israel of tomorrow is of the land that lies southward from Beersheba.

"Go south, go south," he continually tells the youth of Israel, and he practices what he preaches. When he left the prime minister's office temporarily in 1953, he and his wife, Paula, settled in the desert at Sde Boker, a small kibbutz some thirty miles south of Beersheba. The stream of official cars and tourist buses from Beersheba to Sde Boker looked like pilgrimages to Hyde Park, and Ben-Gurion kept his finger in every political pie. Yet he worked as a full-fledged member of the kibbutz. He was the shepherd and his wife, whom he had met during World War I when she was a nurse in Newark, was a nurse in the kibbutz.

Israel's advance upon the Negev is spearheaded from Beersheba, the Biblical desert town where Abraham dug his wells. A few years ago, the air of Beersheba was that of the Wild West in the

Gold Rush—with dusty streets and men without women. Today
Beersheba is a metropolis bursting its seams as it spreads its concrete and cement in all directions across the desert sands.

Jewish settlers of the wild south are pushing up modern white
and colored apartment houses for thousands of new immigrants.
They are opening new chemical plants and steel industries. They
have built movies and restaurants and cafés. H.I.A.S. (the Hebrew
Immigrant Aid Society) has put up a hostel that looks like a ranch
in Palm Springs, several new hotels have been opened; there is a
large shopping center and an ulpan where students can come to
learn Hebrew. To some of the population living in the outposts of
Nahal Oz and all the border defense settlements, Beersheba is Tel
Aviv, Paris, and New York rolled into one desert center of movies
and electric lights. Here people from all over the country come
every Thursday to trade with the Bedouin Arabs in the most colorful market day in all of Israel.

Beersheba is the capital of the Negev desert and it is booming.
Each month six hundred or more new immigrants come to live in
the heart of Beersheba or its sprawling desert suburbs. Whole new
villages of Hungarians, Poles, Moroccans, have sprung up. One
thousand houses are built each year. A hundred and twenty-five
new citizens are born here each month in the Chaim Yaski hospital. Last summer ninety-six children were graduated from Beersheba's elementary school: eight hundred new ones entered.

During the Sinai campaign, Beersheba's hospital was turned overnight into an army hospital for Egyptian as well as Jewish casualties. We had not known, when the hospital was opened in 1948,
what a role it was to play in 1956. Hadassah started the hospital in
a courtyard of some old buildings, naming it after Dr. Chaim
Yaski, who had been killed by the Arabs in the terrible slaughter
of seventy-three doctors and nurses on their way to Hadassah's
hospital on Mount Scopus.

I went to visit the hospital in Beersheba shortly before it was
opened. An attractive, dark-haired young Englishwoman, Dr. Pearl
Ketcher, was to head the hospital. I had first met her when she

was healing the people of the *Exodus 1947*. Dr. Yaski's widow was with us, when we heard someone knock.

Dr. Ketcher opened the door. A new immigrant said quietly, "May we come in? My wife is going to have a baby."

"But the hospital isn't open. We don't have proper equipment yet."

The man repeated, with enormous dignity, "My wife is about to have a baby."

"Of course, of course," Dr. Ketcher said. "Come in."

A son was born and the new immigrants named him Chaim, after Dr. Chaim Yaski and because Chaim means "life."

During the Sinai campaign, the Beersheba hospital was completely converted from peace to war in twenty hours. Mattresses and cots were rushed from Jerusalem to the Negev hospital. Volunteers, too old or too young to serve, put up emergency wards. Operating theaters were erected. Within a day, the Yaski hospital was binding up the wounds of boys and girls from Yemen, from Iraq, from Cochin, from western Europe and eastern Europe, sabras from the soil of Israel, Egyptians from Cairo and the villages along the Nile.

The mayor of Beersheba was David Tuvyahu, a large man with white hair, green-gray eyes, a weather-beaten face, and a soft, probing voice. He was a friend of Mrs. Roosevelt, who visited Beersheba each time she came to Israel. "She had true greatness," he told me, "and she showed it in her concern with little things. The first time she was here she asked me to take her to the homes of new immigrants. I took her to see a Moroccan family, living in a one-room shack.

" 'Why did you come?' she asked the Moroccan.

"He became angry. 'Why? I'm a Jew. I came home to the land of my fathers.'

"Three years later Mrs. Roosevelt came back to Beersheba. She remembered the Moroccan family. She described the house they had lived in to help me remember them. 'I want to visit them again,' she said.

"Now we found them in a fine apartment with a clean kitchen

and nice furniture. The father was not at home. He was working. The mother and the children were home. Mrs. Roosevelt saw the progress they had made."

Like many of Israel's leaders, Mayor Tuvyahu was a mixture of realist and dreamer, builder and sociologist. "If I could have a wish," he told me, "I would like to walk around Beersheba fifty years from now. I would like to see what kind of culture we have created from the ingathering—Yemenites, Moroccans, Iraqis, Rumanians, Poles, Russians, Germans. I would like to see what relationship there will be between Israel as a Jewish center and other Jewish centers in America and in Europe."

The road to the Dead Sea begins in Beersheba; it is a beautiful curving highway that was built in 1953 through the canyons and mountains of the Negev. It passes some of the sites of the Nabateans, a people who lived in the Negev at the beginning of the Christian era.

About six miles before the sudden descent to the Dead Sea, there is a stark pillar of stone. In Hebrew, the inscription says:

MONUMENT TO THE PIONEERS OF THE ROAD TO THE DEAD SEA
WHO DID NOT LIVE TO SEE THE ROAD COMPLETED.

Beneath the inscription are the names of the men who were killed by invading Arabs as they built the road. This is the final high point. From here, you can see the dry yellow-white craters of the Arawa, looking the way the world may look after the atomic bomb. You can see the salt and chemical beds of the Dead Sea, bulldozed out of the sea so that the water could evaporate and leave behind the precious chemicals of this strangely named strange sea. Below you lies the Dead Sea itself, glistening blue in the sunlight, and beyond it lie Jordan and the Hills of Moab, turning crimson and violet and pink in the afternoon light.

The descent from the monument seems almost like a roller coaster. Suddenly you are on flat land 1,286 feet below sea level, passing the potash factory, the salt beds, and now the sea itself, the Dead Sea looking strangely gentle and alive.

The Sea is full of salt and throbbing warmth. It is so buoyant that no swimmer can drown in it. It is so salty that even if you dip only your foot or your finger in it, you seem to taste the salt.

Here are the ruins of Sodom and Gomorrah, the two wicked cities of the Bible. All that one sees of them are tall cliffs, looking like crystallized castles in the rocks. The Israelis have decided that one of the cliffs, separated like an estranged woman from the rest, is a pillar of salt. They call it "Mrs. Lot." A large sign erected by the Government Tourist Office, tells the story of the two sinful cities on the Dead Sea:

SODOM IS THE LOWEST POINT OF
HABITATION IN THE WORLD.
1286 FEET BELOW SEA LEVEL.

SODOM, PRIMITIVE SCENE OF THE MOST TERRIBLE JUDGMENT ON HUMAN SIN, WAS THE DWELLING PLACE OF LOT, "ABRAHAM'S BROTHER'S SON," BEFORE ITS CLASSIC DESTRUCTION WITH ITS SISTER CITY GO-MORRAH.

"THEN THE LORD RAINED UPON SODOM AND UPON GO-MORRAH BRIMSTONE AND FIRE—AND HE OVERTHREW THOSE CITIES, AND ALL THE PLAIN, AND ALL THE INHABITANTS OF THE CITIES AND THAT WHICH GREW UPON THE GROUND." Genesis 19:24-25.

TODAY SODOM IS THE CENTER OF ISRAEL'S POTASH PRODUCTION.

The Dead Sea inspired not only sin but asceticism and purity of spirit and religious faith. It was to this desert air of silence and retreat that the Essenes, the sect of the Dead Sea Scrolls, came to live their strictly disciplined communal life, away from the temptations of Jerusalem.

Most of Israel's mineral wealth lies in the canyons and the sands of the desert. To extract that wealth, she has built roads all through the Negev. Her explorers, taking off from Beersheba for the wild, uncharted places, no longer look only for copper and gold. They look for uranium in the rocks and for land that will grow cotton and for grass where cattle can graze. There are some who prospect for oil, but many more who look for water.

"In the wilderness," Isaiah had prophesied, "shall waters break out, and streams in the desert. And a highway shall be there, and a way, and it shall be called the Way of Holiness. . . . The redeemed shall walk there."

The victory of Sinai did more to make Isaiah's prophecy come true than two thousand years of history.

When the Israel army captured Nasser's illegal guns in the Straits of Tiran, it opened the southern Negev for commerce and freed the port of Elath from the deadly Arab blockade.

At the southernmost tip of Israel, a new city took shape on the sands of Etzion-Geber. "And King Solomon made a navy of ships in Etzion-Geber, which is beside Elath, on the shore of the Red Sea."

Like Israel itself, Elath (pronounced Ay-lot) is out of a children's book of wonders. Here are the romance and mystery of the Bible. It was from this harbor that Solomon sent the wealth of ancient Israel to the markets of his Biblical world. Here in Etzion-Geber, Solomon's artists and engineers, working in his heavy industries, processed the copper and minerals from his nearby mines. Here the romantic king welcomed the beautiful Queen of Sheba and her entourage to his Jewish kingdom.

The colors of Elath are fantastic. She has painted sand and blue and pink and mauve hills. In summer or winter the days are hot and the nights cold. Even in the Arctic I have never been as cold as I was one January night in the desert cold of Elath. Yet next day it was once again hot enough to go swimming.

Elath is fast becoming the most exotic tourist mecca in Israel. Travelers drive down on the desert road from Beersheba or fly down from Tel Aviv. For sports enthusiasts, Elath makes the Riviera look pale. Frogmen with rubber fins, masks, and snorkels look like spacemen out of science fiction. Skin-diving is Israel's newest craze, and young and even middle-aged tourists from Israel and abroad are now diving into the Gulf waters, knowing that these same waters wash the coasts of India and Ceylon, Ethiopia and Madagascar.

Fisherman tell real fish tales about the sea of Elath, for life there is almost as colorful as life along the beach, with iridescent small fish and big game fish swimming among the coral jungles and the Almog trees of the Bible.

In 1948, when Israel was born, Elath was a tiny, forgotten harbor on the Gulf of Aqaba with a few huts made of baked earth and a police station with a lovely name, Umm Rashrash. Now it is a boom town of some seven thousand people, most of them new immigrants. There are schools for Elath's children, who keep increasing the boom. Canadian Hadassah has built a marine hospital here. Ships from far-flung nations of the world sail in, to bring oil and meat and timber and to take out the finished products of Israel's new industries.

One hundred is a mystic number in modern Israel. It took Israel's army one hundred hours to drive through Sinai to Suez. It took Israel's engineers one hundred days to lay the oil pipeline from Elath to Beersheba. Now the line has been extended to the new harbor at Ashdod, below Ashkelon, where Israeli tankers carry the oil to the refineries at Haifa.

The Suez Canal need no longer be the only lifeline to Europe. Israel's pipeline at present is just large enough for her own oil needs, but a line big enough for all of Europe's needs could be laid along the same route.

"In many ways," Ben-Gurion once told me, "the Negev is the same kind of bridge—though a land bridge—that the Suez Canal is. It links the Mediterranean Sea route to the Atlantic and the Red Sea route to the Indian Ocean and the Pacific. We are the natural crossroads for the East and West. Already we are bridging the two worlds ethnically by our ingathering. Now we will do it commercially with our ships and planes."

He suddenly stopped. "Words are not important," he concluded. "Nations are not built on words. Deeds are important. We have lost two thousand years. We have no more time to lose."

17: The Arabs and Israel

THERE ARE few tragedies in the world greater than the tragedy of uprooted people. Refugee camps have become a familiar sight on the face of the earth. Men, women, and children, torn from their native soil, living in tents, demoralized by the abnormality of camp life—this was the picture of the D.P. camps in postwar Europe and Asia; it is the picture of Arab refugees today.

It is a cruel and inhuman existence, and by all the laws of humanity every camp should be liquidated and every human being should be given a chance to live with decency and dignity.

A camp is a camp is a camp. Even the best camps in the world are ultimately evil. During World War II, I helped run what must surely have been the most idyllic of all camps: the one at Oswego, New York, for the thousand refugees whom President Roosevelt had invited from eighteen countries in war-torn Europe. Every day expressions of love and gifts of all kinds poured in for the refugees, the only European refugees brought to the United States during the war. The Congress of the United States was concerned with the camp. Secretary of the Interior Harold L. Ickes, whose Special Assistant I was, was so moved by the tragedies these people—Catholics, Protestants, and Jews—had lived through, that he did everything a humane and idealistic government official could do to help them find comfort and happiness.

Yet as the months went on, the people grew more and more unhappy, deteriorating psychologically, demoralized by the abnormality of camp life. The only purpose of a camp, I was convinced, was to provide immediate temporary shelter and then be liquidated. The Arab refugee camps are no exception.

To every question there are at least two sides and two explanations. On the Arab side, there has been an injustice. For most of the campers (though not all, since at least a third have been born in the camps or were babies when their parents fled) there is the tragedy of upheaval. People who lived all their lives on the soil of Palestine have been uprooted.

The Israelis, for their part, admit that the Arabs have been uprooted, but point out that they were uprooted because there was a war, not of Israel's making but of the Arabs'. Nor was it only invasion by the seven surrounding sovereign states. It was actual civil war begun by the Arabs of Palestine immediately after the United Nations, on the twenty-ninth of November, 1947, voted to partition Palestine.

The simple truth is that there are Arab refugees today because the Arabs made war on Israel and were defeated. If there had been no war, there would be no Arab refugees.

The Arabs knew exactly what they were doing. They announced to the world that they would defy the United Nations and launch a holy war. The Secretary General of the Arab League declared: "This will be a war of extermination and a momentous massacre which will be spoken of like the Mongolian massacre and the Crusades."

It is now almost universally acknowledged that the Arab refugees were the victims of their leaders' propaganda and flight. They were told to flee the country; that the invading armies from Egypt, Jordan, Syria, Lebanon, and Iraq, with contingents from Saudi Arabia and Yemen, would drive every Jew into the Mediterranean, and the Palestinian Arabs would then return in the wake of the victorious armies.

Monsignor George Hakim, the Greek Catholic Archbishop of Galilee, stated on August 16, 1948: "The refugees had been confident that their absence from Palestine would not last long; that they would return within a few days—within a week or two. Their leaders had promised them that the Arab armies would crush the 'Zionist gangs' very quickly and that there would be no need for panic or fear of a long exile."

A month later Mr. Emile Ghoury, former Secretary of the Arab Higher Committee, declared: "I do not want to impugn anyone but only to help the refugees. The fact that there are these refugees is the direct consequence of the action of the Arab States in opposing partition and the Jewish State. The Arab States agreed upon this policy unanimously and they must share in the solution of the problem."

The British themselves, who were much friendlier to the Arabs in 1948 than they were to the Jews, revealed in secret reports that in Haifa the Arabs were fleeing in small boats to Lebanon and Syria. The Jews of Haifa went down to the boats and begged the Arabs to stay.

The British superintendent of police, A. J. Bidmead, wrote to his government in a confidential document, "Every effort is being made by the Jews to persuade the Arab populace to stay . . . (but) Arab leaders reiterated their determination to evacuate the entire Arab population."

To the Arabs' amazement, and to the amazement of the British and most of the world that put its money on forty million Arabs defeating a nation of six hundred and fifty thousand Jews, the war ended with Israel victorious. The tragedy that the Arabs had sought to inflict on the Jews was averted, though it took its heavy toll on both sides.

Wars cannot be taken lightly. Much of the parchment of history is written with the blood of war. The war that the Arabs began was paid for with precious lives. Each of the Arab states lost thousands of soldiers. The newborn state of Israel lost six thousand soldiers—the boys and girls it needed most because they were the bravest. Twenty thousand more were wounded or maimed, some of them invalided for life.

With such a price in human life, a new chapter in history was written: the sealing of independence, the routing of the enemy, and the flight of the Arabs who were to become refugees. As a result of the battle whole Arab villages were demolished under fire. In the soil where some of the Arabs lived, the grass has now grown over the graves of Jewish soldiers. The years 1948 and '49 were not a vacuum that Israel and the world can cavalierly forget.

In exchange for some six hundred thousand refugees who fled, Israel has taken, among the million newcomers, five hundred and fifty thousand refugees from the Arab world. These were Jewish refugees who were also victims of the Arab-Israel war. By every definition of refugee, they were entitled to world sympathy and United Nations aid. But Israel welcomed them, fed them, housed them, integrated them into her economy. To be sure, Israel received help from abroad, particularly from the United Jewish Appeal. So, too, did the Arabs.

The Jewish refugees from the Arab world who came into Israel were moved out of the camps and tent cities as quickly as possible; some of them never lived in camps at all.

The Arab refugees are by no means unique. Since World War II over thirty-five million people have become refugees, uprooted by the tragedy of war and revolution and the rise of nationalism. Among them are the thirteen million refugees in East and West Germany, the eight and a half million Hindus and Sikhs who had fled from Pakistan to India, the six and a half million Moslems who fled from India to Pakistan, the three million people who fled from North to South Korea, the three hundred and fifty thousand Volksdeutsche in Austria, the four hundred thousand Karelians in Finland, the four hundred and fifty thousand Jewish refugees who fled from Arab lands into Israel, and the nine hundred thousand who are now Arab refugees.

The population figure of nine hundred thousand in the camps many experts believe is somewhat exaggerated. With the natural increase in the birth rate the number of refugees today would probably be closer to seven hundred and fifty thousand. But the refugee families generally neglect to report their dead. When these names are not taken off the relief rolls, the ration cards of the dead continue to be used and counted. Also, local indigents have joined the refugee camps; in some cases living conditions are better in the camp than they are at home, with better food, better schooling, and better medical care.

Almost all of the refugees have been assimilated in their host countries. It is an astonishing fact that only the nine hundred thousand Arab refugees have been refused refuge by the Arab nations in which they are unwelcome guests. The Arab states have kept them isolated in camps as festering sores, despite the fact that the refugees speak the same language and practice the same faith as their inhospitable hosts.

For many years the Arab states have been growing wealthier with oil royalties, yet they have contributed nothing to their tragic co-religionists. The world community through U.N.R.W.A. (United Nations Relief and Works Agency for Palestine Refugees in the Near East) is still feeding the refugees, housing them, healing them, and running schools for the children who keep swelling the camps' populations, and for whom Israel is a completely unknown land.

In July, 1957, the Carnegie Endowment published its survey of the Arab refugee problem; Dr. Elfan Rees of the World Council of Churches wrote: "The history of UNRWA has been a clinical study in frustration. No agency has been better led or more devoutly served, but the organized intransigence of the refugees and the calculated indifference of the Arab States concerned have brought all its plans to nought. By chicanery it is feeding the dead; by political pressure it is feeding nonrefugees; its relief supplies have been subjected in some instances to import duty; its personnel policies are grossly interfered with, and its constructive measures necessarily requiring the concurrence of governments have been pigeonholed. The net result is that relief is being provided in 1957 to refugees who could have been rehabilitated in 1951 with homes and jobs without prejudice to their just claims."

The two possible solutions are repatriation or integration. Repatriation means returning these people to Israel after they have been fed for ten years on the poisonous doctrine of extermination and death. Integration would mean being accepted by the Arab states as Israel has accepted the Jewish refugees whom the Arabs expelled.

The Carnegie Institute studied both possibilities and concluded that repatriation would be unwise. Dr. Rees wrote: "It needs to be clearly stated that a persistence in this view (repatriation) is dangerous stupidity on the part of the refugees themselves and criminal lunacy on the part of their leaders. No large-scale refugee problem has ever been solved by repatriation and there are certainly no grounds for believing that these particular problems can be so solved. Nothing can bring it about except wars which in our time would leave nothing to come back to. It appears . . . Arab refugees are prepared for this risk . . . war has never solved a refugee problem and it is not in the books that a modern war would."

Repatriation would be disastrous. Israel could never swallow nine hundred thousand refugees. With the tremendous Arab birth rate, the Arabs would soon outnumber the Jews in a Jewish state. Israel would be strangled. There would be economic, social, and political chaos. Most of the Arabs would certainly not be coming in as friends, ready to live as peace-abiding citizens in a sovereign Jewish state. Many would be coming in as hostile fifth columnists. And in the world refugee picture, there might then be two million Jewish refugees from a disrupted Israel.

Integration, in the minds of most observers, is the only solution for the tragic problem. Israel might very well be willing to accept up to a hundred thousand Arab refugees if that were part of a general peace agreement. For most of the other Arab refugees, the solution may well be the one which former President Herbert Hoover proposed, that the refugees be resettled in the rich, fertile Euphrates Valley in Iraq. This valley, believed to be the site of the Garden of Eden, could not only support the refugees but in turn could become once again a bread basket for the Middle East.

Israel has already taken a number of steps toward a solution. She has integrated forty-eight thousand five hundred Arab refugees from the refugee camps into her economy and has allowed 40,000 Arab refugees with immediate families in Israel to return. She has released nearly $10,000,000 in frozen bank accounts and returned their safe deposit boxes. The United States suggested in 1957 that an international loan would be set up to help Israel pay compensation to the Arabs. Israel accepted. The Arabs refused.

There are two hundred thousand Arabs living in Israel today, and Israel has been determinedly making them a living part of the Jewish state. Arab girls and boys go to school (education is free and compulsory for all children in Israel). Babies are born in free hospitals, cared for in free clinics. Veiled women as well as Arab men go to the polling booths to vote.

Each year Israel has raised the standard of living of whole Arab communities. On a bright Sunday afternoon in 1955, water came to Nazareth. There had been some water before in this city of Mary and Joseph, but every year there was a shortage, and in the years of drought, there was almost no water at all. Now there would be water every day, water running through new pipelines into everybody's home.

Moshe Sharett, who was then prime minister, drove up from Jerusalem to take part in the celebration. He turned a wheel, gaily decorated with blue and white crepe paper; water gushed up from pipes that had been placed upright in the Nazareth hills, and from everywhere, from the roads and houses and sides of the mountains, children ran to the water, singing and shouting and drenching themselves under the miraculous spray.

Most of Nazareth's twenty thousand Arabs and their friends and neighbors came to watch the water ceremony. A big stadium had been built near Nazareth's quarries. Only men sat in the stadium. On all the mountainsides encircling it, the women and their families sat on the stones or walked on the winding roads, watching the celebration and listening to the speeches carried by loud-speakers. Arab and Jewish Boy Scouts paraded together. A youth orchestra from Haifa played. Jewish boys and girls from a neighboring kibbutz danced Israeli and Arab folk dances.

Perhaps the most unusual feature of this Arab-Jewish celebration was that an unveiled Arab woman addressed the gathering. She won the greatest applause and laughter when she told the people of Nazareth what this water meant to their women. "No longer will we have to go to the Well of the Virgin to draw water. Now we will have water in our taps. No longer will we have to carry water on our heads. Now we will be able to go to the beauty parlor and get permanent waves."

Everyone was happy except the Arab Communists who were holding a rally nearby. Water, the Communist leaders told their

followers, was a Western plot. The government of Israel was bringing water to Nazareth to make the city dependent on the Jewish
state.

In 1956 electricity came to the Arab village of Tayiba, just opposite Jordan. Thousands of Israel's Arab citizens cheered as the
sun went down and in the golden dusk Israel's minister of interior
turned on a switch in the Arab high school. Lights flashed on all
over town. In the school square, gaily lit by a string of colored
bulbs, Arab and Jewish leaders made speeches, telling what electric
power could do for the Arabs of Israel.

Electricity is not only power and light in Israel's Arab villages.
It is politics. There is no electricity in the rural villages of Jordan
that lie a few hundred feet away. Schools across the border are for
the privileged few.

A sense of community and civic pride, such as I have never seen
before, seems now to be growing up in Israel's Arab villages. The
Moslem chairman of Tayiba's local council talked to me proudly
of his village, while we stood in front of his white house watching
Jewish electricians sitting on a high pole stringing electric wires to
bring light into his home. He told me that both his son and daughter were studying to become social workers at the Hebrew University in Jerusalem.

Directly across the road from Tayiba are the offices of the military government in charge of the so-called "Little Triangle" between Armageddon and the Plains of Sharon. To keep check on
potential enemies within the land, Israel has set up military government for a number of defense zones.

Military government in Israel bears almost no resemblance to
military government as seen in Frankfurt or Vienna at the end
of World War II. There, the American Army of Occupation was
everywhere. Here, the military governor and a handful of officers
do their governing unobtrusively. Their office, away from the
villages, is a small compound of brown wooden huts, surrounded
by barbed wire and some guards. But like that of the American
military government, their work is more than maintenance of

security. Theirs is the task of bringing Western civilization and the democratic way of life to the Arabs.

The military governor, Lieutenant Colonel Zalman Mart, who looks more like a self-effacing doctor than a soldier, sits behind a simple wooden desk beneath a portrait of Theodor Herzl, the father of Zionism. He is the governor of the "Central Area," a narrow strip of land on the eastern frontier running some thirty miles north from Petakh Tikvah to Armageddon, and ranging from half a mile to five miles wide. There are thirty Arab villages in his area, with 37,500 Arabs.

"My job," he told me in excellent English, "is not defense. That is the task of the frontier police and the Jewish farming villages along the border. My job is controlling the Arab population of the area as long as there is no peace. We know that the great part of the population is loyal. But we also know that another part is not loyal, and they must be checked, patrolled, and supervised.

"They are free to move anywhere they want inside this Central Area. But to leave it, they must have permission from the military governor.

"In a number of incidents within the past year," he continued, "the footsteps of the infiltrators went through these villages. A few months ago, some Jordanian Arabs blew up a house in Kfar Yahvitz, and the footsteps went through Tayiba. But we believe the Jordanians went there on purpose to bring harm to our villagers."

The colonel invited us to eat a typical Arab lunch in his hut, prepared and served by a young Arab boy from Tayiba. Then we crossed the road to visit one of Tayiba's wealthiest farmers. Hassan Baransi's house was a modern villa on the outskirts of Tayiba, utterly unlike the old Arab houses inside the village. Baransi himself met us at the door, dressed in a long woolen Arab gown and a modern jacket.

We followed him up the steps of the veranda into the large living room furnished in modern Arab fashion, with sofas and upholstered chairs lining all the walls. With typical hospitality, he graciously motioned Colonel Mart and me to a sofa.

Since Baransi spoke little English, his sons and two Israeli officers who came with us acted as interpreters. I wanted to know what changes there had been in his life since Israel became a state. Were things better or worse for him than before 1948?

He smiled. "That's a very straight question." He paused. "There is a great difference between then and now. Now the government helps us. She takes from us in high taxes, but she helps us. Before, under the British Mandate, the government didn't take from us, but they didn't give us anything either. Now the government sends us machines for farming and teaches us new ways to farm. The government tells us in advance what is needed—it is a great help in knowing what to plant."

It would be untrue to say that the Arabs are happy under the military government. But they are certainly not tragic figures like the refugees in the Arab states. They are earning their own bread with dignity. Many of them are richer now than they were under the British before 1948.

Yet for Israel, the two hundred thousand Arabs represent a profound security problem. They are 10 per cent of her population. Some of them are the villagers who preferred to stay in Israel. And there are the Druses, a minority who fought with the Jews against the rest of the Arabs. But most of the two hundred thousand did not aspire to live in a Jewish state. They are citizens of Israel simply because they did not run away.

How loyal are they? Are they hiding terrorists sent in by President Nasser? How much smuggling of military information goes on between Israel's Arabs and the states that surround her in an iron ring of hatred?

The possibility is ever present that the Arab citizens who live on the Jordan frontier may be asked to grant hospitality and asylum to an infiltrator from Jordan, a saboteur who may even be a relative. Hospitality is one of the Arabs' noblest traits.

Israel does not contend that her Arab citizens are traitors or fifth columnists, but she is constantly aware of the possibility that they may be forced to become hosts to fifth columnists. Thus far, their loyalty has not been tested.

Israel is aware of the security problem that her Arab citizens present. Despite the danger, she is determined to give the Arabs a chance to live with decency and earn their livelihood. She is aware that there is a risk in not considering the Arabs as potential fifth columnists, but it is a calculated risk.

If the borders remain quiet and the Arab states make no overt efforts to turn Israel's Arabs into saboteurs, Israel is planning to lift the regulations of military government, and to abolish it completely in the not too distant future.

Meanwhile Israel is doing for her Arab population what few Arab states are doing for their own citizens, or for the Arabs who are refugees inside their borders.

18: None Shall Make Them Afraid

BEFORE THE man-made moons began to orbit in the space age, there were two ways to defend a land—with a mobile army and through territorial defense.

An army is on wheels or planes or ships. It can be moved around like a fist, punching in any direction, feinting, shadow-boxing, guarding.

Territorial defense is stationary. In Israel it is a chain of border settlements that are steady, rooted, unyielding. They are the human granite wall against the enemy.

The frontier settlements are planned for defense. They are set in the weakest and most vulnerable spots along the frontier. They are the epitome of home defense—the defense of wives, of children, of treasured homes, and beloved soil. The defense that can, if need comes, be turned into scorched earth to slow up the enemy.

Both these concepts are part of Israel's defense scheme. Hers is a strange army, perhaps the only one of its kind in the world today. There is no "regular army" in Israel. It is a reservist army, made up of inductees. All boys and girls of eighteen, except orthodox girls and married women, must serve in the army, the boys for two and a half years, the girls for two years. Every man up to the age of forty-nine is part of the reserve, and is called up thirty days a year for training or active duty.

There are no career soldiers below the rank of sergeant. To be sure, there is a nucleus of professional officers and technicians, but even they are civil servants who sign a contract that may commit them for a year or perhaps for five years. Israel's former Chief of Staff Moshe Dayan was under contract for several years. When he resigned his post in January, 1958, he registered at the Hebrew University to study history and political science.

It is a "citizen's army" whose purpose is to make citizens of its soldiers and soldiers of its citizens. Its major task is of course defense. But to defend the country with a strong army, it had to integrate thousands of new immigrants into the land.

Breaking in recruits is the job of most Western armies: teaching them hard discipline, instant obedience. The Israel army couldn't "break in" most of its soldiers. Some of them were completely shattered from the life of oppression they had led abroad. Yemenite soldiers had to be taught not to cringe. To rebuild them, the army had to teach them to talk back, to have khuzpeh. They were so weak and undernourished that they had to be built up, not broken in.

It was a unique school. The army taught them how to tie their shoestrings and how to eat with a fork and a knife and how to sleep in a bed. It was a common sight to see Yemenite soldiers on a long march take off their shoes and tie them by the strings around their necks. When their officers asked them at first why they did it, they said, "We're not used to shoes. Besides, this is a long hike. You have to save shoe leather."

Yemenites became sharpshooters, but they had a lot of trouble at first. To shoot a gun, you have to wink one eye. Winking, which in most countries goes with wolf-calls, is apparently not part of Yemenite culture. The Yemenites simply could not wink. At the army camp in Sarafand, you could see scores of Yemenites walking around with a black scarf tied over one eye, training the eye to stay closed.

The army found itself teaching everything from raising vegetables to piloting a jet plane. It had to teach many of the newcomers to read and write, and almost all of them how to speak Hebrew. It had to teach people who came out of the Middle Ages how to live and fight and defend their land in the twentieth century. Its success was fantastic. Yemenites, just up from slavery, became ace pilots. Moroccans from the narrow fetid mellahs of Casablanca made first-rate infantry men. Iraqis from shops in Bagdad made fearless tank drivers. Paratroopers came from the free soil of Israel and the imprisoned countries of terror and pogrom. The ingathering was molded into an army that gave its newcomers dignity and pride. Through the army, the new citizens gave the state the precious gift of youth and courage.

Two of the most important and unusual phases of the army program are Nahal, an abbreviation of three Hebrew words meaning "fighting, pioneering, youth," and Gadna, formed from two Hebrew words meaning "youth groups." Nahal is a part of the soldiers' regular stint. The soldiers have a choice of serving their full two and a half years in an army camp or dividing it and spending half in the army and half in an agricultural or fishing village.

Gadna is a program for high school boys and girls. Each summer the Gadna youth spend two weeks in a camping-out adventure. There are Gadna camp sites all over the country; the most adventurous one is in Israel's southernmost frontier at Beer Ora just above Elath. Beer Ora, which means the "Well of Light," is one of Ben-Gurion's favorite projects in the Israel he hopes will emerge. "Go down to the Negev and see Beer Ora," he told me one day. "That is our future. It is one of the great achievements of our time."

A few days later I flew down to see a graduation in Beer Ora, twelve miles from Elath and surrounded within a few tight uneasy miles by Egypt, Jordan, and Saudi Arabia. We drove in a truck across a washboard road through desert and mountain country that looked like Colorado. We turned in a road, drove through a wooden arch, and entered a Youth Republic.

The desert was transformed by youth. Hundreds of boys and girls of fourteen to eighteen were walking, dancing, singing, running, marching. Some were growing vegetables, raising ducks and sheep and chickens on the desert sand. In neat rows, tied securely against the cold night winds, stood their tents.

They did not live here. They came in different groups every two weeks, in bus loads of two hundred, from the high schools of the country, down the long Negev road. They worked the land, fed the chickens, planted trees, prospected for minerals near King Solomon's ancient mines, and then returned to their schools in the towns and farm settlements of the north, to make room for another two hundred.

The colonel responsible for this youth program showed us through the agricultural station with great pride. We walked through rows of red cabbage and cauliflower. The high school youngsters had dug wells, found ample water, and were now raising experimental crops. The chief gardener, a pretty blond girl in a white shirt and blue shorts, led us to their experiment in hydroponics. In tanks filled with water and chemicals they were raising tomatoes, cucumbers, peppers, eggplants, beans, radishes, and onions.

"And when our two hundred chickens lived and flourished all summer in this heat," the colonel said, "we knew then that chickens could live in the southern desert. Now we could experiment with domestic animals."

It was symbolic of Israel that an army colonel should be talking of development and growing vegetables and raising chickens, since it is peace that even the army is striving for.

Nahal is perhaps the most extraordinary example of an army striving for peace. By offering the soldiers a chance to spend half their army stint as farmers or fishermen, under army discipline, the army is accomplishing a twofold peacetime mission. It encourages youngsters who have come from all over the world to live on the land in Israel. And it encourages them to build their own settlements on the borders after they leave the army.

From the Gaza Strip on the west to the Syrian border in the north and the Jordan border in the east, the country is now being strung like a necklace with a chain of Nahal settlements.

In the new defense villages live the minutemen of Israel. They are the sons and daughters of Israel's doctors and lawyers and supreme court justices, of her farmers and workers. They could have gone back home after their army service, to college or to jobs in the cities or to life in the older and by now secure kibbutzim. But they chose to keep their army group together and settle permanently in a village of their own making. They were forging the chain of Israel's territorial defense.

They knew what they were building for, and what they might one day be actively fighting for. But they built with laughter. They lived in one-room huts and slashed their land with great gashes of trenches. But they sang while they worked and while they guarded, and at night they joined together and played chess and read books and listened to recordings of fine operas and American musical comedies.

Some of them undoubtedly had their days of doubt and loneliness and perhaps even fear. Anyone who wanted to, could leave the settlement and return to a less vulnerable spot. But those who stayed took a kind of vow from the Prophet Micah, that "none shall make them afraid."

Barely six months after the invading Arab states were defeated by Israel in 1948 and 1949, the Arabs began guerrilla warfare. They infiltrated. They murdered. They sought to strike terror. Some of the Arabs were saboteurs, some were spies, some were smugglers, some were plain robbers, some were just hungry. Whatever the motives, they filled life on the borders with sudden death. Israel retaliated. After each retaliation, the border would be quiescent for a few months, only to flare up again.

In the spring of 1955, Colonel Nasser created the *Fedayeen*. They were terrorist gangs, with a regular military organization. They generally struck in small units. They were trained in sabotage, in blowing up trains, mining roads, killing people in buses, stealing irrigation pipes, tossing hand grenades into cottages. They were carefully schooled in the fine art of murder.

The Fedayeen were Nasser's brain child, his claim to a new kind of warfare. They differed from other guerrillas in that they were actually under the Egyptian army command with regular bases in the Gaza Strip and the Sinai Peninsula, from which they launched their attacks.

The war by Fedayeen began officially in the summer of 1955. On August 31 Nasser's government issued a communiqué dealing with his new kind of war:

Egypt has decided to dispatch her heroes, the disciples of Pharaoh and the sons of Islam, and they will clean the land of Palestine. That we have decided and that is our belief. There will be no peace on Israel's border because we demand vengeance, and vengeance is Israel's death.

The same day the Egyptian government issued another communiqué boasting of their success in invading Israel and terrorizing its people:

The Egyptian Fedayeen have begun their activities inside the territory of Israel after the repeated clashes on the border during the past week. The Egyptian Fedayeen have penetrated into Israel's settlements, spread out in the Negev until Beersheba and Migdal Ashkelon, at a distance of 40 kilometers from the Egyptian border and have taught our aggressive enemies lessons that they will not forget. The Egyptian Fedayeen sowed fear and consternation amongst the citizens of Israel.

A few days later the Egyptians were claiming an advance on Tel Aviv: "The forces of the Egyptian Fedayeen moved toward Israel, approached her capital, and caused heavy casualties along the border between Gaza and Tel Aviv."

During the summer of 1956, while I was covering the story of life in the border settlements for the New York Herald Tribune, hardly a night passed without Fedayeen raids. One evening raiders penetrated and tossed a hand grenade into a children's home in the hills of Judea just outside Jerusalem. It was sheer miracle that the bomb fell in the corridor instead of one of the bedrooms. Two watchmen were captured by Fedayeen and their ears were chopped off. A young man took his girl driving one Friday night, and, in the universal manner of young men, parked his car in a dark spot not far from the Lydda airport. Suddenly three Fedayeen, dressed in Israeli army uniforms with packs on their backs, accosted the couple, forced them out of the car, and killed the young man. The girl stayed alive by using her wits. She spoke to the Fedayeen in English and told them she was a Russian Christian girl. The Fedayeen believed her and set her free.

At Nahal Oz on the Gaza Strip, a few hundred feet from the

Three generations guarded the pilgrim's hostel near the Holy Synagogue of the Ghriba, a "Jewish Lourdes" on the Island of Djerba

The people of Djerba fleeing Arab nationalism on a ship to Israel

Woman of Djerba. On their wedding day, the women become queens placing the Djerban diadem on their hair

Little boys at school in Djerba, learning Hebrew. The making of rabbis is Djerba's chief industry

Mrs. Trabelsine at home in Djerba, dressed in the clothes of David's song: "clothed in scarlet . . . with ornaments of gold"

A Djerban printer at work printing the works of the great scholars of North African Jewry

The road from Beer-sheba to the Dead Sea is guarded constantly against Arab infiltrators

Fishermen in Elath, the most exotic tourist mecca in Israel, catching iridescent fish swimming among the coral jungles and the Almog trees of the Bible

Egyptians, where the minutemen look into the guns of the Arabs and watch the Arabs watching them, there had been a handsome boy in 1955, Roy Rothberg, a boy with shining eyes and a laughing voice, who talked not of arms and war but of music and books. Roy had said to me, "I know there's nothing here now but desert. But you come back in five years and you'll find Tel Aviv."

In 1956 Roy was on guard duty riding his horse one night in the fields of barley when he saw some Arab infiltrators from the Gaza Strip. He chased them across the border. The next night the infiltrators returned. This time they did not wait for Roy to chase them. They shot him, dragged him off his horse, and pulled him into the Gaza Strip. There they gouged out his eyes, dismembered his body, and tossed it back into Nahal Oz.

When the Israel army captured Gaza in the fall of 1956, they found the Egyptians who had tortured Roy. The man who had worked on the eyes—eyes seem to have special significance for this kind of terror—was a doctor. He was captured the first day.

The Israelis tried the men in a court-martial. Most armies would have found the men guilty and shot them. But the case was not clear-cut; and the Egyptians were turned free.

For eight years everyone in Israel lived within five minutes of potential danger. Everyone knew that the whole of his land was borderland. Infiltrators could penetrate from any direction. Everyone knew that nightly propaganda broadcasts from Cairo were inciting the Arabs to "burn, murder, and destroy and to prepare for the great battle ahead."

Guerrilla warfare was mounting. The Fedayeen were becoming more efficient. They penetrated deeper into Israel. They killed more people. They grew bolder in their objectives. They blew up the radio tower of *Kol Israel*, the Voice of Israel, south of Tel Aviv. They were paralyzing civilian life, blowing up conduit pipes beneath the roads, dynamiting bridges and reservoirs, attacking small houses on the fringes of the border settlements and then falling on centers of population. Members of a wedding party at Patich in the Negev were killed. Outside of Tel Aviv a school was attacked and the children and their teacher murdered.

"There is no reason why the faithful Fedayeen," Egypt's minister of religious properties declared on April 11, 1955, "hating their enemy, should not penetrate into Israel and transform the lives of its citizens into a hell."

In the fall of 1956 Israel decided that the Fedayeen had gone far enough in trying to turn life in Israel "into a hell."

19: Victory in Sinai

ON MONDAY, the twenty-ninth of October, 1956, Israel's army marched into the Sinai Peninsula.

There were several immediate reasons for this action. The Arab Fedayeen were operating from bases in Sinai as well as Gaza. Israel wanted to destroy those bases.

On October 22, the Egyptians, the Syrians, and the Jordanians concluded and signed a military alliance, putting their armies under Egyptian command. They announced frankly that their objective was to encircle Israel with a steel ring and then annihilate her. By destroying Nasser's army, the best equipped army of the three, Israel hoped to cripple the tripartite alliance.

Her third major objective was to stop Egypt before the Russians gave her enough arms to build an efficient war machine. Russia had sided with Egypt in 1955, through the subterfuge of the "Czechoslovakian arms deal," and had given Nasser, at bargain rates, Mig-15 jet planes, Stalin and T-34 tanks, destroyers, huge artillery, mortars, antitank weapons, light machine guns. Nasser rushed a great part of this equipment into Sinai and Gaza, building a tremendous offensive base for the steel ring that was to encircle Israel.

Nasser made it clear that he did not need Mig-15's to raise the standard of living of the fellahin along the Nile. Nor did he need Stalin tanks to fight communism. His aim was to destroy Israel. Like all dictators, he dreamed of extending his empire, in this case from North Africa on the Atlantic to Asia in the Pacific. He described this dream of conquest in his book *The Philosophy of Revolution*.

The Israel defense forces, in a brilliant campaign, slashed into the Sinai desert. Their speed took even the Israelis by surprise. In four days, their soldiers knocked out Nasser's Sinai army completely. This was one-third of Nasser's total army of one hundred fifty thousand men. The Israel forces captured all of the Soviet material that he had stored in Sinai and Gaza. They took some fifty-five hundred prisoners, among them three hundred officers ranking from major generals down to second lieutenants.

With victory in Sinai, Israel destroyed one myth of Nasser. She revealed the emptiness of Arab military unity, since no Arab state had come to Nasser's aid. She paralyzed Nasser's army for at least a few years. She destroyed the bases in Sinai and Gaza from which the attack on Israel was to be launched. She restored normal civilian life in all of Israel, especially in the border settlements by eliminating the Fedayeen. She destroyed temporarily at least the alliance between Egypt, Syria, and Jordan. She captured the Straits of Tiran, which Nasser had illegally fortified to prevent ships from entering Elath. Now, with Elath open, Israel has a window in the south, a port to the markets of India and the Orient, to East and South Africa, and when peace comes, to Arabia itself.

Israel lost some two hundred soldiers in the campaign, but Egypt took only one Israel prisoner, a pilot whose plane was shot down and who baled out over Egyptian territory. Not one Israel soldier surrendered or ran away.

The four-day war taught the Israelis that a reservist army could fight a real war. Sinai was fought by a conglomerate army whose leaders were veterans of the war of 1948, but whose soldiers were mainly youngsters who did not know the war of independence, and new immigrants who had arrived since Israel was born.

The question, spoken and unspoken, was: how well would the youngsters and especially the new immigrants fight? Sinai showed that you did not have to be born in Israel to be willing to die for it.

No Israeli soldier found the fighting so critical that he could not continue fighting. Yet the war was not without tragedy for Israel. The two hundred boys and girls were brought home from Sinai and buried either near their homes or on Mount Herzl in Jerusalem, in new fresh rows beside the victims of the war of independence. Hadassah's hospital in Beersheba, and other hospitals throughout the land, filled up with six hundred wounded, some of them maimed for life.

Israel's army gives no medals. Most armies think medals are essential in building morale, that officers and enlisted men will fight better if they know they may get a Croix de Guerre, a Congressional Medal, a Victoria Cross or even a Purple Heart. But Israel does not decorate its heroes. Yet in the four days of fighting, many soldiers performed deeds far beyond the call of duty. There was the Yemenite infantryman who leaped upon a roll of barbed wire and bore it down with his body so that the other soldiers could hurry over him in their march forward.

There was the young commander of an armored unit, composed of tanks and half-trucks, who was to attack a fortified position. His half-trucks traveled faster than the tanks, and he knew the enemy position had to be taken by surprise. He attacked with half-trucks and was wiped out with his entire command. But he softened up the enemy and the tanks took the position for which he had given his life.

There was Yehuda, just twenty, one of the paratroopers who landed with jeeps and equipment in the Mitle Pass, some twenty-five miles from the Suez Canal. It was a canyon-like area with a road leading to steep hills, an important point strategically because it controlled a large area of the Sinai desert. When the paratroopers reached the canyon, they were caught in heavy cross fire by the Egyptians, entrenched in caves on both sides of the road. The paratroopers made several moves forward. They were shot down. There were a number of casualties. Twilight came. The commander of the unit asked for a volunteer to drive a jeep on the road through the canyon, to serve as a moving target to draw enemy fire. The entire unit would attack as soon as they saw the enemy positions.

Six volunteers stepped forward. One was a battalion commander. Four were officers and soldiers. The sixth was Yehuda, the unit commander's driver. The commander hesitated. Yehuda was a devoted soldier, with great promise. The mission meant certain death.

Yehuda fought for the job. "I'm the youngest. I have no family. I should be given preference."

He drove the jeep into the canyon. The whole company watched.

He drove slowly so that the Egyptians could not possibly miss him. They didn't. He drew all their fire, all the bullets that a small jeep could take. He drove about two hundred feet, and then rolled out of the jeep. The enemy positions were now crystal clear to the paratroopers. They attacked. When the commander reached Yehuda, he was still alive. He died on the way to the hospital. He received no posthumous medal, but he is a living legend in the Israel army.

The Battle of Sinai was a four-day victory and a four-month retreat. While the Israel army was taking the desert, England and France attempted to wrest the Suez Canal from Nasser, who, after nationalizing it illegally, could almost decree how much tea every Englishman should drink and how much gasoline every Frenchman could use in his car.

The United Nations met in sessions that lasted through the night, and the battle moved from Egypt to the East River in New York. The nations of the world recognized that there had been ample provocation for Israel to go into Sinai and for England and France to stop Nasser at the Suez Canal. The smell of Munich was still strong in many nostrils. They knew that dictators feed on their own greed. To appease Nasser was no different from appeasing Hitler, and in Europe, appeasement had taken far more lives in 1944 than courage would have taken in 1934.

"There has been aggression in the Middle East," Israel's ambassador said, summing up the conflict for England and France as well as for his own country, "but we are its victims, not its authors."

The U.N. voted that all troops should be moved out of Egypt, and that the Suez Canal should be completely rebuilt for Egypt. Nasser's head, which had been practically rolling in the sand, was carefully picked up, dusted off, and placed on his shoulders again. The world solicitously handed him a political victory to assuage his humiliating military defeat.

After four months of debate, Israel's foreign minister, Golda Meir, announced at the U.N. that Israel would move out of the Gaza Strip and the Straits of Tiran on the basis of a number of "assumptions." It was a diplomatic word for concrete promises. Promises that the Egyptian army would not re-establish its offensive base in Gaza. Promises that the United States and other maritime powers would keep open the shipping lanes in the Gulf of Aqaba.

The world had feebly protested two years earlier, and had done nothing, when Nasser placed his guns illegally in the Straits of Tiran and successfully strangled all shipping to Elath. In a swift overland operation from Sinai down to the Straits, Israel's Ninth Brigade had captured and silenced the Egyptian guns. The blockade was over.

Immediately after Mrs. Meir's speech, the United Nations Emergency Force entered Sinai and Gaza, and then went on to Sharm el Sheikh in the Straits of Tiran, filling in the vacuum created by the retreating Israel army.

The retreat sent Israel's political stock soaring. At the United Nations, her statesmanlike withdrawal had a remarkable effect on American and world public opinion. It was now transparently clear that Israel had not gone into Sinai for any expansion of territory. She had gone in to destroy the Fedayeen nests, end the blockade of Elath, break the Egypt-Syrian-Jordan alliance, and maim the enemy before he could carry through his threat of destroying her.

The world now realized that Egypt's plan for war against Israel was not a war for victory but a war for total annihilation, and suddenly nations of Asia and Africa, small powers without armies and arms, felt a warm surge of friendship and sympathy toward Israel.

But for Israel itself, the retreat was a bitter chapter in the life of the state. For the army and the youngsters in the frontier settlements, it was a hard and hardening lesson.

It is one thing for an army to advance and capture and be victorious. It is quite another to be victorious and retreat. The army retreated in an orderly fashion, but with heavy hearts. The exultation at knocking out Nasser's Sinai army was dissipated by the sober realization that the Russians would rearm him swiftly.

Moshe Dayan, then chief of staff, who participated in a number of the major battles of the campaign, took part in every major phase of the retreat. Reporters in El Arish asked him why he came to each ceremonial lowering of the Israel flag. "The High Command," he replied, "must swallow the bitter part of the campaign along with its victories."

The Egyptians, of course, were ecstatic over their political victory; and Nasser carefully neglected to tell them of their military defeat. But there were a few Egyptians who regretted the retreat. While Israel was in Sinai and Gaza, she had tried to bring new standards of living, of health and education to the villages. Uri, a young Israeli lieutenant, was military governor of the village of E-Tor on the eastern coast of the Sinai Peninsula and south of the Suez Canal. Uri knew Arabic and had a real feeling for the villagers and for the Bedouins who roamed in the area. He reopened the schoolhouse and turned it into a modern school. He gave the people food. He brought in a doctor and a nurse from Israel. The people were astonished. The government was coming to them, taking care of them, instead of taking from them.

When the Israel army retreated, many of the people of E-Tor wept at Uri's leaving them.

The retreat was hardest on the settlers on the borders. During the months that Israel was in the Gaza Strip, life in Nahal Oz and the other border settlements had been almost without tension. Egyptian guns did not look piercingly into the settlements by day and by night. The barbed wire was down. The watchtowers were empty. The children had been able to play freely. The sirens that had been used to send the people rushing their children into the bombshelters to spend a fitful night were now used only to call people to lunch. Life on the border was as free as life in Tel Aviv.

After the retreat, the settlements returned to the old tensions. The barbed wire went up. The watchtowers were manned every night. Huge searchlights played on the fields, fingers of light searching for Fedayeen. The children went back to sleeping in the bombshelters. All was normal again. Everyone lived within five minutes of potential danger.

Perhaps the most telling lesson of Sinai was Israel's treatment of her fifty-five hundred Egyptian prisoners. Israel knew what Cairo propaganda had been telling the Egyptians of life in Israel—that it was a country of armed beggars, tottering on the brink of economic and physical collapse because of the "successful" Arab boycott and blockade.

The propaganda was not only on the radio. It was printed. The army was indoctrinated with a sense of superiority and hatred toward Israel. In Sinai, the Israelis captured numerous copies of *Mein Kampf* in Arabic.

Top-secret military documents were found on the Egyptian prisoners. One was addressed "to Commander of the Egyptian zone in Palestine":

Par. 3. Every commander should be prepared and prepare his troops for the unavoidable war with Israel, in order to achieve our supreme objective, namely annihilation of Israel and its complete destruction in as little time as possible, by fighting against her as brutally and cruelly as possible.

Par. 5. Our objective always is the annihilation of Israel. Remember that, and act for its fulfillment.

Certificates of merit were found honoring soldiers who had "fulfilled their holy mission" of killing Jews. One, bearing the picture of an Egyptian soldier, was marked boldly:

CERTIFICATE OF MERIT

RANK: A volunteer sergeant

NAME: Al Sayed Hasan Dahasmah

I, Captain Tala'at Souleiman Ghalabei, Commander of the Aretz position, hereby declare that the above mentioned has fulfilled his holy mission in the land of Palestine on May 28, 1956, in a perfect way. He acted on Israeli soil with exemplary courage, valor and bravery, and maintained excellent discipline, the highest morale, and a noble behavior. He is a man who understands and appreciates discipline and reveres it.

SIGNED: Captain Tala'at Souleiman

Because of this hate-Israel propaganda in Egypt, the Israel army decided to try a new prisoner technique. They could, of course, have tried brainwashing the prisoners as the Red Chinese did with Americans, hammering them with radio programs in their barracks and lengthy conversations at headquarters, forcing them to read propaganda books, holding out preferential treatment for quislings. Or they could have tried, as most armies do, to extract as much military information from the prisoners as possible by any method, however brutal.

They decided instead to embark on a highly unmilitary program. It was a long-range program of enlightenment. They wanted to get the message of Israel across to the leaders of the Egyptian military machine.

There were of course officers who said that the only way to handle the Egyptian prisoners was by force. They argued that the only language the Arabs understood was the language of guns. "If we try anything else," they said, "the Egyptians will say we're weak."

Ben-Gurion, as prime minister and minister of defense, agreed that the army should try the unique program of enlightenment. It became official government policy. The Egyptians were to see that Israel was not a country of warmongers on the one hand or starving beggars on the other. They were to see that Israel was a young, dynamic, fertile land, whose economy was being strengthened from day to day. They were to see that Israel was not an armed camp, that its strength lay in the spirit of its people. The Egyptians were to see that the Arab boycott, though it was annoying, was actually an incentive for Israel to raise its standards of production to compete in world markets.

The objective was not to boast of prowess to the Egyptians, but to give them a sense of reality, to end the ludicrous caricatures of Arab propaganda, to show that Israel wanted to live at peace with its neighbors.

Egyptian officers and soldiers were allowed to go out with unarmed escorts. Tours were arranged in cars and buses for some thirteen hundred of the prisoners. No one was forced to go. At first the Egyptians were reluctant to go. But after the brave ones began, the others followed. In the beginning the Egyptians wore their own khaki uniforms, and the people of Israel knew these were prisoners. When the Egyptians pointed out that they were uncomfortable, the Israelis gave them civilian clothes, so that they would not be conspicuous. They were taken to factories, farms, cities, kibbutzim, and were even invited to people's homes for dinner.

The wife of one of Israel's staff officers told me she nearly fainted one night when her bell rang and an Egyptian colonel in full uniform stood at the door. Her husband, in the time-honored tradition of husbands, had forgotten to tell her he was bringing guests to dinner.

It was a remarkable dinner party. The guests included the Egyptian colonel, who had been chief operations officer at Khan Yunis in the Gaza Strip, three Israeli officers, and the American military expert, Brigadier General S. L. A. Marshall.

The conversation was general and polite. The Israelis were determined not to embarrass the Egyptian colonel in any way. He was their guest. After dinner they played a kind of chess game, reconstructing the battles that the Egyptian had commanded at Khan Yunis. They asked each other questions concerning motives, tactics, strategy. They evaluated each other's moves—which were good, which were bad.

General Marshall, knowing that Nasser was telling his people they had won the war, asked the Egyptian prisoner: "Do you believe that the Egyptian army was not beaten in Sinai?"

The Egyptian colonel, who had seen his own troops take flight and who knew there were over five thousand prisoners in Israel, said, "I do not know if we were beaten. How can I be sure?"

Toward the end of the evening, the host asked the Egyptian colonel, "Would you be willing to tell me your opinion of us? You have been told that we are a barbaric people. And you tell that to your troops. Do you still believe it?"

The Egyptian answered, "I have been treated well here. And so have the prisoners in the other camps. But that still does not prove that what we are told and what we tell our troops is not true."

The Israelis knew that they could not undo years of Arab

propaganda overnight. They were willing to settle for raising a few
doubts in the minds of the Egyptians.

One of the captured officers, part of the military clique that had
brought Nasser into power, was taken on a tour of the kibbutzim
around Haifa. He was driven in a car by an Israeli officer of equal
rank. At Mishmar Ha-Emek, a kibbutz in the north that is a garden
spot, the Israeli officer told the Egyptian that he was free to go
wherever he pleased, and talk freely to anyone. The Egyptian spoke
fluent English.

He stopped a farmer in front of one of the pretty white stucco
houses. "Pardon me, I am an Egyptian."

"Yes," the farmer said simply.

"Are you willing to talk to me?"

"Why not?"

"I want to know how you feel toward us."

"You're people, aren't you? You don't have horns. How should I
feel?"

"You mean to say you don't hate the Arabs?"

"We've got two hundred thousand Arabs living with us. They're
our neighbors. Good farmers too, the ones up north here, and good
neighbors."

"But you must hate the Egyptians. We just had a war."

"Why should I hate you? I don't like Nasser. He's a dictator.
But maybe some day you'll throw him out and get a decent democratic government. Then maybe our two governments can sit down
together and talk peace, and we'll be able to live together. Who
needs war and hate? There are too many things to do around here."

The Egyptian walked back to the Israeli officer. "You've laid him
on. He's talking straight propaganda. He doesn't believe a thing he
told me."

The Israeli officer shrugged his shoulders and said nothing. They
drove to Haifa, enjoying the magnificent view along Panorama
Road as their car climbed to the top of Mount Carmel. The Egyptian pointed to a café on the mountain and asked if they could
stop for some coffee.

They entered, and once again the Egyptian was given his freedom to visit. He chose a group of attractive young women sitting at a table.

"Pardon me. I am an Egyptian officer. May I talk to you?" He addressed the prettiest young woman at the table.

"Of course," she said.

"I would like to know if you hate the Egyptians."

"The Egyptians? They're people. Why should we hate them?"

"Would you like your children to go to school with Egyptian children?"

She laughed. "Why not?"

Once again the answers were so free of anti-Arab venom that he returned to the Israeli officer. "You've planted them all."

The Israeli officer said quietly, "This is a free café. You chose it. Stop anyone who comes in."

They sat for a while. Then a young man entered with a heavy growth of beard and a sailor's pack. He looked as if he had just come off a ship.

The Egyptian walked over to him. "Pardon me. Do you mind if I talk to you? I am an Egyptian officer."

The sailor said, "Buy me a drink first."

The Egyptian who, in accordance with the Geneva convention, had been given some pocket money, said, "*Tfadel*" (Be my guest). Then he began the same questioning. "Do you hate me?"

The sailor finished his brandy. "No. I don't hate you. Even in spite of what your government did to me. I was on the *Bat Galim* and was taken by force in the Suez Canal long before the Sinai campaign. Sure, I'd like to get my hands around the necks of the guys who beat me up. But you can't blame all the Egyptians for some S.O.B.'s."

The Egyptian officer returned to his Israeli guide and for the rest of the trip said nothing at all.

The policy of enlightenment did bear some fruit. When the fifty-five hundred Egyptians were exchanged for four Israelis, three of whom had been taken prisoner before Sinai, there was complete silence in Egypt. Prisoners of war, on their return home, usually denounce their captors. But of all the fifty-five hundred prisoners, only one, Major General Digwi, who had been governor general of Gaza, complained that he had not been treated well. He had had his hemorrhoids removed.

But Nasser succeeded in turning the military disaster of Sinai into a political victory. In 1958, two years after his army was defeated, he created the United Arab Republic in a loose federation with Syria and Yemen. In 1961 the federation became a shambles with a Syrian anti-Nasser coup. Nasser, realizing he would be thoroughly trounced if he marched into Syria, quickly withdrew.

He spent the next years reforming an Arab federation, working always toward two objectives—control of the Arab world from Casablanca to the Persian Gulf, and the destruction of Israel. He equipped himself well, determined not to have another military disaster. He built a standing army estimated at 100,000 men with a potential of 160,000. From the Soviet Union he received Mig-17 and Mig-19 jets, submarines, destroyers, motor torpedo boats, and guided missiles. From Germany, he imported scientists, some of whom had worked with Hitler and were perhaps happy to have another crack at the enemy Hitler had not quite vanquished. The Germans built him ground-to-ground offensive missiles that could wipe out whole sections of Israel. The United States continued its aid program, with millions of dollars in surplus foods.

To keep the delicate balance of arms in the Middle East, the United States permitted Israel to buy Hawk missiles, defensive antiaircraft missiles which are ground-to-air, not ground-to-ground. The French allowed Israel to buy jet planes. Their cost was astronomical. "And when I think," Ben-Gurion told me one day, "that every plane we have will be obsolete in two years, I cannot sleep at night."

Preparing for defense, Israel still went about the business of building a nation. She sought to remain an island of stability in a sea of dictatorships, assassinations, and political chaos. An island of sanity in a nightmare world.

20: The Dead Sea Scrolls

FEW DISCOVERIES in our time have excited scholars and laymen as much as the discovery of the Dead Sea Scrolls. The words themselves are magic. The earliest known writings of the Bible, the source of man's faith, man's hope, were suddenly available to be looked at, to be touched. Scrolls on which holy men had written the holy words some two thousand years before in the Holy Land, had suddenly come home.

The drama of Israel's own birth had its counterpart in the drama of the discovery of the scrolls. It seemed almost an act of destiny that both occurred on the same day.

In New York, on Saturday, the twenty-ninth of November, 1947, the United Nations was calling the roll. The nations of the world were voting to partition Palestine and create a Jewish state.

In Jerusalem, Dr. Elazar Sukenik, Professor of Archaeology at Hebrew University, was hurrying home from Bethlehem with the sacred scrolls wrapped in paper under his arm. He opened them in his study, and began excitedly reading the writing on the ancient leather.

There are few dramas as breath-taking as the story of their discovery. In 1947, a group of Bedouin Arabs had been wandering with their goats in the desert near Qumran, along the northwestern shore of the Dead Sea. A goat strayed into a cavern. One of the Bedouin boys threw a stone into the cave. The boys were surprised to hear the sound of something breaking. Pottery, perhaps. The next day they returned to the cave and crawled in. They found a group of earthenware jars in which there were bundles of parchment, some of them wrapped in linen. They wandered around for weeks, showing the bundles to other Bedouins. Then they took them to Bethlehem to see if they could get any money for these strange leather things.

A Christian merchant thought the writing might be ancient Syriac and took the bundles to the head of the Syrian church in Jerusalem, Metropolitan Mar Athanasius Yeshue Samuel. (Metropolitan, the term for the regional head of the Greek Orthodox Church, is the equivalent of a Western archbishop.) Trying to obtain expert opinion, Metropolitan Samuel found everyone skeptical. Two scholars, authorities in ancient writings, said the scrolls looked as if they had been written at the time of the second Temple and of Jesus Christ, which was obviously incredible. Therefore what they had seen could not be true.

Meanwhile, Dr. Sukenik, who had been in the United States on sabbatical leave from the Hebrew University, returned home. On November 23, an Armenian dealer in antiquities sent a message to the University asking Dr. Sukenik to call him immediately, even though it was Sunday. These were the last days of the British in Palestine. Everyone knew that the phones were being tapped. The Armenian dealer could tell Sukenik only that he had something urgent to show him. They arranged to meet the next morning at the gateway to Military Zone B.

Jerusalem had been split by the British into military zones. Barbed wire and "dragon's teeth" divided the city; armed sentries guarded the zones. We jested in those days that Jerusalem was the only place in the British Empire where the British barricaded themselves behind barbed wire. Most of Jerusalem was out of bounds to the soldiers. And everyone now needed an official pass to go from one zone to the other.

Dr. Sukenik met his friend at the barrier, and they talked across the rolls of the barbed wire. Through the wire, the Armenian dealer held up a piece of parchment with Hebrew script, and told Sukenik the story of the discovery. Sukenik listened with mounting excitement. His friend said the scrolls were now in the hands of an Arab antiquities dealer in Bethlehem. Were the scrolls genuine, he asked Sukenik, and would he buy them for the Museum of Jewish Antiquities of the Hebrew University?

Dr. Sukenik peered at the parchment. He forgot the barbed wire. As he gazed, the letters began to take shape. They looked like the letters he had seen on coffins and ancient tombs that went back to the period before the Romans destroyed Jerusalem in 70 A.D. He became convinced that these were probably the oldest Hebrew documents in the world. He decided to buy the scrolls for the University, and asked his friend to bring more samples from Bethlehem.

They met again and decided to go to Bethlehem together to buy the scrolls. It was now the twenty-eighth of November. Mrs. Sukenik was frantic at the thought of her husband making the dangerous trip to Bethlehem.

That afternoon, Dr. Sukenik's oldest son, Yigael, dropped in. Yigael, who had taken the Hebrew surname of Yadin ("He shall judge"), was chief of operations of Haganah, the Jewish self-defense movement. Yadin had gone to Jerusalem to see how the city was prepared to defend itself against possible Arab riots, if the U.N., then in session, voted to create a Jewish state.

Yigael was not only a soldier. He was an archaeologist who had interrupted his studies to lead the Haganah. After visiting Haganah headquarters, he went to see his parents. His father excitedly told him the story of the scrolls. "What shall I do, Yigael? Shall I go to Bethlehem in the morning?"

Yadin was torn. As head of Haganah, he could not permit anyone, let alone his father, to make the dangerous journey through all-Arab territory on this of all days. As archaeologist, he yearned to go on the journey with his father, to feel the parchment, to look at the writing, to know the ecstasy of discovery. The soldier-son told the archaeologist-father that he must not go. Fortunately, the father disregarded the son's advice, and on the fateful morning of November 29, without telling anyone, he entered Zone B, met his Armenian friend, and together they took an all-Arab bus to Bethlehem.

They went directly to the attic of the Arab dealer, Feidi Salahi. After the usual Arab amenities of drinking coffee and talking of their families and the weather, they finally came to the business at hand. Salahi showed Sukenik two jars and the leather scrolls. The archaeologist was so excited he could hardly read the magnificent Biblical Hebrew.

He told Salahi he would probably want to buy them, but he needed to study them further at home. Salahi wrapped the two scrolls in paper, and Dr. Sukenik and his friend took the tense Jerusalem bus back to the Jaffa Gate.

While he was examining the scrolls in his study, his youngest son, Mati, who later became a pilot and was killed during the war of independence, kept tuning the short-wave radio to Lake Success in New York. After midnight, Mati rushed in to tell his father that the world had voted to give the Jews a home of their own. The Jewish state was about to be born.

Dr. Sukenik bought three scrolls for about a hundred dollars. His diary records his growing conviction that the scrolls were one of the greatest finds in the Holy Land. On December 1, 1947, he wrote:

I read a little more in the "parchments." I'm afraid of going too far in thinking about them. It may be that this is one of the greatest finds ever made in Palestine, a find we never so much as hoped for.

December 5: More killings. The [Arab] strike was over today, but not the violence. The find leaves me no peace. I'm bursting to know what will come of it all. It might turn out that the neighborhood has many things of this sort. Who knows what surprises still await us?

December 6: Night. I sit and think and think about the scrolls. When will I see more of them? Patience, patience.

December 21: Days of awe. I contacted X. We're to meet tomorrow at noon near the gate [to the Security Zone].

I came. I bought another scroll in very bad condition.

January 13, 1948: I went to the main post office [near the border]. X came. He promised to get in touch with Bethlehem. I said the Hagomel blessing as I left [a blessing said upon being saved from mortal danger].

The Bedouins now realized there was a good commodity in the caves. They became amateur archaeologists. More scrolls began to turn up. But relations between the Arabs and Jews deteriorated. Travel between Jewish Jerusalem and Arab Bethlehem became impossible. A Syrian friend, Anton Kiraz, wrote Dr. Sukenik from a short distance away in the Arab quarter of Jerusalem that he had some additional scrolls. They decided to meet at the Y.M.C.A. building in Zone B.

The Arabs sitting on the wide stone verandah of the Y., which was used almost entirely by Arabs, must have been astounded in those tense days, to see a Jew enter. Sukenik had put some books under his arms as a pretext that he was planning to use the library. Kiraz showed him several new scrolls from the same cave in Qumran. Once again he trembled with excitement. One of the scrolls looked like the whole book of Isaiah.

Dr. Sukenik took the scrolls home to show them to the University and to raise the money for their purchase. He promised Kiraz to return them within a few days if he could not get the money. By this time the Jewish Agency, the shadow government of the Jewish people under the British Mandate, had moved to safer ground in Tel Aviv. Travel between Tel Aviv and Jerusalem was almost at a standstill. Only convoys climbed the Hills of Judea to Jerusalem. The Arabs, sitting in the hills, blasted away at the cars and trucks that dared bring food and men to the holy city. Dr. Sukenik was unable to reach the leaders in Tel Aviv, to raise the money he needed.

The dark day came when he had promised to return the second batch of scrolls. On Friday, February 6, 1948, he went to the Y.M.C.A. in Zone B, carrying the scrolls back to the Syrian. When he returned home, he found an executive of the Jewish Agency waiting for him. The following Sunday word was brought to Ben-Gurion in Tel Aviv and in about two weeks Dr. Sukenik was told to buy the scrolls immediately. He could have any amount of money he needed. Sukenik wrote a letter to Anton Kiraz. But by this time, the Syrian Metropolitan had decided to shop around to get a better price. Sukenik was heartsick. "Thus," he wrote in his diary, "the Jewish people have lost a precious heritage."

There were four remaining scrolls. The Metropolitan showed them to scholars in the American School of Oriental Research in Jerusalem, whose headquarters was in the Arab sector of the New City of Jerusalem, near the Damascus Gate and the Rockefeller Museum. The director of the School then, Professor Millar Bur-

rows of Yale, was in Iraq, but his assistants, Dr. John C. Trevor
and Dr. William H. Brownlee, realized the importance of the
scrolls. Trevor made his way with difficulty to the Old City of
Jerusalem to see the Metropolitan. He persuaded the Metropolitan
to let him photograph the scrolls. Scholars, he explained, would
then learn of them and their price would skyrocket. (The price
Metropolitan Samuel paid for the scrolls has never been revealed,
but it is generally believed to have been about two hundred dollars.)

The American School kept the scrolls for weeks, made hundreds of photographs, and later published a number of texts. The
Metropolitan now decided to take his scrolls out of Jordan. The
Jordanians said he "smuggled" them out but actually there was no
safe place to keep them in war-torn Jerusalem. He went to America
to sell them to the highest bidder.

The scrolls were a secret no longer. In the spring and summer of
1948, Dr. Sukenik talked of the great discovery to some of the foreign correspondents who were covering Israel's war. I was fortunate
to be one of them. Those were hard days to think of archaeology.
Israel had been invaded by the Arabs. She was sealing her independence with blood. Front-page stories were being made in the
battles of Negba, Lydda, Ramle, not in archaeological finds.

I was living a few houses away from Dr. Sukenik in the Rehavia
suburb of Jerusalem, the guest of Hannah Ruppin, Yadin's
mother-in-law. The Haganah had now become the Army of Israel,
and General Yadin, thirty-three years old, was Chief of Operations
under General Yaakov Dori. He was later to become Chief of Staff.
We saw Yadin whenever he had a moment to say hello to his parents and to his wife's mother. We talked of the scrolls, but we
talked far more of the victories against the invading Arab states.

Elazar Sukenik was to continue working on the scrolls for five
years until his death in 1953. But the drama of discovery was not
yet over.

In 1954, Yadin and his wife Carmella came to the United States
on a lecture tour. One morning the telephone rang in their New
York hotel. Monty Jacobs, a former Jerusalem correspondent, who

was in the United States working for an Israel newspaper, asked
Yadin if he had seen the *Wall Street Journal.*

Yadin, with no interest in stocks, was amazed. Why should he
be looking at the *Wall Street Journal?*

Monty explained that there was a small advertisement about the
Dead Sea Scrolls. Metropolitan Samuel had obviously not yet
found the price he wanted. He was now offering his four Dead Sea
Scrolls in a most unlikely place for scholars, but a good place for
financiers.

Yadin was now to know the ecstasy of discovery in New York
that had been denied him in Bethlehem. Through intermediaries
and in utmost secrecy, to prevent the Arab League from blocking
the sale, he raised the money with private and government funds.
He was greatly helped by the America-Israel Cultural Foundation,
and particularly by its president, Sam Rubin. An American philan-
thropist, the late D. Samuel Gottesman, arranged to meet the
Metropolitan's price of two hundred and fifty thousand dollars. He
jestingly told me at dinner one night that he now called himself
Dead Sea Scrolls Gottesman.

The four scrolls were sent carefully to Israel. On February 13,
1955, Yadin, then in London, received a cable from Teddy Kollek,
director general of the prime minister's office in Israel: "At this
memorable moment the Prime Minister [Moshe Sharett] is telling
the country and the world about the homecoming of the scrolls.
Excitement and joy are great."

The excitement and joy spread from Israel around the western
world. As the scrolls were translated and published, laymen were
drawn into speculation about them. At first, there were extremists
who said that the scrolls might shake the foundations of Christianity. That fear has now been thoroughly scotched. Archaeological
finds cannot change the foundations of Christianity, which are
based on faith.

People began to ask why the scrolls were so long in being discovered. The reason lay in the inaccessibility of the caves. They
were a perfect hiding place for buried treasure. For twenty cen-

turies, until the famous goat was lost, no one dreamed that the limestone cliffs contained penetrable caverns.

The scrolls' preservation was as miraculous as their discovery. We have ample proof that scribes were busy writing scrolls for centuries. But the climate of Palestine was not dry enough to preserve them. The only completely dry area was the desert and narrow shoreline around the Dead Sea.

Preserving scrolls in jars was common practice in Biblical days. "Take these evidences [lit. these books]" Jeremiah says, in chapter 32, verse 14, "and put them in an earthen vessel, that they may continue many days."

The cloth wrapped around the scrolls was examined by the new carbon-dating test that determines the age of objects made of vegetable matter. The test definitely placed the cloth's origin in the period between 100 B.C. and 100 A.D. This was further evidence that the scrolls were authentic.

But the final proof came when an archaeological expedition under Père de Vaux of France and Gerald Lankester Harding, Curator of Antiquities for Jordan, unearthed the ruins around the Qumran caves and discovered the buildings in which the sect of the Dead Sea Scrolls had lived.

They found the scriptorium, the writing room in which the scrolls were written. They found three inkwells, one of bronze and two of pottery, and in them the remains of ink. The scientists were able to compare this ink with the ink used on the scrolls. They uncovered the assembly hall in which the sect lived its ascetic communal life. They even found the pottery shop where the potters made the clay jars in which the scrolls were placed for safe-keeping.

Now there could be no question that the scrolls were authentic. Elazar Sukenik's hunch that November day, when he first peered at the writing through the barbed-wire fence, was completely vindicated.

It is now almost universally accepted that the people of the Dead Sea Scrolls were the Essenes. There is almost incontrovertible similarity between the description of the Essenes by the early historians Josephus and Philo, and the lives of the people described in the scroll called "The Manual of Discipline." The archeological findings, too, point to the Essenes—the assembly hall, the scriptorium, especially the cisterns that were used for purification rites in some form of immersion or baptism. But perhaps the best proof comes from the Roman historian and geographer Pliny the Younger, who wrote that the Essenes lived above Engeddi. "Above" means to the north, and the Qumran caves and their community building on the shore of the Dead Sea are about ten miles north of Engeddi.

The scrolls and fragments of scrolls have yielded the whole book of Isaiah; a fascinating Commentary on the Biblical book of Habakkuk; Commentaries on the Psalms, on the prophet Nahum, and other minor prophets; the "Thanksgiving Scroll," a collection of hymns in the style of the Psalms; and the "War Scroll," which tells the story of the war between the Sons of Light and the Sons of Darkness. The scroll that is perhaps of most interest to laymen is "The Manual of Discipline," which describes the self-imposed laws by which the Essenes lived. For sheer poetic beauty, there is the "Scroll of the Apocryphal Genesis," written, not as most of the others were, in Hebrew, but in Aramaic, with new stories and a new description of Abraham and Sara. The scroll has been superbly translated by General Yigael Yadin and N. Avigad of the Hebrew University.

In this scroll, based on Genesis, Abraham himself tells the story of how he went into Egypt with his wife Sara. She was so beautiful that the princes of Egypt brought her to the palace where Pharaoh, captivated by her beauty, took her as his wife. Through a dream, God told Abraham to hide Sara's identity so that Sara could save him from death at the hands of Pharaoh:*

'How . . . and (how) beautiful the look of her face . . . and how . . . fine is the hair of her head, how fair indeed are her eyes and

* Translation from *The Message of the Scrolls*, by Yigael Yadin. Copyright © 1957 by Yigael Yadin. Reprinted by permission of Simon and Schuster, Inc.

how pleasing her nose and all the radiance of her face . . . how beautiful her breast and how lovely all her whiteness. Her arms goodly to look upon, and her hands how perfect . . . all the appearance of her hands. How fair her palms and how long and fine all the fingers of her hands. Her legs how beautiful and how without blemish her thighs. And all maidens and all brides that go beneath the wedding canopy are not more fair than she. And above all women is she lovely and higher is her beauty than that of them all, and with all her beauty there is much wisdom in her. And the tip of her hands is comely.'

And when the King heard the words of Horkanosh and the words of his two companions, for all three spoke as one man, he desired her exceedingly and he sent at once to bring her to him and he looked upon her and marvelled at all her loveliness and took her to him to wife and sought to slay me. And Sarai spoke to the King, saying, 'He is my brother, that it might be well with me (that I might profit thereby). And I, Abram, was saved because of her and was not slain. And I wept, I, Abram, with grievous weeping, I and with me, Lot, my brother's son, wept that night when Sarai was taken from me by force.

That night I prayed and entreated and begged and said in sorrow, as my tears fell, 'Blessed art Thou, Most High God, Lord of all worlds, because Thou art Lord and Master of all and ruler of all the kings of earth, all of whom Thou judgest. Behold now I cry before Thee, my Lord, against Pharaoh-Zoan, King of Egypt, because my wife has been taken from me by force. Do Thou judge him for me and let me behold Thy mighty hand descend upon him and all his household and may he not this night defile my wife. And men shall know, my Lord, that Thou art the Lord of all the kings of earth.' And I wept and grieved.

That night the Most High God sent a pestilential wind to afflict him and all his household, a wind that was evil. And it smote him and all his house and he could not come near her nor did he know her and he was with her two years. And at the end of two years the plagues and the afflictions became grievous and strong in him and in all his house. And he sent and called for all the wise men of Egypt and all the wizards and all the physicians of Egypt, if perchance they might heal him from that pestilence, him and his house. And all the physicians and wizards and wise men could not rise up to heal him, for the wind smote them all and they fled.

Then came to me Horkanosh and besought me to come and to pray for the King and to lay my hands upon him that he might live, for in the dream . . . And Lot said unto him, 'Abram, my uncle, cannot pray for the King while Sarai, his wife, is with him. Go now, and tell the King to send away his wife to her husband and he will pray for him and he will live.'

And when Horkanosh heard these words of Lot he went and said to the King, 'All these plagues and afflictions with which my Lord, the King, is plagued and afflicted are for the sake of Sarai, the wife of Abram. Restore her, Sarai, to Abram, her husband, and the plague will depart from thee and the evil will pass away.'

And he called me to him and said to me, 'What hast thou done unto me for the sake of (Sara)i, that thou hast told me "She is my sister," and she is indeed thy wife, and I took her to me to wife. Behold thy wife who is with me, go thy way and depart from all the land of Egypt. And now pray for me and all my house that this evil wind may depart from us.'

And I prayed for . . . this swiftly (?) and I laid my hand upon his head and the plague departed from him and the evil (wind) was gone and he lived. And the King rose and said unto me . . . and the King swore to me with an oath that cannot (be changed . . .) . . . And the King gave him a large . . . and much clothing of fine linen and purple . . . before her, and also Hagar . . . and appointed men for me who would take me out. . . .

And I, Abram went forth, exceedingly rich in cattle and also in silver and in gold, and I went up out (of Egypt and Lot), the son of my brother, with me. And Lot also had great possessions and took unto himself a wife from . . .

It is "The Manual of Discipline," one of the non-Biblical scrolls found in the first of the Qumran caves, that gives us a new insight into the life and thinking of the sect who wrote the scrolls and who lived in the period between 100 B.C. and 100 A.D. Certainly the people of the sect influenced the religious thinking of their time. The Manual throws new light upon the Talmudic period of Jewish life and the atmosphere in which Christianity was born. In minute detail the scroll describes the initiation rites into the sect, the rules of daily behavior, the punishments for infringement of the rules, and under what conditions a man could be excluded from the sect. The Manual is exciting to us today because this sect lived just before or during the lifetime of Jesus.

All those who became members of the sect were called "Sons of Light." Their enemies were called "Sons of Darkness." In their initiation, they pledged "to love all Sons of Light, each according to his lot in the Council of God, and to hate all Sons of Darkness, each according to his guilt in the vengeance of God."

All members were required to rid themselves of all their worldly goods and to contribute—note the order—"all their knowledge and strength and wealth into the Yahad [community] of God."

Their life was strictly disciplined. Punishments were harsh for any infractions of ethics or the law:

If there is found among them a man who lies about his wealth intentionally they shall exclude him from the midst of the purified of the superiors for one year and he shall be deprived of a fourth of his food . . . And he who answers his fellow in stubbornness, or speaks with a quick temper . . . he shall be punished for one year . . . and if he has spoken in anger against one of the priests registered in the book . . . he shall be punished for one year and set apart for himself. . . . But if he spoke unintentionally, he shall be punished six months. . . . And if he shows himself negligent so as to cause damage to the property of the Yahad, he shall repay it in full; but if he is not able to pay it he shall be punished sixty days. . . . One who bears a grudge against his fellow without justification, shall be punished six months . . . And he who shall utter an obscene word shall be punished three months. And for him who breaks into the words of his fellow—ten days . . . and he who shall lie down and sleep in the public session —thirty days. . . . And he who shall walk naked before his fellow without being gravely ill shall be punished six months; a man who will spit in the middle of the public session will be punished thirty days. . . . And he who shall laugh foolishly and loudly shall be punished thirty days. . . .†

The scrolls have proved that the Jews did not stop their creative writing after the Bible was finished. "The Scroll of the War of the Sons of Light Against the Sons of Darkness," written in a

†*Ibid.*

beautiful hand, is a unique book in both Jewish and Christian writing. It contains a prophetic vision of a war between the forces of good and evil, represented by Israel and its enemies. In the end good triumphed. The war itself is described in minute details of men, arms, and strategy. Since the dream of this prophetic war was based on the kind of arms and armies known to the author or authors of the scroll, we now have an excellent description of the army organization and the methods of warfare that existed two thousand years ago. It is the "modern" concept of the war that is so startling, for today's wars are still fought between the forces of good and evil, and God is always on the side of the righteous. The scroll is written with much the same realistic, almost eyewitness approach that we find in many of the books of the Bible.

Of special interest to treasure hunters are the Copper Scrolls, which were found in another Qumran cave in 1952. For some years, no one could unroll these two metal scrolls, for they had become fragile with age. Finally, they were carefully sawn into sections. Upon being read, these were found to constitute one scroll, which must have been cut into two parts and rolled when the Essenes apparently fled in haste from persecution.

The Copper Scroll tells of fabulous treasures of gold and silver and incense. The places where the treasures are buried are named and even the depths at which they are buried is given. The scroll has not yet been published in full, but the excitement about the treasures keeps mounting. Some scholars believe that this may have been a record of the treasures of the Essenes, a list embossed on copper and hidden before they fled. Others argue that it is inconceivable that the Essenes, who gave up all their wealth when they were initiated and then lived in poverty, would have had such treasures. They think it likely that the scroll describes some Solomonic treasure that belonged to the Temple. Further study of the scroll, it is hoped, will settle these questions.

The Bedouins continue to search along the Dead Sea for other caves that may have eluded detection. Cave 12 was discovered in 1956, and archaeologists continue to turn up new and valuable treasures.

In 1960, Dr. Yohanan Aharoni of the Hebrew University began to dig in some caves near En Geddi. He found parchment sections of tiny scrolls, coins, a woman's comb, pieces of clothes, and human bones. He had unearthed fragments of one of the great periods of Jewish resistance fighters, the revolt of Shimon Bar Kochba and Rabbi Akiba, who led some half million Jews against the Roman Emperor Hadrian in 132 A.D.

Bar Kochba was at first spectacularly successful. With guerilla tactics and men ready to die for their homeland, he captured fifty towns from the Romans. But the Emperor sent strong legion re-enforcements under the well-known General Severus. After two years of resistance and bloodshed, the Romans drove Bar Kochba and his men to the caves of the Dead Sea, where they bottled up the warriors until they starved to death.

Bar Kochba's story, known in history, had never been substanti-ated. Ben-Gurion decided this was the moment to substantiate history. He turned the task over to Yigael Yadin and the army. They planned a search of the caves with the thoroughness of an army of invasion. They used helicopters, mine detectors, jeeps, and walkie-talkies; soldiers, mountain climbers, volunteers, kibbutzniks, and skilled archaeologists. After hair-raising experiences and narrow escapes, they found baskets with human bones—the remains of Bar Kochba's fighters. Then they began to find their treasures—utensils, beads, raw wool, and at last, a small package of papyri. The papyri, slowly unwound and unraveled, were Bar Kochba's letters, fifteen in all, in Hebrew, Aramaic, and Greek. In one, Bar Kochba scolded two of his regional commanders for "sitting, eating, and drinking the property of the House of Israel," unconcerned for their comrades in arms. In others, he ordered his commanders to help the people get food, repair their houses, and celebrate the festival of Succot.

Now at last Israel had proof that one of her great heroes of re-sistance had really lived. The remains of the courageous fighters were buried on Mount Herzl in Jerusalem. Like the Dead Sea Scrolls, Bar Kochba's men had come home.

21: Saddle the Sun, Sweeten the Sea

WHAT IS Israel's place among the nations of men? How does she see herself? What lies ahead in her relationship with the Western nations and with Russia, with the Arabs and the Asian-African world? What is her meaning for Jews outside of Israel, and for people of all faiths?

For thousands of years, people have sought to destroy the Jews and each time have failed. The Egyptians failed under the Pharaohs. The Romans failed under Titus. The Spaniards failed in the Inquisition. Hitler failed in World War II. The Arabs failed in 1948.

All over the world, when Israel was reborn, Jews felt a new dignity and a new pride. They could walk two inches taller down the streets of their own beloved cities. Anti-Semitism, which feeds on weakness, was given a body blow. Jews had shown that they could fight. They did not start the war, nor did they want it. But when the Arabs invaded, they fought back and they fought brilliantly. No longer would people say, "Jews have no guts. We have to pull their chestnuts out of the fire." The Jews fought and won.

They continued to live by the ethics of the Fathers. "If I forget thee, O Jerusalem," the Jews sang in exile in Babylonia, "may my right hand forget its cunning." They never forgot, and now, from seventy countries, they have come home. In ten history-laden, time-squeezing years, Israel has become a refuge for the homeless, while she built a democratic state.

Among the nations of men, Israel now plays a strategic role in the battle of the East-West giants, a far greater one than any other nation of her size. The United Nations has a favorite phrase for problems with which it is occupied: it is "seized of them." The world has been "seized of Israel" for a decade. The Western giant, the United States, has been a friend of Israel and of the Arabs throughout these years. The Eastern giant, the Soviet Union, has switched from being a friend of Israel to an outspoken foe.

Broadly stated, Russia sided with Israel against the Arabs in 1948 because she wanted to get the British out of the Middle East. She is openly siding with the Arabs against Israel to get the United States out of the Middle East. It is not that she loves the Arabs more; they are simply better tools in her plan of Middle East conquest.

The battle is greater than for the spoils of the Middle East; the battle is for Western Europe too. It was Secretary of State John Foster Dulles who told the world in 1958 why the West cannot afford to lose the Middle East. "It will be the greatest victory that Soviet communism could ever have gained because if they get this area, they, in effect will have gotten Western Europe without a war."

The military and economic aid that the Soviet Union is now giving Egypt and Syria poses a threat to Western civilization and Christianity. It is part of the dynamics of history that the tiny Jewish state has proved to be (with Turkey, of course), the best friend that Christianity has in the Middle East.

The race between the East and West is not for the territory of the Middle East but for the minds and souls of the Arabs. The West offers the Arabs economic aid, military aid, royalties for their oil, and the democratic ideals of social progress. The East offers them economic aid, military aid, political backing at the United Nations, and, most important of all, support in the one issue on which all the Arabs are united: the destruction of Israel.

There is no bidding for the minds and souls of the Israelis. Russia has written Israel off. From her very birth, Israel has made it clear that her lot is with the West. She is a democratic ally in the East-West war.

Democracy is not a shibboleth in Israel; it is a way of life, the very web of her life. She was born of a democratic vote in the United Nations. Many of her leaders had fled tyranny abroad to find and establish democracy on this holy soil.

She is paying a high penalty for being part of the free world. If she were a backward or uncommitted country, she would probably not have been singled out by the Russians for their enmity.

Yet in this penalty, in this very weakness, lies her strength. If the Soviet Union should decide to take Israel over, alone or through an Arab satellite, she would have to conquer Israel by force. Such an act would be pure aggression. If the Western World were to allow this to happen, no small country would feel that it could rely on the West against Eastern aggression. The uncommitted and even many of the committed countries would fall like plums into Russia's hands.

Israel is here to stay. She has no intention of allowing herself to be conquered. If the Arabs should attempt such a conquest, even with the vast equipment the Russians have given them, Israel could fight back. But if Russia herself attacks, Israel would obviously be no match for the giant that sent Sputnik into the air and shock waves of anxiety through the Western powers until the United States launched her own astronauts.

During the last few years in the United Nations, Russia has voted with the Arabs on every single Middle Eastern issue; yet Israel has maintained her independence without succumbing to fear or blackmail or dubious neutralism.

"This small nation," Ben-Gurion declared in the Knesset, "burdened with so many problems, besieged, blockaded, and threatened, not only by her neighbors, is not for sale."

Israel has firmly established herself as a voice of eloquence and thoughtfulness in the halls of the United Nations. She has become a center of democratic confidence on which the West can rely.

The great reservoir of American friendship toward Israel began at the very moment of her birth, when President Truman signed a formal document, and the United States became the first country in the world to recognize the Jewish state. In 1956 I called upon former President Truman in his office in Kansas City. He talked of the birth of Israel and of his friendship for the Arab states as well as Israel.

"Some people have said that my administration was pro-Jewish and anti-Arab when we recognized Israel. That's a lie. We were being fair to all of them. The United Nations (the Arabs, remember, were members of the U.N.) voted to partition Palestine. We went along with that decision. It was my responsibility as President to see to it that our foreign policy fit in with the foreign policy of the world. Besides, after what Hitler did to the Jews, and after the reports I got when I sent Earle Harrison to make a study of the D.P. camps and found that the Jews wanted to get out of Europe and go to Palestine, I felt that the Jews ought to have a democratic home of their own."

Behind Mr. Truman's desk in Kansas City was a bust of Israel's first president, Dr. Chaim Weizmann. There was an ancient oil lamp unearthed in Israel. And there were informal and happy pictures of Mr. Truman and his great friend and former haberdashery partner, the late Eddie Jacobson. Just as Mr. Truman's name is written large in the history of the birth of Israel, so too is Eddie Jacobson's, for Eddie was the "ambassador of his people" to his friend the President. He had the same qualities that Truman had, the same unswerving loyalty, the same fierce courage. Eddie even looked a bit like Truman and talked like Truman. When Eddie had died of a heart attack in 1956, Mr. Truman told me, "He was the best friend any man could have."

The tangible aspects of the friendship that began with Harry Truman have continued until today. The United States, throughout this decade, has sent experts, money, equipment to strengthen the young state. American Jews have poured forth their help as never before in history.

The miracle of Israel's rebirth brushed off on the rest of the world. Jews particularly felt it, and grew ennobled. It had been given to their generation to see the Jewish people reborn. The dream was real. The future was the present. Israel lived.

Israel came into existence with the help of Jews throughout the world; American Jews had played an important role in all the stages leading up to that birth since the days of Justice Louis Brandeis, and even earlier. After the state was born, they continued to be a kind of senior partner in the great task of rescuing homeless Jews. The small community inside Israel could never have assumed the whole job of rescuing almost a million people. American Jewry, by far the largest Jewish community in the world and the wealthiest, underwrote most of the cost of rescue.

A new spirit arose in America. The Jews felt a new sense of destiny, an ecstasy and pride, an intimation that "the spirit of the Lord God was upon them. . . . He had sent them to bind up the broken-hearted, to proclaim liberty to the captives and the opening of the prison to them that were bound."

Israel, for her part, had a responsibility to the rest of the world. This land, which had given the world the Book, was now the land to which millions of people looked for new spiritual and dynamic leadership.

The first stage had been one of ingathering, of rebuilding the land and securing it against the enemy. And while she gathered and repaired, she began to help other small nations repair their land and people too. Her friendships spread around the world.

A robust child, seeking to find her own way, she became teacher as well as student. She set up her own Point Four program. It began with Burma. Israel's first minister to Burma, David Hacohen, so completely won the confidence of Prime Minister U Nu, that U Nu visited Israel in 1955 on his trip to the West. U Nu was deeply moved by the ticker-tape parades and the great outpouring of love that the people of Israel showed him. He was the first head of state to visit their young land. He became a symbol of their own nationhood.

The two countries discovered striking parallels in their history. Burma won its independence from Britain in 1948, the same year that Israel did. Both countries were land bridges, and for centuries armies had marched across their faces to conquer them.

Israel's contribution to Burma was more than know-how. It was her mind and heart; it was the fearlessness of her spirit and the joyousness of her youth. The bright air of pioneering that infused every town and settlement in Israel, was the spirit with which Israel infused Burma. The Burmese might be suspicious of foreign aid from the great powers, fearing they might want to buy her loyalty, but they could not be suspicious of aid that came from Israel. Friendship grew between the two small powers without strings and reservations.

A top-level governmental mission, headed by David Hacohen, went to Burma to set up the Point Four program. The projects included an exchange program: Burmese students and technicians went to Israel to study; Israelis went to Burma to teach and to establish joint projects in industry and farming. Israel sent technicians to Burma to teach such things as modern methods of farming, town planning, sewage disposal, maternity care, and preventive medicine.

At Burma's request, Israel set up a large managerial model farm in Burma, like "Sam's Farm" in Beit Shaan, to show the Burmese American-Israeli methods of farming and pipe irrigation. The Russians are Israel's chief competitors in Burma. They have set up a Russian-type farm next to the Israeli farm, with Russian methods of farming and channel irrigation. The Israelis won out when they put on a big water display with fancy revolving sprinklers in Rangoon itself.

Ghana, in its very first year of statehood, turned to Israel for technical aid. The brand new Negro republic in British East Africa sent a delegation to Israel in the summer of 1957. Once again, a young nation found its own dream crystallized in the dream that was Israel.

With the unadulterated honesty of youth, one of the members of the Ghana delegation told a public meeting in Tel Aviv why Ghana had come to Israel for friendship and aid.

"Ghana is interested in rapid industrialization and in the development of her quarries and her agriculture. She needs assistance and is interested in receiving it from Israel, because you do not intend to exploit us."

A large delegation of representatives of all the Ghanaian ministries dealing with industry, agriculture, finance, health, and welfare arrived in Israel to set up an Israeli Point Four program for Ghana. They traveled with Ehud Avriel, then minister to Ghana, who, like David Hacohen in Burma, was an unstuffed-shirt diplomat who won the confidence and friendship of President Kwame Nkrumah.

Nkrumah tells the story of the "shopping list" he gave to each of the sixty or more diplomats who came representing their countries on Ghana's Independence Day.

"There was one fellow," Nkrumah reminisces, "who spoke a kind of English, who took a crumbled notebook out of his pocket and wrote down what I said in some strange characters. Six months later, his country—Israel, the first country in the world—delivered the goods. A flag was hoisted over the first Ghanaian-African ship in history."

Nkrumah and Israel worked out a partnership pattern which Israel was to follow with all the small nations that came asking for help. The Black Star Shipping Line was created with sixty per cent of the capital put up by Ghana and forty per cent by Israel's Zim Navigation Line. The National Construction Company was established the same way, a joint venture with Solel Boneh, the industrial arm of the Histadrut. Each contract contains a clause allowing the host country to decide when it wants to take complete control. The clause is not an empty one; after two years, Ghana bought out Israel's interest in the Black Star Line and in 1961 in the National Construction Company. But Ghana uses Israelis to manage and supervise the companies.

To be sure, Nkrumah causes political soul-searching in Israel each time he joins with Nasser in signing anti-Israel proclamations. But these are the days of *Realpolitik*. Even while Nkrumah embraces Nasser, he sends teams of Ghanaians to study in Israel, and invites Israelis to build his nautical college, his fishing harbor, set up the machinery for his census, and advise him on medicine, public health, industry, and agriculture. About a dozen Israeli doctors are working across the country fighting malaria, tuberculosis, venereal diseases, and directing the departments of pediatrics, surgery, gynecology, and internal medicine in the hospitals at Accra and Kumazi. Israel's Dr. Brachott is Nkrumah's advisor in the Ministry of Health. Another team of Israelis is working across the country in agriculture, and Israeli engineers are teaching in the Technical College in Kumazi.

The new nations soon discovered that independence was only the beginning; that a president and a flag and a vote at the U.N. were only the honeymoon. The long days of setting up a nation, with little or no experience, lay ahead. Impatient with their colonial past, restless, sometimes overwhelmed, like a distraught mother with a swarm of little children, many of the new nations turned to a country they could easily identify with, young in nationhood herself, to help them with the whole housekeeping of government.

The requests were often poignant. They needed everything. Big things and little things. Kindergarten teachers. A school building. A bank. A post office. Plumbing. A city sewage system. Breeding chickens. Building industries and labor unions. Dams. Ports. Fisheries. Hotels. Some of the colonial powers had built hotels as farewell gifts before they departed. "Please send us hotel managers," the new nations now write to Israel constantly.

The world has been alerted, and has come to help. All the agencies of the U.N.—WHO, UNICEF, UNESCO, Special Fund —the U.S., the U.S.S.R., the former colonial powers, all have sent men and money and invaluable aid. Yet little Israel is doing one of the outstanding jobs—not in money; she has little herself. Not in equipment or gifts. But in terms of human beings who are extending their sense of dedication and pioneering, the *Chalutziut* which built Israel, to helping other nations pioneer.

Of all Israel's exports, doctors are perhaps the most welcome. Israel has the greatest ratio of doctors in the world—one to about every 450 people. Africa ranks among the areas which have the fewest doctors in the world. The burden of immigration has enriched Israel; doctors, fleeing from countries in Eastern Europe and even from Argentina, come to Israel, often with nothing in their suitcases, but with a wealth of skills. While these new doctors are retrained to fill the gap at home, Israel sends her most gifted men and women to help small nations in need.

The needs are staggering. In remote areas of Tanganyika, one out of every two babies dies. Thousands of Africans are blind from dread eye diseases. Now a whole generation is being saved from blindness and infectious eye diseases in countries where eye clinics were almost unknown a few years ago.

In Liberia, Hadassah's now world famous Dr. Isaac C. Michaelson, Chief of the Department of Ophthamology, helped President William Tubman set up a crash program to fight eye disease. The first eye hospital was built in Monrovia in 1960, followed soon by another eye clinic in Las Palmas. The hospital is so urgently needed, that patients come not only from Liberia, but from neighboring countries like Sierra Leone, Guinea, and the Ivory Coast. Some walk. Some come by bus or truck. Some come on small boats. None are turned away.

Three Israelis, a husband and wife team, Dr. and Mrs. Eliahu Neumann and Dr. Hanan Zauberman run the hospital, examining more than twenty thousand patients and performing over one thousand operations each year. Among their assistants are two Liberian doctors and several nurses who were trained in Hadassah's hospital in Jerusalem. Mrs. Neumann, who is the optician, has set up a workshop for a whole retinue of Liberians who can now fit and grind prescription glasses. It used to take weeks while glasses were sent out of the country to be ground; now patients can have eyeglasses while they wait.

His Majesty Haile Selassie I, the Lion of Judah, invited Israel to send doctors to staff his hospital in Addis Ababa and the new Haile Selassie Hospital in Massawa. His Technical College in Addis Ababa has been adopted by the Haifa Technion as a sister college, and is directed by Israelis.

A kind of chain reaction of aid has spread through Africa and Asia. Tanganyika sent a group of veterinarians to study veterinary medicine in Israel, and two male nurses to train in the treatment of eye diseases; at the same time it invited two surgeons to work in Tanganyika. In Singapore, Israelis are teaching at the medical school. In Liberia, a public health specialist from Israel is reorganizing the health services, and a tuberculosis expert is directing a campaign in the prevention and cure of TB. In Leopoldville in the

Republic of Congo, several Israeli doctors are teaching at the University; the head of the ear, nose, and throat department is Dr. Rudi Werth, famous in his own right as well as in being the proud husband of Dina Werth, commanding officer of the Chen, Israel's Women's Army Corps.

Nor was it enough to send doctors into Africa and Asia; doctors had to emerge from the new nations themselves. The Hadassah-Hebrew University Medical School began a six-year training course for medical students from the developing countries, with courses given in the beginning years in English. Because of the importance of this program, both the Israel government and the World Health Organization provide funds and scholarships to the medical students. It is everyone's hope that some of these students will become medical teachers rather than practitioners, so they in turn will teach medicine in their own countries.

Israel's speed in answering calls for help has become legendary. When the Belgians left the Congo in 1960, they took all their doctors with them. The Republic of Congo (Leopoldville), in the agonies of birth, appealed to the nations of the world to send some doctors. Israel, within forty-eight hours, assembled a team of doctors, nurses, surgeons, and anaesthetists and sent them on a swift, direct flight by El Al to Leopoldville.

Some of the students come speaking French and an African language; others come speaking English and a different African language. The only language some of the students have in common is Hebrew, and they are learning to talk Hebrew, "Pinglish," and "Sleng" with zest. It is still an unforgettable experience to hear tall Africans in regal white robes talking about nudnicks and schlemihls.

Two diplomats from Sierra Leone boarded an El Al plane in Europe on which I was traveling to Israel one summer; they were C. B. Rogers Wright, Minister of Housing, and Olu Wright, Director General of the Ministry. Their mission, they told me, was to try to get Israel to put up a parliament building for their independence day celebration. Every construction company they had asked in Europe had refused, saying it was impossible to build a parliament in eight months.

Barely a week later, I waved the two men off as they flew home —mission accomplished. Solel Boneh would help them. The hill site was cleared in Freetown while the blueprints were still being drawn in Jerusalem. Eight months later, on April 26, 1961, Sierra Leone became an independent nation and its flag flew on top of its new parliament building.

On September 1, 1962, an earthquake in western Iran killed 12,403 people and wrecked 25,000 homes in 294 villages. The earth reared in more than 80,000 square miles, an area being developed in co-operation with Israel in the Iranian land reform. Israel had already sent sociologists, economists, legal and farm experts to help bring this primitive section of Iran into the twentieth century. One hundred farmers and their families were already living in small moshavim and kibbutzim modeled after Israel's.

Now the earthquake had wiped out all their work. Iran's Minister of Agriculture sent a cable to Israel's Minister of Agriculture, Moshe Dayan, asking if he could come immediately.

Two days later, Dayan was in Teheran. The two men took off in a helicopter for the disaster area. Below them lay total destruction.

Dayan, the soldier-hero of the Sinai Campaign, turned to the Iranian.

"You and I," he said, "are men of action. Our job is to rebuild this valley immediately. Out of evil there must come some good; the old things you were trying to undo have been wiped out. Now you have a clean slate on which to start. This is the time to implement your new agriculture, your new industry, your new village co-operatives; and doing it, you will rebuild the morale of your people. Israel will help you."

A crash program to rebuild life above the devastation was begun. Within a few days, top experts from Israel flew to Iran. Iranian families flew to Israel to live and work in the settlements. Helping to rebuild the shattered valley became Israel's biggest project in foreign aid.

In Burma, Hadassah's Dr. Moshe Rachmilewitz was told of a strange anemia that affected Burma's pregnant women. He offered

Israel's help. Every week a test tube was flown from Rangoon to Lydda Airport and from there was rushed to a Hadassah laboratory. Within months, the cause of the anemia was discovered and, with it, the cure.

Burma meanwhile has been sending more than one hundred Burmese ex-veterans, most of them noncommissioned officers with their own commanding officers, to live for a year or more in the moshavim and kibbutzim. They learn how to farm by day, and guard their settlements, if necessary, by night. Most of them come with their families, for women too must understand the new social concepts their husbands are learning in Israel. The experiment in teaching men to become new farmers cannot succeed if their wives do not travel the new road with them. In Israel, the Burmese women learn to work together in a co-operative village; they learn to entrust their children to nurses and teachers while they work in the fields, as they will later do in Burma. "And each year," the Burmese Ambassador to Israel told me, "we have a whole batch of Burmese sabras born in the moshavim."

Now the Lachish Plan has come to Burma. In Namsan in northern Burma, about 150 miles from the Chinese border, a human TVA is springing up. A huge area was surveyed by the Burmese government with Israeli engineers and economists and farm experts. Radiating around one central village, like Kiryat Gath, more than twelve co-operative villages have been built. The Burmese farmers and their wives, returning from Israel, are the instructors and leaders, teaching the army veterans who could not go to Israel, the lessons they learned in the Galilee and the Negev.

A high point in Israel's relations with Africa and Asia was reached in August 1960 when the Weizmann Institute of Science convened the "International Conference on Science in the Advancement of New States." One hundred twenty delegates came from forty nations to attend this first confrontation in history between the political leaders of brand-new nations and scientists from the older western world.

It was not the scientists but the young Africans who set the tone of the Conference. The teachers who had come to teach stayed to be taught. Just before the Conference started, several of the scientists told me, "Some of the Africans will surely ask us for a little nuclear reactor to take home in their suitcases—a little atomic power to catapult them into the twentieth century."

But they were wrong. The Africans did not want nuclear power; they wanted to know how to keep their babies alive. They did not want to reach the moon; they wanted to know how to wipe out black magic and superstition. It was young Dr. Solomon B. Caulker, who had been born in a jungle village in Sierra Leone, who brought the whole conference into the focus of Africa's crushing problems of hunger, illiteracy, diseases, and death.

Israel itself, its landscape, its desert, its people, became the teacher. The delegates, in all the costumes of Africa and Asia, traveled around Israel to learn how to bring water to the desert, how to make cotton grow, how to keep mothers and babies alive. They discussed with the experts from the west how to sweeten the salt water of the sea and saddle the sun, how to get their young students home to face the frustrations of little or no equipment, how to wipe out the dread tse-tse fly, and feed the hungry in a population explosion.

"Civilization is running a race with famine, and the outcome is still in doubt," Walter C. Lowdermilk said like a modern-day Jeremiah, while David Ben-Gurion warned the world that "the peace of the human race will not be secure" until "the gap between rich and poor nations is wiped out."

The Conference bore fruit. Many of its proposals were carried to the U.N. and in February of 1963, the United Nations held a similar conference in Geneva called the "United Nations Conference on Science and Technology." Israel's Eban, then Minister of Education and Culture, one of the vice-presidents of the Conference, described for the fifteen hundred delegates the methods by which Israel had become a free university for thousands of young people, technicians, and government officials from Asia and Africa.

Opening the Foreign Policy debate in the Knesset on May 6, 1963, Prime Minister Ben-Gurion told the nation that "hundreds and thousands of young people from thirty-six countries in Africa, fourteen in Asia including India, the Philippines, and Japan, five in the Mediterranean basin, Cyprus, Greece, Iran, Turkey, and Malta, and recently twenty countries in Latin America and the Caribbean area have come to Israel to study methods of agricultural settlement, the labor movement, youth education in the Nahal and Gadna, vocational training, and co-operation and various branches of science in the Hebrew University in Jerusalem, the Technion in Haifa and the Weizmann Institute in Rehovoth; and 890 Israeli experts are active in Asian, African and Latin American countries."

It was not too surprising that the Republic of the Congo (Leopoldville), with the military assistance of eighteen member nations of the U.N. available, asked Israel, which was not one of the eighteen nations, to train her paratroopers. Israel had won her confidence; she had meticulously abstained from becoming involved in any country's internal problems.

Her friendship with the emerging nations was tested at the U.N. In both the sixteenth and the seventeenth General Assemblies, held in 1961 and 1962, the new nations took the lead in introducing resolutions for peace in the Middle East between Israel and the Arab States. In the sixteenth Assembly, of the sixteen sponsors nine were African nations, five were from Latin America, and one was from Europe—the Netherlands. The resolution was defeated in committee. Undaunted, the next year, twenty-two nations introduced the peace resolution; this time twelve were Africans, six were Latin Americans, and three were Europeans—the Netherlands, Luxembourg, and Iceland.

Even though the resolution never came to a vote, some of the Africans turned their speeches into testimonials of friendship.

When Ahmed Shukairy, Saudi Arabia's delegate, lost his temper and accused the Ivory Coast of having "been bought" by Israel, Ambassador Arsène Usher reminded the world that it was the Arabs who bought and sold Negro slaves. "The representative of Saudi Arabia," he said movingly, "may be used to buying Negroes, but he can never buy us."

"Israel," the delegate from Upper Volta told another U.N. session, "has shown us that the desert can be used for better things than the parking of Cadillacs."

There have been problems, to be sure; there have been trials and errors. Some of the emerging nations, countries like Algeria, Mali, Guinea as well as Mauretania, Somalia and, of course, Ghana have joined with Nasser in denouncing Israel. Yet even among these detractors are nations who send their youth and their farmers to Israel, and who request Israeli participation in most of their development projects. Israel not only has active diplomatic relations with Mali, Guinea, and Ghana through its embassies, but has strong trade relations with them, and economic partnerships.

In the first years of the African program, when African visitors were a novelty in Israel, some of the children called the Africans *cushi* or *negro*. The Africans resented it, even though the word is not truly derogatory. It is in fact a Biblical word for the people of Africa, and the land of "Cush" in the Bible in the time of Solomon and the Queen of Sheba is believed to be Ethiopia. Yet Israel is so attuned to the sensitivity of its African visitors that it has initiated a program in all the elementary schools of the nation to teach children to use the word "Africans" instead of *cushi* and to explain the whole Afro-Asian program to them.

"Working with other small nations," an Israeli who accompanied President William Tubman of Liberia to Israel told me, "is a kind of Biblical fulfillment. It is as if this is a continuity of our mission in life. The mission of redemption—of constantly redeeming and purifying ourselves—this comes to us from the prophets in the Bible. We are not proselytizing, but we are redeeming. Redeeming ourselves while we help new nations redeem themselves too."

Redemption is no one-way street. Israel is not only the giver; she is the receiver, too. Trade has started with the new nations. The Israelis who go to build in the hot sands of Africa and the mountains of Asia come back better builders in the sands of the Negev and the mountains of Galilee. They come back, for the most part, better human beings, too; learning much from the spiritual purity of the gentle Buddhists in Nepal and Burma, and from the gayety and the joy-in-life of the Africans.

Presidents, prime ministers, cabinet members and their wives have begun visits of state to Israel. Tom Mboya, the young and dynamic leader of Kenya, took his beautiful bride Pamela Odede to Israel for their honeymoon. Pamela had studied for two years in the United States before their marriage, training to do social work among her people.

The President of Upper Volta, Antoine Yameogo, told an Israel diplomat, "The French have done great things for us, and they are still doing great things. They are trying to bring the twentieth century to us. But now we want to bring ourselves into the twentieth century. The white people who can help us are the Israelis. They are able to understand us because of their sensitivity, because they had to build their own country so quickly, and because both they and we have suffered from oppression."

There are no textbooks for bringing people from the bush on to the highways of this century. But Israel is writing a living textbook, not only on the fields, but in the hearts of many of the Africans. "Every African who has visited Israel has his heart full of admiration for Israel," the Ivory Coast's President Felix Houphouet-Boigny told the Israelis. In the hills of Judea he planted the first trees in a forest soon to have ten thousand trees. "We will help you," he said, "to make peace."

In the grand design for peace, Israel continues her work and her goals and her dreams—harnessing the desert; building new towns and cities; advancing education and research in science; co-operating with the new nations; and taking in tens of thousands of immigrants each year.

The prophecy that Ben-Gurion had made to me that day in 1948 is being fulfilled. The Negev is blooming. The hills are covered with trees. New towns have sprung up. Children, beautiful children, are everywhere. And they have not forgotten their Bill of Rights—"to love your fellow human as yourself."

Appendix

Go See for Yourself

PEOPLE ARE constantly asking me, "Do you think I ought to go to Israel on a trip? Do you think I might like to live there for a while? What's the hotel situation like? Could I have fun there on a long vacation?"

My answer to all of them is: go now. Go now if you are ready to trade off the plush carpet for the magic carpet. Go now if you want to know what America must have been like in the first flush of independence. Go now if you want the excitement and adventure of seeing an ancient land and an ancient people reborn.

Israel has fascination for all people: for Jews and Christians; for those who have relatives or special ties to the land, and for those who have none; for those who want to walk on the soil where the people of the Old Testament and the New Testament lived; for those who want to see a modern democracy come into being; for those who want to compare today's pioneering spirit in Israel with yesterday's pioneering spirit in the United States; and for those who simply want a comfortable, luxurious vacation in one of the most exotic and exciting settings in the world. Israel has something unique to offer to every kind of traveler.

"Israel, the Mid-East Riviera," is now a reality. Here are all the comforts and pleasures of the Riviera or Florida, from the sun and the beaches to the nightclubs and cafés.

The tourist can swim or sail or drive along vast stretches of the 110 miles of glistening, unspoiled Mediterranean beaches.

But even more exciting than the Mediterranean, unique in the world, he can swim or sail in the Sea of Galilee or the Dead Sea, the latter 1,286 feet below sea level, the lowest surface water on earth.

He can fish for marine giants or rainbow trout. There is deep-sea fishing and underwater fishing in the Red Sea at Elath, whose translucent waters have some many varieties of beautiful, multicolored tropical fish and coral reefs. Game hunters can go boar-hunting in the hills around the Huleh.

Amateur archaeologists can dig all through the country. There are scores of mounds all over, called tells, that are signposts to the archaeologist. If he chooses well, he can dig up treasures from cities built by Crusaders, Persians, Romans, Greeks, Babylonians, Assyrians, Philistines, Israelites or Judeans, Canaanites, and on down the far reaches of history through the calcolythic and neolithic eras when prehistoric man made the first beginning of what we call civilization.

Painters, sculptors, and photographers can find an Israeli Provincetown in the new artist's colony at Ein-Hod, south of Haifa, or in the winding streets of Safad, high in the mountains above the Sea of Galilee.

Israel is like America. You can find almost everything you look for. If you have hopes, they will doubtless be fulfilled. Should you have prejudices, they will probably be confirmed. If, that is, you look for squalor and slums, you will find them. If you look for adventure and excitement, for the brush of nobility and greatness that comes from opening your arms to fleeing people, you will find them too.

What you need to put in your baggage are humor, humility, and the Bible. The need of humor is obvious, humility is desirable, and the Bible is a must.

You need humility in visiting any land, however large and self-sufficient, but you need it especially in visiting a small frontier land making brave new experiments. There are few things more offensive than the traveler who tells everyone just what's wrong with a place. In any town, even in America, the phrase "Can't compare with what we've got back home" is an open declaration of hostility, if not war. The Israelis know they are making mistakes; they err, dream, squabble like the rest of us, and save themselves from falling too often on their faces by a healthy affirmation of humor. Most of them are eager to have American know-how. But they want to be sure the know-how is offered by people who really know how.

The Bible is a necessity. It is not only the history of the past, but the Baedeker to the present. Jerusalem, Safad, Tiberias, Nazareth— Bible names that we learned in childhood—are living places here, where people eat and drink and sleep and fall in love and die. There is a tie to this land is each man's heart. And every return to it is a return to the Bible.

You can travel to Israel by sea or air, or a combination of both. Airplanes fly directly from New York to Tel Aviv; you can fly nonstop to Israel or make stopovers in Europe. El Al Israel Airlines—the name "El Al" means "Onwards and Upwards" or more freely, "To the Skies" —flies planes daily directly to Israel. Its jets have cut the flying time to ten and a half hours.

The new economy group fare to Israel, $535 round trip, is probably the cheapest fare in the world. It can be arranged through any travel agent, who can give you the dates when a group of forty or more people who may never have seen each other can leave together. You can fly with a group that will stay a couple of weeks or a couple of months. There are hundreds of departure dates to pick from. On the way home, you can make a stopover in Europe at any place the group decides. But you must take the same plane that the group takes home.

For people with lots of time, who love ocean voyages, there are steamships and passenger-carrying freighters which sail the high seas between New York and Haifa. Israel's Zim Lines now has a whole fleet of luxury liners like the *Israel*, the *Zion*, and the *Shalom*, with everything from swimming pools and air-conditioning to antirolling stabilizers. The ocean voyage eastbound takes thirteen and a half days and makes calls en route at such ports as Madeira, Gibraltar, and Piraeus, Greece. Westward-bound, the ships call at Cyprus, Naples, Marseilles, Gibraltar, and sometimes Halifax, Nova Scotia, on their way to New York.

You can combine air and road and sea travel by flying to Europe, driving to Marseilles or Naples, and there boarding one of the Zim lines that ply the Mediterranean, the sisterships *Jerusalem* and *Theodor Herzl* or the M/S *Moledet*, a one-class thrift ship. Traveling on these Mediterranean ships, you may find your fellow passengers are not only Americans, Europeans, and Israelis, but new immigrants, fleeing persecution from North Africa and Eastern Europe. If you begin to know these passengers and hear their stories of anguish and rescue, you may find yourself understanding better what makes Israel tick, and understand a feeling which may not come in the first days of strange and perplexing sensations, but which begins to grow after a few days in the land—a feeling of returning to one's roots even as one returns to the birthplace of three religions.

PASSPORTS AND VISAS

To travel to Israel, if you are a United States citizen, you will need a valid passport. Write to the Passport Division, State Department, in Washington, D.C., or, if you live in one of the large cities, apply to the local office of the Passport Division. Citizens of the United States or Canada do not need a visa for Israel.

If you are not a citizen of the United States, you must apply for an Israel visa, in person or by mail, to any of the following:

Israel Embassy
   1621 22 Street, N.W.
   Washington, D.C.
   Tel.: Hudson 3-4100

Israel Consulate General and Passport Service
   11 East 70th Street,
   New York 21, N.Y.
   Tel.: Trafalgar 9-7600

Israel Consulate and Passport Service
   659 South Highland Avenue
   Los Angeles 36, Calif.
   Tel.: Webster 8-3691

Israel Consulate and Passport Service
   936 North Michigan Avenue
   Chicago, Illinois
   Tel.: Whitehall 3-0265

Israel Consulate and Passport Service
   795 Peachtree Street N.E.
   Atlanta, Georgia
   Tel.: Trinity 5-7851/2

Consulate General and Passport Service
1555 McGregor Street
Montreal, P.Q., Canada
Tel.: Wellington 7-3937

Israel Embassy
45 Powell Avenue
Ottawa, Canada
Tel.: Central 2-5305

If you are in Europe and need an Israel visa, apply to the local Israel Legation or Consulate. If your stay in Israel is prolonged, you can have your visa renewed by applying to the District Immigration Offices:

Jerusalem: Generali Building, Shlomzion Hamalka Street *Tel.:* 4611
Tel Aviv: 138 Allenby Road. *Tel.:* 3025
Haifa: 61 Derech Ha'Atzmaut. *Tel.:* 4248

INOCULATIONS

A smallpox vaccination is the only inoculation Israel requires; the United States also requires it for re-entry. To enter Israel, you must have a certificate proving that you have been vaccinated against smallpox within three years of your trip.

If you want to play safe, you might also get inoculations against typhus, typhoid, and paratyphoid fever. For a few hours you may feel like a candidate for the Purple Heart, but it's probably worth it.

DRUGS

As in every country in the Mediterranean, beware of eating unwashed fruits or vegetables unless you peel them yourself. Though no one should recommend drugs from the pages of a book, I carry sulfaguanadine pills the way an Englishman carries an umbrella. The moment I feel any symptom of what our G.I.'s called "G.I.'s" and what Israel calls "*shilshul*" I take the sulfaguanadine. It is a specific that hits the dysentery bug right on the head.

CLOTHING

If you plan to go to Israel in the summer, take summer-resort clothing. For the winter, take a good warm suit and a heavy coat. In
Jerusalem one winter I left my hotel each morning at about eight,
wearing a woolen suit and a heavy fur coat. By ten, I took off the
coat. At eleven, I stripped off my suit jacket. At noon I wished I were
wearing a bathing suit. At four I had the suit jacket on and at six the
fur coat, buttoned to the neck.

By air you are allowed only sixty-six pounds of baggage free of charge,
if you go first class; forty-four pounds if you go tourist class. By ship
you can carry a good deal of baggage, but it is a good idea to travel with
suitcases that can be handled easily, rather than with trunks. Washable
clothes ought to be high on your list; there are dry-cleaning establish-
ments in Israel, but they are always busy and rather expensive. Drip-
dry cottons that are not stiff and hot are a blessing. They launder easily
and conserve space and weight.

For people who are not certain what they may need in Israel, here
is a list of clothing from head to foot for a one-month stay:

FOR WOMEN

HATS. Most women content themselves with a head kerchief, or a
big floppy straw hat to keep the sun off their faces. But you might
want one or two hats, crushable if possible, for tea parties and afternoon receptions. You will need a variety of bandanas to keep your
hair in place as you drive around the country.

SUNGLASSES. If you wear sunglasses at home, by all means take a
few pairs with you. This is subtropical country and the sun is intense.
It is no tragedy if you forget or lose your glasses. You can buy new
ones in Israel.

COATS. A lightweight coat in the summer; a winter coat for the rainy
winter season. The rains generally fall in November, December, and
January.

SUITS. Two woolen suits for winter, spring, or fall; two lightweight
suits for summer, one gabardine and one seersucker.

BLOUSES. Six blouses, cool cotton or nylon for the summer, silk for
winter. Most nylons do not absorb perspiration; cotton or dacron
blouses are more practical for the subtropical heat.

Sweaters. One pullover and one cardigan for any time of the year. For an overnight trip to Haifa or one of the northern kibbutzim in the summer, you may want to leave your coat with your luggage in Tel Aviv or Jerusalem and take just a sweater for the cool evenings.

Dresses. Six dresses, including three or four simple cotton or dacron resort dresses for all seasons and one or two afternoon dresses, perhaps of nylon or silk. In the winter fewer cottons are needed and at least one dress should be warm wool. Cotton sunbacks are useful, especially on the beach. But it is best not to plan to appear on the streets without a jacket. Women dress more conservatively in Israel than in America, so don't appear in décolletage unless you like wolf calls.

Evening Dresses. Take one if you expect to be invited to a diplomatic or government function; otherwise you can probably get along, even if you're invited to an elaborate party or a dance, with a cocktail-length party dress.

Lingerie. Since lingerie, especially nylon, doesn't weigh much, take the lingerie you would ordinarily need for a month. In winter, add two pairs of woolies for the cold damp days. You will need a lightweight robe that can be laundered easily and needs no ironing.

Stockings. Take along a dozen pairs for any season, though you probably won't wear them all summer. You can always make somebody happy by a gift of nylon stockings.

Bobby Socks. Two pairs of socks or peds if you can't bear to wear your shoes without stockings.

Shoes. One pair of good walking shoes for winter; one pair of summer sandals; two pairs of dress shoes, and a pair of folding washable or leather bedroom slippers. Shoes are heavy, but if you need extra shoes, cut down on other clothes.

Rainwear. Galoshes are unnecessary in the summer, but light rubber ones are advisable for winter. An umbrella is a nuisance and generally weighs more than it's worth. If you are a confirmed umbrella carrier, take a small folding one. It would be more sensible, though, to take a plastic shawl for your head and a plastic or some other lightweight raincoat.

Bathing Equipment. In summer or winter, take along two bathing suits, since you can swim in all the seas in the summer, and in the Dead Sea and at Elath (the Red Sea) in the winter. No beach robes unless you go by ship. They weigh too much for air travel. Your light-weight robe can double in brass for the beach.

SLACKS. Not essential, but if you like slacks, take one warm pair for winter, a lightweight pair for summer. Shorts are part of a girl farmer's equipment, so you will feel quite at home in the country in shorts.

HANDBAGS. Two handbags. One large one, either to be worn over the shoulder or hung from your wrist. It should be roomy enough to hold your passport, your tickets, and all the documents you need, as well as the fifty-seven varieties of things most women throw into their handbags. The second bag, for dressing up, should take little room in packing.

JEWELRY. Don't take much, especially if it's heavy. If you have family heirlooms, leave them home. Wear only what you need. You'll probably want to buy Yemenite jewelry in Israel anyway.

COSMETICS. Figure out how much cold cream, powder, lipstick, nail polish, tissues, shampoo, soap flakes, and suntan lotion you use in a month and carry that much with you. Put your cosmetics into small plastic nonbreakable bottles and jars. You will find that the beauty parlors of Israel follow American and French styles closely and that some of the women of Tel Aviv are as well coiffured as any woman on Fifth Avenue.

LUGGAGE. Two suitcases and a hatbox, all lightweight. The hatbox can be used as a suitcase for short overnight trips.

FOR MEN

Men's wear in Israel is casual. Polo shirts and tennis shirts are common and neckties are rare. It's perfectly proper in Israel for men to wear shorts on the city streets. One of the sights I shall never forget was when two distinguished American visitors, one of them five feet two and the other six feet three, hurried over to a men's haberdashery in Tel Aviv and bought khaki shorts, polo shirts, and long khaki socks. In their new sartorial splendor, they called on the Prime Minister and Foreign Minister at the very moment the Soviet Ambassador, dressed in tails, was presenting his credentials.

Israel's Knesset is an open-necked, tieless, tea-drinking parliament. Ben-Gurion arrived at the Knesset one day in pinstriped tails and apologized: "Excuse me, gentlemen, for coming here in my working clothes."

HATS. Useful to keep the sun off your head, and for cold weather. A canvas hat with a sun visor is highly practical.

COATS. Warm, all-weather coat in winter. Light topcoat for the rest of the year.

SUITS. Two. Wool in winter, lightweight in summer. An extra suit of washable material is practical. A tropical suit for afternoon or evening functions. Evening clothes only if you expect to be invited to diplomatic functions, and even then tourists are generally considered properly dressed if they wear a business suit.

SHIRTS. Six. Colored and white cotton; at least one should be nylon or dacron. Four polo shirts.

SHORTS AND SLACKS. Two pairs of shorts for the summer and one pair of slacks for any season.

SWEATERS. Two. A heavy one for winter; a thin one for summer.

TIES. Half a dozen to a dozen. You can always leave your extra ones as gifts.

UNDERWEAR. Take the underwear you would ordinarily need for a month. A lightweight robe; a pair of traveling slippers.

BATHING TRUNKS. One or two pairs for summer or winter.

SHOES. Two pairs, plus a pair of sandals for summer and a pair of rubbers for winter.

SOCKS. A dozen pairs.

SCARVES. One silk scarf for warmth.

RAZOR. Don't take an electric razor, unless you want to carry a transformer with you. You can get blades and shaving cream in Israel, but the price is high. Better stock up with a month's supply.

INCIDENTALS. Sunglasses, drugs, a ball-point pen, or at least one that doesn't leak when you're flying, a large passport case to hold your passport, tickets, extra passport photos.

CUSTOMS IN U.S.A.

If you have been away from the United States for at least 48 hours, you may bring back, duty free, one hundred dollars' worth of items for personal use and gifts, including one gallon of alcoholic beverages. This does not include gifts for resale. While overseas, a tourist is allowed to send a ten-dollar gift a day to a different person back in the States.

If you take a foreign camera out of the United States, be sure to register it with the United States Customs as you leave. Otherwise you may have to pay 100 per cent import duty on it when you return. You don't have to register an American-made camera.

MAIL AND TELEGRAMS

Air-mail letters to Israel cost 25 cents; you can also buy an 11-cent "air letter" at any United States Post Office. Air-mail to and from Israel takes four days to a week or longer, depending on planes and weather. Straight ship mail takes about a month or longer. Packages may take several months. Telegrams and cables from Israel are sent at national post offices in all the cities and villages. You can also speak to Israel now by telephone.

ELECTRICITY

Electric power in Israel is 220 v. A.C., so that for many American appliances, you need a transformer, a resistor, or a resistor cord.

CURRENCY

The official rate of exchange of Israel currency is three Israel pounds for each $1.00. But it is wise before going to Israel to check the current rate of exchange. The Israel pound is written as I£.

The Israel pound is divided into one hundred agora and there are coins of one, five, ten, and twenty-five agora. Banknotes are used for fifty agora, or half a pound, one, five, ten, fifty, and one hundred pounds.

Tourists are no longer required to declare the amount of foreign currency in their possession on their arrival in Israel. You can change your currency at the airport, in banks, hotels, or stores authorized by the Government Tourist Corporation. You can exchange Israel Bonds at any bank.

You may bring in as much currency as you like, but don't exchange it all immediately into Israel pounds, because on leaving the country, you can reconvert up to $300. You cannot enter or leave Israel with more than I£100 in one or five pound notes. You can also take out a souvenir amount of one Israel pound in coins.

Tourists who fly in are met at Lydda Airport by an attractive hostess in a blue and silver uniform, who enters the plane and says in Hebrew, "Welcome! Blessed be he who cometh." She leads them across the airport, takes them through customs, and, while they are waiting, treats each visitor with a glass of orange juice.

CUSTOMS OFFICIALS

As in most countries, the customs officials in Israel are amateur psychologists. If they think you have an honest face they may just skim through your bags. But sometimes they decide that you might be smuggling an extra carton of cigarettes for your Aunt Sarah and go through your baggage with a fine comb. The Israelis are old hands at customs inspections. They learned a lot working under the British and they taught themselves a thing or two about smuggling during the illegal days. Some of them even had to unlearn old tricks. There was a story, apocryphal no doubt, about a customs official who cased every ship to see what he could smuggle off if he wanted to. He never did smuggle anything, but he was like a dog who couldn't break an old habit. Some tourists resent Israel's customs inspectors and the duty they are asked to pay. Others pay up without complaint. "After all," I have heard them say, "it's a new state. The country needs money."

You are allowed to take in, customs free:

    a. Old and new wearing apparel and personal effects, in reasonable quantities.

    b. Binoculars, photography equipment, cameras, typewriters, and sports accessories (excluding firearms), provided they have been used and the customs officer is satisfied that they are part of your personal belongings.

    c. Implements, instruments, and tools for your professional use.

    d. Intoxicating liquors up to half a pint.

    e. Nine ounces of tobacco or 250 cigarettes.

    f. Twenty-two pounds of assorted food per person. It is advisable to include only small quantities of spices, instant coffee, and tea, worth up to $10. After that, you have to pay duty.

    g. A bicycle, a baby carriage, golf clubs, and other sport accessories, even a caravan trailer, kitchen utensils and portable musical instruments can all come in free. They may even be sent, along with your personal effects and tools thirty days before or after your arrival. But they must all be sent out again at the end of your stay.

    h. You can bring bona fide gifts for your friends and relatives up to $40. If you want to bring more, your gifts of $100 above the duty-free $40 are exempt from import licenses, but you have to pay duty on them.

i. Though you may bring in your own radio and phonograph, with twenty-five used records, if you plan to leave them in Israel, you will have to get an import license and pay duty on them. The same requirements are made for refrigerators, washing machines, playing cards (except two packs), merchandise in any form except commercial samples, and a TV set.

j. You can bring a pet in without any permit. But it's wise to give your pet antirabies shots before you come, and to bring along a certificate of proof. Otherwise you can get shots at the Ministry of Agriculture in Jerusalem.

You may bring a car with you for your own use without paying customs duty or tax if you follow either of two procedures:

a) By signing an agreement that you will take the car out within three months. If you stay longer than three months, you will have to deposit in cash 10% of the duty, which will be refunded to you if you take the car out within a year.

b) By giving the Collector of Customs a valid "Carnet de Passage" or "triptique" issued by any internationally recognized automobile club and valid for Israel.

You may of course leave your car in Israel or sell it there, but then it is subject to full payment of customs duty and purchase tax.

TOURIST INFORMATION

There are Tourist Information Centers in Tel Aviv, Jerusalem, Haifa, and Lydda. The one in Tel Aviv occupies two large, friendly rooms on Mendele Street, a few blocks off the sea. On one of its green walls hangs a map of Israel; pamphlets describing the cities, the country, and life in the new state are strewn on a reading table. Officials sit at various desks answering inquiries. One desk deals only with finding accommodations for the night, another helps to arrange tours through the country. Other officials answer questions and make appointments for you with various government officials or business and professional people to whom you may have letters of introduction, or with whom you may want to discuss investments, new businesses, etc.

The offices of these Tourist Information Centers, conducted by the Government Tourist Department throughout the country, are at:

Lydda Airport. *Tel.*: 228
7 Mendele St., Tel Aviv. *Tel.*: 23266
Haifa Port, Shed 3. *Tel.*: 3188
2 Balfour St., Haifa Town, *Tel.*: 66521
Jerusalem, 5 Ben Yehuda St., *Tel.*: 3420 or 5954
Elath, Airport.
Tiberias, 8 Nazareth Street.
Beersheba, Mif'alei Hanegev Square.
Nazareth, Casanova Street, *Tel.*: 144
Kiryat Gath, Beit Ha'am, *Tel.*: 57
Ashkelon, Clock Tower, *Tel.*: 309

Leaders of the Tourist Department, as well as other government agencies concerned with the welfare of visitors, are constantly making plans to put more roofs over your heads, set more food on your tables, have hostesses meet you at the airport, give you polite and efficient officials to hurry you through customs, and arrange tours to all the points of interest for travelers making their first pilgrimage. Israel hopes to be put under siege each year by over 100,000 pilgrims, tourists, students, teachers, businessmen, pleasure seekers, and innocents abroad.

HOTELS

The sound of hammering is rapidly replacing the voice of the turtle heard in the land. Many new hotels have been built and there is constant expansion and refurnishing of older ones in order to provide the tourist with the most comfortable and up-to-date accommodations. Tourists will be surprised to find so much luxury and beauty in Israel's new tourist hotels. Many are luxury hotels of the highest international standard; the rest are smaller, comfortable hotels or pensions with modern décor and facilities. Many of them are air-conditioned; many have private beaches along the Mediterranean; others have swimming pools; still others are set in Biblical hills or valleys; most have first-class dining rooms, open-air cafés or gardens, and a number have bars, night clubs, and dance floors. Some outstanding hotels are the following:

DAN CARMEL, Haifa: brand-new and glamorous.

SHERATON, Tel Aviv: one of the newest luxury hotels.

DAN HOTEL, Tel Aviv: a sumptuous modern establishment over-looking the Mediterranean.

RAMAT AVIV HOTEL, outskirts of Tel Aviv (some 10 minutes from the center of town): modern, tastefully furnished cottages, surrounded by flowers and gardens; in the center of the grounds is a large swimming pool.

ACCADIA GRAND HOTEL, Accadia Beach, 15 minutes from Tel Aviv: all rooms face the sea; hotel has its own private Mediterranean beach, a beautiful terrace, patio, and other glamorous facilities.

SHARON HOTEL, Herzlia-on-Sea, 15 minutes from Tel Aviv: private beach on the Mediterranean; excellent cuisine.

TADMOR HOTEL, Herzlia-on-Sea: music and dancing nightly in its fashionable Topaz Club.

KING DAVID HOTEL, Jerusalem: world famous and ranks with almost any first class hotel for comfort; unforgettable sunset over the Old City is seen from its balconies and windows.

EDEN HOTEL, Jerusalem: only a short distance away from the Knesset (Israel's Parliament), and you can run into an M.K. in the Eden's lobby or restaurant.

PRESIDENT HOTEL, Jerusalem: comfortable luxury hotel; private swimming pool.

ZION HOTEL, Haifa: in the heart of the city, within easy access of beautiful Mount Carmel and the Haifa port area.

DOLPHIN HOUSE HOTEL AND COUNTRY CLUB, Galilee: a charming place; rooms face the sea; swimming pool; horseback riding; music and dancing.

GALEI KINNERETH, Tiberias: a sumptuous hotel overlooking the Sea of Galilee; luxurious comforts and exquisite views.

Besides these hotels, there are charming smaller places and pensions in all these cities as well as in Nathanya and Nahariya, popular vacation centers. Noteworthy are the beautiful Dagon Hotel in Ashkelon and the modern Hias Hostel in Beersheba. A number of kibbutzim operate rest homes as an extra source of income; some of the more famous ones are at Givat Brenner, close to the Weizmann Institute in Rehovot; Ein Kharod, on the Plain of Esdraelon; Ayeleth Ha Shakhar, in the

Upper Galilee; Kfar Giladi, in the Galilee, a favorite hideaway for the Habimah theatre folk.

A vacation in the kibbutzim offers the tourist the opportunity of witnessing communal living among Israel's farmers, and by and large the rates are cheaper than in the hotels. Kfar Giladi's American plan— three meals with an additional mid-morning snack of fruit and yoghurt, mid-afternoon tea, and fruit at night—comes to about $5.00 a day.

RESTAURANTS

Most of the better hotels have their own dining rooms. Some of the restaurants are kosher; most are not. You can find cooking from every kind of cuisine in Europe. In the Tnuva restaurants you can get vegetarian light meals with borsch, potatoes, sour cream, a variety of salads, and, invariably, *leben* (a variety of yoghurt). For dietary observers, the Rishon Cellar and Mines are famous in Tel Aviv; in Jerusalem Goldschmidt's and the Egged Café are well known; and in Haifa the Balfour Cellar is charming and fairly inexpensive.

American corn lovers may buy corn from vendors who sell it piping hot from pushcarts or little stands in the best Coney Island tradition. The Israel version of hamburger is *felafel*, an Arab-inspired delicacy of vegetable paste fried in fat and served on *peeta*, a flat, unleavened Arab bread.

The newest rage with Israelis is Oriental cooking. In all the cities there now are restaurants that serve food straight out of Africa and the Orient. Here is a list of some of the food you might order in such a restaurant:

Taheena: a flavorful paste of ground sesame seeds, oil, and garlic, eaten with *peeta*.

Hummus: similar to *taheena*, though the basic ingredient is ground chick peas.

Shashlik: pieces of lamb or beef charcoal-broiled on a skewer.

Kebab: ground meat broiled on a skewer.

Leben: curdled milk often served as a side dish with meals.

Yoghurt: cultured milk, taken after meals as a dessert, sometimes garnished with honey or fruit syrup.

Burekas: buns of flaky paper-thin crust filled with cheese or spinach, usually eaten with a hard-boiled egg.

Mahshi: peppers, squash, or eggplant, stuffed with rice, ground meat, and tomatoes.

A meal ordinarily costs between $1.00 and $1.50. A la carte meals in first-class or de luxe restaurants will run between $2.25 and $4.00. Drinks additional. A half-bottle of wine is 55 cents. Restaurants charge 10 per cent for service, plus 10 per cent for municipal taxes.

TIPS

Tipping can sometimes be a ticklish problem in a country consciously overturning the economic pyramid. In the kibbutzim, you would insult anyone by offering him a tip. Taxi drivers tell you the amount of the fare, since the cities are zoned. Most will expect no tip.

Here and there, you will find drivers who look upon a tip as degrading. A group of Americans who traveled through the country for several days with one taxi driver made a pool at the end of their trip and offered their driver I£10. The driver refused to accept the money. "I thought we had become friends," he said. "How could you do this?" Their insistence was useless. Finally the leader of the group asked the driver if there was anything at all he could give him, perhaps for his wife and children.

The driver thought for a few moments. "Yes, something personal. Maybe some buttons, just so I'll have something to remember you by. But no money."

You are expected to tip porters at hotels for carrying your bags, just as you would in the States. Also, if you have stayed for any length of time at a hotel, you tip your waiter and chambermaid. Hotels and restaurants automatically add a 10 per cent service charge to your bill, but most people leave something extra for the waiters. At the docks in Haifa and Tel Aviv and at the airport at Lydda, a standard porterage fee is placed on each piece of your checked baggage, but you will probably want to give an extra tip to the porter who carries your bags to the taxi or limousine. By and large you tip for the same services in Israel that you do in the United States, and for any special services for which you feel you want to show gratitude.

TRAVEL

Most traveling around the country is done in taxis and buses. The Egged Bus Company travels across all the routes of the country, linking cities with towns and settlements. Though buses and trains are undoubtedly the most interesting and intimate form of travel in Israel, most tourists use the public taxi services, called *sheroot*. These run between the big cities, carrying four to six passengers, and leave at specified hours.

The taxi fare is slightly higher than the bus. You can hire a taxi for about $40 a day. Inside the cities you can use buses and taxis that have fixed rates for zones, as in Washington, D.C. On Saturday, when the buses don't run, you can use the *sheroot* taxis. These follow the bus routes, and are more expensive than the buses but considerably less than private cabs. You can also hire a taxi to take you on a trip through the country, or you can join a group on a trip organized by travel agencies.

SHOPPING

What to buy is almost no problem in Israel. You will probably want to stock up on blouses embroidered by Yemenites, and their exquisite silver jewelry. You may like the new leather work introduced by the immigrants from Germany, the new ceramics, or the small pottery figures that capture the style and verve of the sabra, the kibbutznik, and the orthodox lovelocked believer. In the three big cities, you will find shops run by W.I.Z.O. (Women's International Zionist Organization), which farms out all its products and sells them for the benefit of the craftsmen. W.I.Z.O. and other souvenir shops are along all the main streets in Haifa, Tel Aviv, Jerusalem, and the smaller towns.

You may want to purchase some of the suits, coats, tablecloths, or rugs woven by new immigrants and sold by Maskit, a government sponsored agency for handicrafts.

Many tourists now consider buying at least one Israel knit suit a "must" since they are beautifully styled and comfortable for nearly year-round wear. Furs too are popular among tourists, who can pay with American traveler's checks at authorized furriers.

WHERE TO GO

Whether you are planning one quick week in Israel, a full month's visit, or a prolonged visit of a year, you will want to divide your time between the cities and the farming villages.

For a one-week visit, you might plan one day in Tel Aviv, one day in Jerusalem, one day in Haifa, one day visiting the Negev, two days driving through the Galilee, and the last day to catch your breath, do your shopping, and perhaps revisit some spot that particularly intrigued you.

A two-week visit, of course, gives you much more time to dig around the country. You can plan to spend at least two, perhaps three, days in each of the cities and the rest of the time touring. Be sure to include a visit to Elath, Israel's bustling Red Sea port. There are numerous daily flights from Tel Aviv to Elath, and a most interesting side trip from Elath to King Solomon's Mines. The tourist bureaus in Israel will help arrange motor trips so that you can really get the feel of the land, from Dan to Elath.

If you are interested in the processes of government, you will want to spend extra time in Jerusalem and watch the Knesset at work. If you are interested in industry, you may want to spend more time around Haifa Bay. If commerce, beaches, shopping, night clubs, and the theatre are your passion, then make Tel Aviv your headquarters.

You may want to visit some of the archaeological digs and excavations at places like Hazor in the Huleh region where Canaanite fortifications and a whole city have been uncovered. Or you may want to visit Beit Shearim outside of Haifa with its catacombs and sarcophagi where famous rabbis were brought even from Yemen to be buried. You may want to see the sixth-century mosaic floor in the synagogue of Beit Alpha, or the Roman theatre excavated at Beit Shan.

Interested in archaeology or not, you will surely want to visit Caesarea named for the Emperor Augustus Caesar and founded about 22 B.C. The Roman theatre recently excavated is now used for concerts given by men like Pablo Casals. Caesarea has been turned into a tourist's paradise, with a restaurant, beach, tennis courts, and fishing. Israel's only golf course is here at Caesarea, and even though the golf club has some fifteen hundred members overseas, tourists can rent clubs and play on the eighteen-hole course.

If the kibbutzim and the cooperative farms are your special interest, ask the Tourist Information Office to help you arrange a tour by car or bus through the country, so that you can see the various kinds of farms—private, semiprivate, cooperative, and collective—in different stages of development.

You may spend as much time as you want on the grounds of a kibbutz, without imposing on the kibbutz, by staying at one of the rest houses already mentioned. If you have friends or relatives in a kibbutz who have invited you to spend some time with them, by all means do. But remember that a kibbutz is a home—a collective home for a lot of people, and you are their guest. You will be invited to eat with the whole kibbutz family, which may mean eating with five hundred or a thousand people. You will probably deprive some kibbutznik of his bed and room. But he will never complain to you. The golden rule in a kibbutz is to act as you would in a friend's home. You might bring a gift with you, or send a gift after you leave. But don't offer to tip anyone, except at a kibbutz rest home. The girl working in the kitchen may have a Ph.D. from Smith; your driver may be a famous engineer; the shepherd tending his flock on the hill may be a well-known poet or philosopher. All that they ask is that you come with your eyes and your heart open. For theirs is a country that means it when it says ISRAEL WELCOMES YOU. BLESSED BE HE WHO COMETH.